Bannockburns

To all who live in Scotland,
to Scotland's friends,
and in memory of Gavin Wallace
(b. Willerby, Hull, 1959; d. Burntisland, Fife, 2013),
a friend to writers

Bannockburns

Scottish Independence and Literary
Imagination, 1314–2014

*to Lloyd
with best wishes,*

Robert Crawford

*Robert Crawford
Stirling 2014*

EDINBURGH
University Press

© Robert Crawford, 2014

Edinburgh University Press Ltd
22 George Square, Edinburgh EH8 9LF

www.euppublishing.com

Reprinted 2014

Typeset in 10.5/13 pt Sabon by
Servis Filmsetting Ltd, Stockport, Cheshire,
and printed and bound in Great Britain by
CPI Group (UK) Ltd, Croydon CR0 4YY

A CIP record for this book is available from the British Library

ISBN 978 0 7486 8583 7 (hardback)
ISBN 978 0 7486 8584 4 (paperback)
ISBN 978 0 7486 8585 1 (webready PDF)
ISBN 978 0 7486 8586 8 (epub)

Contents

Acknowledgements

For love and sustenance from the first to the last minute I thank Alice, Lewis and Blyth. While almost nothing of the original survives, this book began with a talk about poetry and the visual arts given to the Scottish Arts Club in Edinburgh. I am grateful to Ian MacKenzie and to Duncan Thomson for their encouraging comments afterwards. Part of Chapter 2 was given as the Lewis Walpole Library Lecture at Yale University in 2012; warm thanks to Margaret Powell and Ruth Yeazell for inviting me to speak. Part of Chapter 4 was given at a conference on 'Classics and Class' at the British Academy in 2010, at the kind invitation of Edith Hall. Considerably recast, some of the material on Edwin Morgan and on Alasdair Gray in Chapter 5 draws on my chapters in *About Edwin Morgan* (co-edited with Hamish Whyte) and *The Arts of Alasdair Gray* (co-edited with Thom Nairn) for Edinburgh University Press, as well as on a lecture on Morgan to the Scottish Universities International Summer School in Edinburgh in 2012. Though all garblings remain my own, I am especially grateful to Alice Crawford, Christopher MacLachlan, Susan Manly, Kylie Murray, Rhiannon Purdie and Neil Rhodes for commenting on chapters and parts of chapters; to Celia Hawkesworth for advice on Serbia; to my colleagues and students in the School of English at the University of St Andrews for many discussions; to Jackie Jones at Edinburgh University Press for prompt responses and really good editorial advice; and to the two anonymous readers commissioned by the Press, whose pertinent suggestions were very helpful. Thanks are due, too, to the staff of Glasgow University Library, the

National Library of Scotland, the National Trust for Scotland, the Scottish Poetry Library and St Andrews University Library. Poems by Hugh MacDiarmid are reprinted from his *Collected Poems*, edited by Michael Grieve and W. R. Aitken, by permission of Carcanet Press.

Introduction

1314–2014

'Should Scotland be an independent country?' That question, put before Scottish voters in a national referendum on 18 September 2014, has been wrangled over for centuries. Some stubborn people thought it had been answered decisively by the Scots' unexpected victory in June 1314 on the battlefield at Bannockburn – a triumph celebrated in epic and still sung about today. Other, equally stubborn people were sure that the question had been given a more modern but just as dusty answer when the Scottish Parliament – encouraged, as Robert Burns put it, by 'English gold' – voted for Union along with the English Parliament in 1707.[1] A third group of folk, uncertain and wearied by the promises and counter-promises of Scotland's twenty-first-century 'neverendum', wonder if the issue may go on being argued about for at least the next 700 years.

Yoking the medieval Battle of Bannockburn to Scotland's 2014 political arguments is asking for trouble. Yet in modern democratic politics the very terms used – campaigning, tactics, contest, struggle, jousting, victory – carry persistent military undertones. Always mobile, whether in reports or in stories, language skids through implications and ambiguities in directions that we cannot entirely control. Similarly, voters' attitudes are guided on occasion by think-tanks' and journalists' supposedly neutral facts and figures, but at least as often by myths, beliefs, jokes, cherished ideals. It is naïve to regard this as foolish. Mythology, imagination and the play of literature are not separate from real life: they are important parts of the historical process because they encapsulate and engender values, losses and gains. Our stories matter. They help make us who we are both at individual and societal levels. They should not be dismissed as 'mere stories'.

Codifying what we love, loathe, laugh at, or are excited by, literary imagination defines us more fully and subtly than does any economic balance sheet or political slogan. History and imagination combine in surprising ways. For connoisseurs and casual observers of sport in Scotland, the date 2014 means Glasgow's proud hosting of the Commonwealth Games. For an international assortment of admirably bookish people it signals the 200th birthday of Walter Scott's globally influential Scoto-British novel *Waverley*. But for far more folk with Scottish interests the date 2014 marks the historic political referendum on national independence, which just happens to coincide dismally with the centenary year of the outbreak of World War I – and, perhaps more mischievously, with the 700th anniversary of the Scots' spectacular victory over that English army at Bannockburn. Like it or not, old and recent conflicts, memories of carnage from Gettysburg to Baghdad, from El Alamein to Culloden, are a stubbornly insistent part of all national narratives. Even in modern-day Europe at least two crucial fourteenth-century battles for independence have gone on playing an ineradicable part in the literature and thought of small nations. That this should be so is at once undeniable and, like a lacerating thistle, rebarbatively hard to grasp.

In Scotland's case no one has set out in detail the way the 1314 battle of Bannockburn reverberates throughout seven succeeding centuries of imaginative writing; yet for Serbia, the literary and political repercussions of the 1389 battle of Kosovo have been chronicled with all too convincing and disturbing results by Branimir Anzulović.[2] Kosovo (a medieval defeat for the Serbs at the hands of the Ottoman Empire) has been at least as important for Serbian literary and political history as has Bannockburn for the Scots. As with Bannockburn, Kosovo was sung in ballads and poems before passing into imaginative and historiographical prose. It continues to be a crucial reference point. In 1985, some time before the most recent outbreak of conflict in the area then known as Yugoslavia, as a young poet and editor I talked with Miodrag Pavlović, a writer influenced by T. S. Eliot as well as by the literary inheritance of his native Serbo-Croat. I was struck by the intensity with which Pavlović's poetry interrogated fourteenth-century havoc. Here was verse convinced that after the historic slaughter of the battlefield, through literature 'our nakedness will be clothed with words'.[3] Verbal art can clothe, memorialise, morph and even prolong conflict. Branimir Anzulović shows how disastrously this has happened in the case of Serbian nationalism. The relevant corpus of imaginative writing runs from medieval celebratory ballads through later epic-length poems including *The Mountain Wreath* (1847) by Vladika Petar Petrović Njegoš to twentieth-century fiction and verse, most notorious of which is the poetry of the former Columbia University creative-writing student and admirer of Walt Whitman, Radovan Karadžić. No poet in history has been more notorious for wartime atrocities. To read about the relationship between literary imagination and Serbian independence is to encounter a 'glorification of genocide' in the Romantic-era *Mountain Wreath*, which between 1847 and 1913 was 'the most widely read literary work among the Serbs', and was known 'by heart' by the Serbian terrorist Gavrilo Princip whose assassination of Archduke Franz Ferdinand sparked World War I. That glorification continues in works including the popular modern Bosnian Serb Vuk Drašković's *The Knife*, with its celebration of the slaughter of Muslims, and culminates in the atrocities of Karadžić and Slobodan Milošević who 'followed' the 'precept' of modern Serbian novelist Dobrica Ćosić.[4] Ćosić argues for the literary importance of 'national mythology' and 'above all . . . the Kosovo myth'.[5]

In writing *Bannockburns*, I have kept in mind the example of Kosovo. This has made it all the more important to confront head-on the bloody and vitriolic anti-Englishness of some of the literary works discussed here, from Blind Hary's medieval *Wallace* to its recent descendant *Braveheart*. Certainly there have been craven celebrations of political martyrology and slaughter in works championing Scottish independence. Overall, however, it would be perverse even for those most opposed to what the Scottish nationalist theorist Tom Nairn terms 'the break-up of

Britain' (and what his British Unionist opponents sometimes term 'Balkanisation') to argue that Scottish independence and literary imagination have combined to produce anything like the atrocities of modern Serb nationalism.[6] True, there are moments of bloodthirstiness to be found even in the work of Enlightenment-era democratic poets including the Robert Burns of 'Scots, wha hae wi' Wallace bled'.[7] Yet the ideals of Bannockburn have been linked to modern warfare less by singers of Scottish independence than by writers committed to imperial British nationalism. Following the 1914 celebrations of the battle of Bannockburn, British 'Kossovo Day' celebrations of World War I (encouraged by such Scottish or Scottish-influenced figures as Elsie Inglis and the writer H. W. Seton-Watson) were designed to bolster loyalty to the militant British Empire. What is so striking about the modern ideal of Scottish independence and its literary imaginings is that no one has died for them. They have advanced not through battlefield bloodshed, but through democratic elections and referenda.

Battles, like democratic nations, are seldom straightforward. My title, *Bannockburns*, uses a plural noun to suggest that the singular occurrence at Bannockburn on 23–4 June 1314 has long since become many Bannockburns. It has been re-envisioned in other contexts by writers in quite different eras. This book's title also winks towards Robert Burns. His 'Bruce to his Troops on the Eve of the Battle of Bannock-burn' made him, almost 500 years after the conflict, both that battle's greatest literary celebrant and the master-poet of modern democratic ideals. The following chapters acknowledge that the contest to preserve Scottish independence in the Middle Ages was, as Burns recognised, persistently bloody. Its masculinist militarism has been an important part of its literary legacies and may have conditioned the temper of its nation. Still, with the notable exception of *Braveheart*, it is noticeable how far recent imaginings of Scottish independence in literature and politics have attempted to carry forward ideals of freedom while moving away from battlefield violence. Modern Scottish literature is as far from Tacitus's Calgacus, that first-century Caledonian freedom-fighter and opponent of Roman imperialism, as it is from medievalising Serbian mythology. If, at first, setting the cultural legacy of Kosovo beside that of Bannockburn provokes thoughts of similarity, ultimately it reveals lasting differences. *Bannockburns*, then, is the first book-length consideration of how the ideal of Scottish independence has spurred, been sparked by and generally come into contact with writerly imaginations. Examining work from eight centuries, much of what follows deals with writing by and about men – some straight, some gay; this preponderance of males may be inevitable (little work by medieval and Renaissance Scottish women survives), but is also emblematic of continuing problems. Polls suggest Scottish independence is more popular among male than among female voters. In the gendering of Scottish identity and political life, some have argued, women are doubly 'decentred': by gender as well as by nationality.[8] I leave that possibility for readers to ponder, and have resisted the temptation to co-opt for my literary-political topic fictions such as those of Janice Galloway, A. L. Kennedy and Alice Thompson which at times imagine in Scottish contexts the pain of the past, yet do not explicitly (or even, perhaps, implicitly) engage with the issue of the independence of the Scottish nation. For different reasons, I have omitted consideration of popular historical works and speculative thrillers such as those of Nigel Tranter, John Connell and Douglas Hurd since several of the best of these have been considered by Craig Buchanan in his contribution to Caroline McCracken Flesher's innovative edited volume, *Culture, Nation, and the New Scottish Parliament* (2007).[9]

Future writers on literature and independence may address the topics of gender, Jacobitism, Gaelic and popular culture in a different idiom and at greater length. Yet whether they take their bearings from the literary quotations set into the Scottish Parliament's Canongate Wall or from theorists as influential as Benedict Anderson or Homi Bhabha, they are likely to conclude that literary imagination is shaped by and helps to configure the political imaginary: the way a group – in this case a nation – articulates itself.[10] Poets are alert to this. The title of at least one modern Scottish poetry anthology – *Dream State*, first published several years before the establishment of the devolved Scottish Parliament in 1999 – sums it up with nice ambiguity.[11] Often, the literary process of recording, dreaming and recounting a story of national independence develops over centuries. Yet there is not one unchanging entity called 'Scottish independence'. The meaning of those words is hardly the same in 2014 as it was in 1314. Nor is there one essentialist 'literary imagination'. Perhaps after the word *Bannockburns* this book's subtitle should have gone on to flourish a knowing plurality of further plural nouns, but I hope that one is enough.

Many of the works discussed here come from Scotland itself. A significant number of them, though, have been produced beyond the nation's borders – whether in England or Canada, Australia or the United States. Though it surveys 700 years of writing, *Bannockburns* does not claim to be fully comprehensive. Literature in the sense of creative writing is at its heart; but the chapters that follow also pay a small amount of attention to film (how could I ignore *Braveheart?*) and to the scripting of history, whether by eloquent medieval chroniclers or by that influential colossus, Walter Scott. About half the volume is devoted to literature written before 1900, the other half to work produced since. In the last century Modernist-era writers did much to shape and inspire campaigns for Scottish self-government, while, more recently, authors from Edwin Morgan, Alasdair Gray and Liz Lochhead to David Greig, James Robertson and Kathleen Jamie have seen their works become part of political debate.

While its idiom is that of literary history, this is not a history of Scottish literature: I have produced that elsewhere, in *Scotland's Books*. Other recent histories include volumes authored by Roderick Watson, and those co-written by large teams of contributors under the editorship of Ian Brown, Marco Fazzini, Douglas Gifford and colleagues.[12] All have shown Scottish literature to be adventurously protean, and some people might argue there is no need for further panoramic surveys of Scottish literary history just now, until Scottish criticism and theory have faced up to so much recent literary historiography. Still, one positive result of this burgeoning of literary histories is that only a fool would argue Scottish imaginative writers should confine themselves to addressing the constitutional position of Scotland.

That is certainly not my contention here. All literatures are resiliently porous; gleefully, imaginations go wherever they like. Yet this book has a deliberate and timely selective focus: it attends to imaginative works that deal explicitly with Scottish independence. Relatively few creative writers have concentrated on this theme. Many of Scotland's most celebrated authors – from Robert Henryson to Muriel Spark and beyond – have avoided it. Nonetheless, Bannockburn and the *topos* of Scottish independence have remained, in the historian Pierre Nora's terms, crucial 'sites of memory'.[13] The literary portrayal and transmission of them is part of that 'cultural identity' which, the theorist Jan Assmann argues, is communicated through 'reusable texts, images, and rituals specific to each society in each epoch, whose "cultivation" serves to stabilize and convey that society's self-image'.[14] Assmann's formulation is useful, but while Bannockburn and Scottish independence have such a function in Scotland, they can work also to unsettle the status quo. Published in the year that marks the 700th anniversary of the battle, *Bannockburns* is intended as a contribution to political arguments about the Scottish nation as well as a focused addition to recent literary scholarship. It aims to add nuance, depth and elements of surprise to vigorous continuing debates.

Twentieth- and twenty-first-century thinkers as different as Jürgen Habermas and Peter Sloterdijk have cherished the importance of literature in the constitution of the public sphere.[15] However, some observers still regard creative writing as peripheral to today's politics. Such readers may have statistics on their side. In their 2012 study, *The Scottish National Party: Transition to Power*, James Mitchell, Lynn Bennie and Rob Johns analyse in detail the findings of a comprehensive survey of the membership of Scotland's principal pro-independence party. The survey was conducted just after the SNP formed the Scottish Government of 2007. That minority administration was followed by the Nationalists' achievement of an overall majority at Holyrood in the Scottish Parliamentary election of 2011, paving the way for the first-ever official referendum on Scottish independence. When asked what aspects of being Scottish were 'important to you personally', only about 20 per cent of respondents ranked 'Scottish art, music and literature' among their top three choices.[16] Modern campaigners place far more emphasis on economics, social networking and digital media than on printed poems and stories. Yet, as the present book demonstrates, literature – from the poetry of Bannockburn eye-witnesses and of Robert Burns to bestselling Romantic-era fiction and modern drama – was and remains powerful in articulating ideals of Scottish autonomy. Writers were to the fore in the founding of the National Party of Scotland, and several continue to portray the cause of independence in addition to supporting the 'Yes Scotland' campaign launched in 2012.

In an earlier book, *Devolving English Literature* (1992; 2nd edn, 2000), I set out among other things Scotland's substantial contribution to the literary articulation of 'Britishness'. *Devolving English Literature* shows how this grew in the eighteenth and nineteenth centuries before declining in the twentieth.[17] Today there is a striking and surely revealing absence of imaginative writing from Scotland that communicates (as Scott and others once did) a positive ideology of Britishness. In some ways *Bannockburns* complements *Devolving English Literature* by showing how, over a longer period, Scottish independence has been presented by creative writers. For many readers the imagining of freedom may provide a 'safety valve', an escape from the immediate present into a fantasy 'dream state'. Imagined Scottish independence may function as a sort of perpetual possibility for a putative and perhaps arrested national psyche preoccupied with 'missing out'.[18]

Maybe such an awareness is a necessary part of the political unconscious; it need not translate into voting patterns. However, in the years leading up to the independence referendum, opinion polls have shown consistently that Scots desire further constitutional change, greater independence, whether or not as part of a modified British state. The imagining of independence in literature is part of this political pressure, fuelling it and fuelled by it. Many opinion polls conducted in Scotland before the 2012 Edinburgh Agreement on referendum arrangements, signed by British Prime Minister David Cameron and Scottish First Minister Alex Salmond, suggested that a majority of Scots favoured a 'Devo Max' option. This would have provided a maximum amount of political and fiscal devolution for Scotland, and would have moved the whole United Kingdom (including that stateless nation, England, currently the only part of the UK without its own parliament) in the direction of a federation. Though Salmond was willing to entertain the idea of a 'Devo Max' option featuring on the independence referendum ballot paper, Cameron and his allies were not. As a result, at that time the majority of Scots lost out. The Edinburgh Agreement, confirmed by the Westminster Parliament in 2013 and subsequent deliberations in the Holyrood Parliament, specified that a referendum must present Scottish voters on 18 September 2014 with a single Yes or No question, whose wording became, 'Should Scotland be an independent country?'

Despite sometimes insubstantial hints of 'Devo More', loss of the popular, if imprecisely defined, 'Devo Max' option led to a more polarised public debate. From the 'Better Together' Unionist camp came warnings that political independence would mean frightening risk, financial peril, pejorative change and no longer hosting a long-term base for nuclear weapons; it would bring, too, a period of scarcely manageable uncertainty, renegotiation of Scotland's relationship with Europe and a revised, smaller UK, plus all the pains of separation. On the other side, the pro-independence 'Yes' camp envisioned a nation regaining greater control over its own affairs, managing its wealth (not least its natural resources) in a more just way, positive change and no longer hosting a long-term base for nuclear weapons; Scotland would become a nation-state like any other, renegotiating its relationship with Europe and a revised, smaller UK, rather than remaining a sort of northern province or what the British Broadcasting Corporation has sometimes termed a 'national region'. The Scottish Government in 2012 claimed independent Scots would each be £500 better off and in 2013 asked for negotiations to clarify the terms of independence; the British Government in 2013 claimed Scots would each be £1 worse off, and refused pre-referendum negotiations. Whether the magnitude of either cash figure was likely to sway voters on the matter of their nation's future is debatable. Having warned in 2012 about the consequences of uncertainty produced by a Scottish independence referendum, David Cameron complicated matters in 2013 by promising a future 'in or out' referendum on the United Kingdom's membership of the European Union

– thereby creating prolonged uncertainties of his own. Many people in Scotland, as elsewhere, have grown cynical about economic forecasts and competing politicians' financial and constitutional spin. The phrase 'lies, damned lies, and statistics' is hard to banish. Implicit throughout this book is the idea that Scottish independence is an issue involving long-term arguments about culture and imagination, not just immediate arguments about cash.

The written context

Over the last century support for Scottish autonomy has grown markedly. Less well understood is the way in which throughout successive centuries literature has shaped and sometimes been shaped by the resilient envisioning of Scottish independence. As a poet and critic this topic has long fascinated me. Like many Scots, I have a vested interest in the debate. In the early 1990s I published my first collection of poems, *A Scottish Assembly*, as well as the prose of *Devolving English Literature*; both were contributions to the cultural climate that led to the 1999 re-establishment, after 292 years, of a Scottish parliament. In successive poetry and prose volumes I have gone on writing about Scottish-inflected themes, addressing Scots and non-Scots alike. No doubt, for good or ill, there are aspects of overlap between my practice as poet and as prose writer, but the two genres have different demands and this book does its best to avoid prose poetry. I am not a politician, or even a member of a political party, but *Bannockburns* makes claims for the lasting importance of literary voices as contributors to political debate. Quite rightly, arguments over whether in fact 'poetry makes nothing happen' will continue to be staged in seminar rooms; but *Bannockburns* provides support for the short-term and long-term efficacy of the literary imagination in politics – not just in Periclean Athens, in Yeats's Ireland, or in modern Tahrir Square, but, more quietly yet still tellingly, in 2014 Glasgow and Edinburgh.[19]

Written in an idiom accessible to a general audience, *Bannockburns* is a work of literary and cultural history that is, too, a political intervention. It aims to find readers outside university departments, but also, I hope, within them. Academic readers will be aware of a body of thought (including work by Anderson, Bhabha, Robert Young, and Deleuze and Guattari in *Kafka: Toward a Minor Literature*) that theorises how nations, not least small ones, assert their distinctiveness in writing.[20] In Scottish contexts some of this has been drawn on in books by critics including Cairns Craig, Leith Davis, Ian Duncan, Susan Manning, Murray Pittock, Alan Riach, Janet Sorensen and Katie Trumpener, though there has been a tendency for many of these commentators to concentrate on particular post-Renaissance periods, especially the Romantic era, rather than thinking across a wider historical spectrum.[21] If only to counterbalance smaller-scale chronological concentration, there is a good case for surveying the whole period from Bannockburn to 2014.

Many different approaches could be taken to such a project. Other writers more thoroughly informed about, say, song or cyberculture, may produce their own. The sparky essay collection *Unstated: Writers on Scottish Independence*, edited by Scott Hames in 2012, brings together a range of authors from Kathleen Jamie to Suhayl Saadi and from James Kelman to Meaghan Delahunt. While not claiming to be representative, Hames's book gives the cumulative and probably accurate impression that if Scottish independence had been left up to creative writers it would have been achieved long ago. *Unstated* as a whole has been too little read and discussed, though (often in distorted form) one of its essays, Alasdair Gray's 'Settlers and Colonists' – considered in Chapter 5 below – has achieved notoriety. Hames's thoughtful introduction apart, there is little extended work by Scottish or non-Scottish literary academics that directly addresses the context of the 2014 independence referendum. Perhaps this is because of the long gestation time involved in cultural study, but it may be due also to the complexly nuanced history of the university subject of 'English' in Scotland; a topic relevant when it comes to long-running arguments about whether or not there should be some compulsory elements of Scottish literature and history in the high-school curriculum. If there was certainly a 'Scottish invention of English literature' as an academic subject, then the development of that specialism, whether at Edinburgh, Glasgow, or St Andrews, or in India, Australia, or America was often bound up with the deliberate suppression of markers of local cultural difference, and its history can be read in terms of cultural – and political – colonialism.[22] Sometimes 'English' academics are reluctant to face up to such aspects of their own discipline's partly colonial or quasi-colonial history, especially when it relates to the immediate society in which they operate. The Australian poet Les Murray's witty line, 'a major in English made one a minor Englishman', has sometimes resonated awkwardly in Scotland.[23]

Increasingly, academic critics and theorists of Scottish writing, including Eleanor Bell, Penny Fielding, Michael Gardiner and Graeme Macdonald, have emphasised the importance of postcolonial approaches to Scottish writing as well as, in Gardiner's case, to the formation of the literature of England in *The Constitution of English Literature* (2013).[24] The 2011 essay collection *Scottish Literature and Postcolonial Literature*, edited by Gardiner, Macdonald and Niall O'Gallagher, is presented by its publisher as 'the first full-length study of Scottish literature using a post-devolutionary understanding of postcolonial studies'.[25] Today questions of national independence feature constantly in postcolonial criticism, often drawing on some of the theorists mentioned in the paragraphs above. A good example of this might be the work of Lorna Burns on Deleuze, postcolonialism and Caribbean writing.[26] But sometimes there has been a reluctance on the part of postcolonial critics to address works which deal explicitly with Scottish independence, while readers outside specialist university studies can be put off by arcane terms such as '*sinathion*'.[27] In Scotland, postcolonial criticism has entered the public and political sphere less readily than has literary history; and, where it has done so, it has generated more heat than light. When the distinguished New York-based postcolonial critic Robert Young, arguing that the 'Scots' goal must be postcolonial nationhood', gave a lecture at the 2010 Edinburgh International Book Festival he invoked the language of historian Michael Hechter's *Internal Colonialism*, stating that 'for many it has seemed that Scotland, like Wales and Ireland, have [sic] always been de facto "internal colonies"'. Young's words were denounced in the press as 'academic drivel', the 'Wallace-like' contentions of a 'maudlin folk singer'.[28] Writing in the *Scotsman*, Scottish historian Keith Brown, author of those last, emotive words, declared his own 'unionist sympathies', scornful of 'emotive, manipulative language' like Young's. Professor Young the postcolonial theorist, Professor Brown implied, was guilty of 'sloppy thinking'.[29] However, to set out in emotive and even manipulative language a sense of national independence is exactly what a considerable number of influential major as well as minor works of Scottish literature do. Particularly now, this deserves sustained attention.

I hope *Bannockburns* may be of interest to historians and postcolonial critics. Yet, rightly or wrongly, I want to sidestep their academic fisticuffs, so what follows is not addressed to them specifically. Moreover, there seems as little point in duplicating the work of Michael Gardiner and his colleagues in *Scottish Literature and Postcolonial Literature* as there would be in repeating the examination of Scottish historiography in William Ferguson's *The Identity of the Scottish Nation* (1998). Other commentators have written on some aspects of the material I deal with in the present book. Most notably, in several literary studies from *The Invention of Scotland* (1991) to *Scottish and Irish Romanticism* (2008) and his more sociologically-oriented account of Scottish politics and history since the 1960s *The Road to Independence?* (2008) Murray Pittock has set forth ideas of Scottish identity involving (especially Jacobite) literary nationalism; building on the work of Marinell Ash, historian Graeme Morton has written on the iconography of William Wallace; Penny Fielding in *Scotland and the Fictions of Geography: North Britain, 1760–1830* (2009) has produced one of the most sophisticated recent investigations of Scotland's relationship with Britain in the Romantic era; Carla Sassi in *Why Scottish Literature Matters* (2005) has authored a succinct and provocative survey; Cairns Craig has been astutely insightful about Scottish fiction, though some of his recent work in *Intending Scotland* (2009) has moved into philosophy and cultural theory and away from the examination of imaginative writing; while the exhumation of Hugh Trevor Roper's elegant relic *The Invention of Scotland: Myth and History* (2008) made me all the more ready to realise that imaginative writers are so important precisely because they are inventive: it is Fiona Stafford's scholarship on Ossian, not Trevor Roper's, which is truly illuminating.[30] In timely fashion Gavin Bowd's political study *Fascist Scotland* (2013) has shown how, especially in the early and mid-twentieth century, extremist rhetoric has fanned potentially dangerous flames on the Unionist and nationalist sides.[31] I have learned from these and other critics, but the focus of this book is different from theirs. Attentive to the past but addressed to the present, it seeks both academic readers and a wider audience interested in the literary imagining as well as the potential realisation of Scottish independence.

'The natives of Caledonia turned to armed resistance on a large scale' wrote Tacitus almost 2,000 years ago. In his *Agricola* the Latin historian put into the mouth of that first-century Caledonian chieftain Calgacus the most ringing defence of independence and resistance to imperialism produced anywhere in the ancient world. Conscious that his proud and resilient northern people are threatened with loss of their freedom, Calgacus denounces Roman colonists:

> Pillagers of the world, they have exhausted the land by their indiscriminate plunder, and now they ransack the sea. A rich enemy excites their cupidity; a poor one, their lust for power. East and West alike have failed to satisfy them. They are the only people on earth to whose covetousness both riches and poverty are equally tempting. To robbery, butchery, and rapine, they give the lying name of 'government'; they create a desolation and call it peace.[32]

While these words (quoted surprisingly little by postcolonial thinkers) resonate widely in terms of later superpowers' interventions, whether in the seventeenth-century Caribbean or in twenty-first-century Iraq, they scarcely apply to present-day Scotland. Not even the most inveterate supporter of independence now maintains that Scotland is being subjected to plunder, butchery and rapine at the hands of an imperial invader; indeed the late Douglas Mack showed nicely how Scottish novelists spoke for British imperialism as well as, at times, articulating a 'subaltern' response to it.[33] Yet it is unsettling to realise that as long ago as the time of Tacitus the resistance of Caledonia could emblematise struggles for self-determination.

Sixth-century Iona, rather than fourteenth-century Bannockburn, is the most resonantly emblematic point of origin for literature emanating from the part of the planet we now call Scotland. Still, Bannockburn retains its literary and political importance. The Bannockburns invoked in the National Theatre of Scotland's *Black Watch* or in James Robertson's sweeping novel, *And the Land Lay Still*, or in the poetry of Kathleen Jamie are very different from those of medieval poet John Barbour or Romantic novelist Jane Porter, but they confirm the continuing importance of the events of 1314 to literary imaginations. Perhaps Bannockburn survives in literature most movingly as a lyric cry, one at once particularly Scottish and universally recognisable.

Before setting out this book's structure in more detail, a word about tone and explication. Some readers, following their particular interests, may use the volume's index and subheadings to select individual sections; the parts of *Bannockburns* can be read on their own. However, the book covers a broad spectrum and has an over-arching design. Experience suggests that several of the works discussed – especially poems in the Scots tongue from the Middle Ages and by Hugh MacDiarmid – are linguistically challenging. Moreover, few folk today have read Blind Hary *and* Margaret Holford, or Hamilton of Gilbertfield *as well as* MacDiarmid. So, throughout, I have assumed little prior knowledge of the literature I deal with, including the Bannockburn passages from the Latin *Scotichronicon* and the Scots poems of MacDiarmid. I have supplied some translations, summaries and glosses. My hope is that, for the sake of the big picture, specialists may tolerate at times an introductory approach applied to their own particular area; this tone is designed to make all parts of an unusually wide-ranging book welcoming to an international readership whose background may lie in literature, in history, in politics, or in none of these fields. I would like to think that a variety of readers will find something new in *Bannockburns*.

A summary of this book

As the first chapter's title suggests, 'Writing Bannockburn' concentrates on how the battle was presented in poetry and prose. My focus here is on the medieval and Renaissance eras. I begin with remarkable, little-known eye-witness poetry, then relate it to the more celebrated 1320 Declaration of Arbroath, still a familiar reference point for supporters of Scottish independence. Chapter 1 also considers later, epic-length celebrations of national freedom by the Scots poets John Barbour and Blind Hary as well as the literary imagination of Walter Bower's ambitious *Scotichronicon*. Through literary craft, the emblematic victory for Scottish independence resounded across the later Middle Ages, even as the ideology of a British Union began to emerge. Apparently unaffected by the Unionist propaganda of that masterpiece *Macbeth*, works celebrating independence continued to be published throughout the Renaissance alongside fresh imaginings of Bannockburn. Sometimes in surprising ways writers, editors and patriotic publishers ensured that the battle and its associated ideals stayed exciting as Scotland entered the early stages of the Enlightenment, and parliamentary union with England drew near.

'Burns and Bannockburns', the second chapter, starts by looking at the literary climate around the 1707 Union. Showing how different accounts of Bannockburn circulated in imaginative writing, it focuses on two poets – one today little remembered, the other globally celebrated. Both writers maintained and developed ideals of Scottish independence. Most of this chapter looks at what the politically loaded word 'independence' meant to Robert Burns. I tease out how his political articulation of that ideal intersected with his enthusiasm for Wallace, Bruce and Bannockburn. However, before turning to Burns, I discuss an intensely popular work that shaped his thinking from infancy: William Hamilton of Gilbertfield's reworking of Blind Hary's *Wallace*. Unpublished south of the Anglo-Scottish border, but enjoying a very substantial audience in Scotland during the decades after 1707, Hamilton's poem, more than the writing of any other author, kept the ideal of independence alive. Taking up themes as well as phrasing from Hamilton, Burns developed the topic. By linking Scotland's freedom-fighting past to the brave possibility of a democratic future, he gave the notion of his nation's liberty an Enlightenment modernity that cut loose from the dangers of nostalgia. This chapter provides the most detailed examination to date of Burns's creative engagement with the ideal of Scottish independence.

Just as Burns's popularity was international, so the theme of Scottish independence was taken up with enthusiasm by writers beyond Scotland – often in unexpected circumstances. Surveying prose, poetry and drama from England to America and Australia, Chapter 3, 'Beyond Scotland', looks at how this happened. Though this part of the book considers Walter Scott and his legacy, it concentrates on the work of English women writers, particularly Margaret Holford and Jane Porter. Published four years before *Waverley* and read with enthusiasm in Europe and America, Porter's *The Scottish Chiefs* was the nineteenth century's most influential imaginative portrayal of Scottish independence. Circulating in many versions, her fiction enthused Americans who identified with the Scots' idealisation of liberty. In Britain there were strained attempts by writers in Scotland and beyond to position Wallace and the victor of Bannockburn as precursors of British Empire rule. Yet in Porter's novel and other works the imaginative excitement lies in a resolute assertion of Scotland's independence. Informed by recent scholarship, Chapter 3 treats Porter's sometimes patronised book as a crafted, long-lived piece of popular writing, rather than simply as an international cultural phenomenon. Noting the work of American authors linked to Porter, this chapter shows how a championing of Scottish liberty from beyond Scotland culminates eventually in the Australian-American-Anglo-Scottish blockbuster, *Braveheart*. Deeply indebted to literary imaginings, *Braveheart* – globally enjoyed, widely attacked and frequently ironised – remains a popular reference point in today's arguments about Scottish independence.

As the next chapter suggests, the roots of modern Scottish nationalism have nothing to do with Hollywood. Instead, they are bound up with print-based literary imaginations. Chapter 4 starts with an overview of early twentieth-century responses to Bannockburn, and with the work of such English-born Scottish nationalists as R. B. Cunninghame Graham and Compton Mackenzie. It then reads Hugh MacDiarmid's often linguistically difficult poetry in the context of his spiky commitment to Scottish independence. Paying tribute to the poet's provocative and often profound imaginative work, my analysis calls attention to serious limitations in his political thinking, especially when set beside that of his 1930s literary ally, the American Scottish nationalist James H. Whyte. Thanks in part to his background, this Jewish-descended, bisexual, English-educated immigrant presented in *The Modern Scot* the most nuanced theorisation of Scottish nationalism. His thinking was developed in conscious opposition to the European Fascism of the 1930s. Whyte supported an important circle of nationalists and other intellectuals; he left a legacy that continued for decades after he left Scotland. Whyte's pluralist nationalism prefigures that of the present-day SNP, while pro-independence sympathies that he nurtured were passed down through several generations of writers and academics. In the 1970s, this legacy conditioned the education of the undergraduate Alex Salmond. That St Andrews student responded enthusiastically to his tutor's presentation of Bannockburn and the Declaration of Arbroath, and has gone on to champion in the twenty-first century a pluralist version of Scottish independence.

This book's concluding chapter, 'Voting for a Scottish Democracy', looks particularly at works produced in the period between the 1979 devolution referendum and the 2014 Scottish independence referendum. It opens with extended considerations of the poetry of Edwin Morgan and the fiction of Alasdair Gray. Morgan's metamorphic imagination has a political dimension that led to support for independence both in his writing and in his posthumous bequest of a million pounds to the Scottish National Party. Gray, on the other hand, has consistently authored fictions whose protagonists battle against kinds of entrapment: viewing this as the situation from which Scots must escape, repeatedly – sometimes subtly and sometimes not – he has set out a case for 'why Scots should rule Scotland'.[34] In Gray's oeuvre the politics of nation are bound up with those of gender; but it is Liz Lochhead's *Mary Queen of Scots Got Her Head Chopped Off* which, more than any other work, has brought that combination of concerns to a wide popular audience. Chapter 5 examines Lochhead's play and the more recent dramas *Black Watch* and *Dunsinane*. Generating controversy, these have become part of contemporary politicians' arguments in the run-up to the Scottish independence referendum. The chapter's penultimate part considers James Robertson's ambitious 2010 novel, *And the Land Lay Still*, which surveys over half a century of Scottish politics and traces the movement of pro-independence activists from the margins of politics into government. Robertson reveals political autonomy as a continuing process; it may be that the achievement of independence remains, as James Kelman (an advocate of Scottish independence, but no nationalist) puts it, 'not an economic decision', but 'a decision to do with self-respect'.[35] Finally, acknowledging that the twenty-first-century literary imagination has found convincing new ways of articulating in cyberspace and on solid ground the struggle for Scottish independence, the book considers contemporary poets' responses to Bannockburn composed for 2014, that milestone year in Scotland's journey.

Chapter 1

Writing Bannockburn

Bannockburn, 1314

The Battle of Bannockburn had a poet-in-residence. Confident his army would subdue Scottish forces led by King Robert Bruce, in early summer 1314 England's King Edward II commissioned a poet to accompany his soldiers, then write a Latin victory celebration as soon as the battle was won.[1] This poem, like the conflict, would enhance Edward's prestige, making clear that the might of one of Europe's great monarchies had put paid to Scotland's tenacious but absurd claims to independence. That was the script, and, given the overwhelming military superiority of the English army, its realisation seemed inevitable.

King Edward's sending a poet with his invading army was far from ridiculous. Today's military knows the importance of public relations, embedded battlefront correspondents and even war artists; in the late twentieth century there was talk of commissioning Scottish poet Douglas Dunn to go with troops to Kuwait during the Iraqi invasion there. In medieval Scotland, though not as familiar as a soldier, a Latin poet was hardly an unknown figure; it is probable that Bannockburn was witnessed by several writers with access to various languages. This chapter is about how that famous military encounter came to be written up in poetry as well as in prose, and how the writing of it has resounded over the centuries, though hardly in the way that England's King Edward intended.

For the better part of a millennium before the Battle of Bannockburn, throughout the territory we now call Scotland, poems circulated in Latin, Gaelic, Old Welsh, Old Norse, Old French, Old English and, eventually, in Scots. Most of these works have religious or military associations. They celebrate the power of God and the Christian church, or redound to the glory of competing kingdoms within the northern part of Britain. Dating from around the sixth century, a poem in Old Welsh whose hero has stood 'Rhag Eidyn' ('Before Edinburgh') tells how 'Mynog Gododdin traethiannor' ('A lord of Gododdin will be praised in song'). Old French verses recount how 'Fergus a trait le bonne espée' ('Fergus drew his favourite blade') when the rusty-armoured Arthurian knight Sir Fergus from the south-western kingdom of Galloway rides to vanquish a dragon dwelling in a north-eastern cave at Dunnottar.[2]

Even before Scotland took form as a nation, poetry hymned its precursor kingdoms. When, around the end of the first millennium AD, an identifiable Scottish nation emerged, the literary imagination played a significant part in its articulation. Poets set forth the character of the kingdom at those most crucial moments in medieval public life: the coronations of monarchs. The new ' "Scottish" kingdom,' argues historian Colin Kidd,

> found its identity in Scoto-Celtic monarchy, whose foremost expression was the royal genealogy recited as part of the coronation ritual by a Highland sennachie or bard ... Genealogies also catalysed pride in a Scottish 'community' by indicating great longevity and a national origin in remote antiquity under a great founding father; at the coronation of Alexander III in 1249 his descent was traced back beyond Fergus MacErch, who brought the Scots to Britain from Ireland, to a patriarchal founder, Iber Scot.[3]

Such pieces of *mythistoire*, enhanced by the bardic literary imagination, were not unusual in medieval nations. Poetry furthered statecraft, as well as inciting troops. To Lachlan Mór, a member of the hereditary bardic MacMhuirich family, is attributed the 'brosnachadh' or 'incitement' poem said to have been chanted to fighters of Clan Donald at the 1411 Battle of Harlaw. With its distinctive rhythms (the brosnachadh is associated with bagpiping), this Gaelic poem is an abecedarian work, its formally patterned lines following the course of the Gaelic alphabet:

Gu h-àirneach, gu-arranta,
Gu h-athlamh, gu h-allanta,
Gu beodha, gu barramhail,
Gu brìoghmhor, gu buan-fheargach . . .

Be at them, be animals,
Be alphas, be Argus-eyed,
Be belters, be brandishers,
Be bonny, be batterers . . .[4]

Today this sort of poetry may seem unfamiliar, but war poetry has not gone away. In medieval Scotland, as across the world in our own era, verse could function as anguished lament or as victory song, propagandistic bluster or high art. An abiding, resolute art-form, it became an important channel for the expression of ideas about Scottish independence. Not only England's Edward II realised the political value of verse.

Scottish poetry was shaped by the Wars of Independence that raged from 1286 until after the middle of the following century. Strife continued to flare up whenever English kings sought to dominate Scotland. This conflict was symbolic as well as bloody: King Edward I of England, nicknamed the 'Hammer of the Scots', had encouraged the destruction of Scotland's national historic records in 1296. That year a great national symbol, the 'Stone of Destiny', associated with the crowning of Scottish monarchs, was pillaged from Scone and taken by English forces to Westminster Abbey where, despite imaginative efforts at repatriation, it would remain for seven centuries. Kings in earlier medieval England had adopted such imperial titles as '*imperator totius Britanniae*' (emperor of the whole of Britain); their political assumptions were bolstered by twelfth-century interweavings of myth and written history such as Layamon's *Brut* and the *History of the Kings of Britain* by Geoffrey of Monmouth which imperiously asserted English overlordship over the entire island.

Englishmen claimed that once upon a time King Arthur had ruled Britain, 'Scandinavia and Gaul'.[5] Scots countered with their own versions of myth and history, yet 'For medieval Englishmen, as for so many of their early modern descendants, an independent Scotland was quite simply a political freak which flew in the face of all that was known about the glorious British past.'[6] The Wars of Independence strengthened 'a Scottish national consciousness' expressed by historians and poets.[7] If the war of myths, symbols and ideas was fierce (and, for the Scottish kingdom, potentially lethal), actual physical conflicts were even fiercer. Along with earlier struggles of the freedom-fighter William Wallace, the decisive victory won by King Robert Bruce at Bannockburn, near the Lowland settlement of Stirling, came to emblematise an unflinching determination to maintain Scottish independence.

From the start, Bannockburn was the most literary of battles. Drawing on earlier verse and prose accounts, the fifteenth-century Latin *Scotichronicon* describes how Edward II brought with him to the fray 'the most famous poet in the whole kingdom of England . . . so that he might compose to the shame of the Scots some verses about the triumph he had gained over them, verses which would remain as an everlasting memorial, since these northern troublemakers (as he thought) were bound to be conquered by him'. This poet, Carmelite friar Robert Baston, was captured by the Scots: 'Brought to King Robert . . . in return for his release he was compelled to compose . . . verses without ambiguity about what had happened.'[8]

Baston's verses might have remained a dusty curiosity had it not been for a surprising twenty-first-century intervention. In 2004, the eighty-four-year-old Edwin Morgan marked his appointment as Scots Makar or National Poet by translating this poem. A committed Scottish nationalist and internationalist, Morgan, who had been a professor of English literature at Glasgow University, argued that the claims made for Baston's poetic eminence 'may not seem too absurd if we remember that he antedated Hoccleve and Gower, Lydgate and Langland: what rivals could he have in 1314?'[9] Certainly in England it fell to the fourteenth-century minor poet Laurence Minot to complain about the 'skottes . . . ful of gile' who had defeated 'king Edward' at 'bannok burn', leaving Minot only to hope that 'at the last Edward sall haue al his will'.[10] Edwin Morgan presents Baston's dark account of slaughter as 'a "horrors of war" poem'. The twenty-first-century version catches a good deal of the original Latin's alliteration and onomatopoeia which are scattered 'sometimes recklessly but often most effectively'.

Hic rapit, hic capit, hic terit, hic ferit. Ecce dolores!
Vox tonat, es sonat, hic ruit, hic luit. Arta modo ores!
What snatching and catching, what bruising and broostling, what
    grief!
What warhorns and warnings, what winding and wirrying, no
    relief![11]

However stylised, Baston's verses give every appearance of emanating from an eye-witness. Mentioning England's wish for 'domination' in the 'double realm' of Britain, Baston does present Robert Bruce as an inspiring orator, but the captured English poet never uses words such as 'freedom' or 'liberty', which are prominent in Scottish accounts of the conflict. He shows how before the battle the English soldiers 'spent the night drinking, bragging how they'd bring down the Scots'. Yet on the first day of fighting, concealed pits in the ground dug by Scottish 'plebs' (Baston uses that Latin word) trap the English cavalry; their horses are impaled on wooden stakes hidden within. By the second day of the conflict 'pain' is piled on pain and the amazed invading force finds itself thrown and mown down in a gory humiliation that reduces the English poet to proclaiming his own sense of traumatised numbness. Bannockburn for Baston is a military disaster. His poem invokes the concept of 'tragedea' – tragedy.[12] The intended victory song is a jeremiad of carnage.

Other poems, too, dealt with the battle. Authored and assembled by monk and historian Walter Bower, and drawing on the fourteenth-century Latin *Chronica Gentis Scotorum* of John of Fordun as well as on further texts now lost, the prose *Scotichronicon* includes extracts from a substantial poem by 'Bernard abbot of Arbroath', a Benedictine monk who served as chancellor to King Robert Bruce from 1308 until 1328. Rhetorically skilled and one of the king's most trusted advisers, Bernard is likely to have been present with Bruce on the battle-field. In Bower's Latin *Scotichronicon* the English king is deter-mined not just to kill Bruce and his supporters but 'to remove their memory from the land'. Edward seeks 'perpetual empire' ('perpetue imperio') over the Scots; like the work of his literary supporters, his military campaign aims to control not just ter-ritory but national memory. The *Scotichronicon* is written to strengthen Scottish resistance to English *imperium*; famously its concluding colophon comments, 'Christ! He is not a Scot who is not pleased with this book!' The work's modern editor, D. E. R. Watt, explains that Bower 'intends to show that the spirit which animated Scots during the Wars of Independence was characteristic of their entire history': Scotland and independence are one.[13]

The *Scotichronicon* circulated in various medieval manuscripts and this 'monumental' production's 'impact' was 'tremendous'.[14] A lover of poetry and of imaginative literary craft, Bower attempts to write Bannockburn into national memory, making it 'an example of destruction' as far as the proud English imperialist Edward is concerned, and more generally a mirror ('speculum') to warn kings and princes. With literary artistry that might be regarded appropriately in terms of a large-scale processional tapestry, Bower presents Edward and his invading army as dauntingly imposing, yet also (Bower has just cited Old Testament examples of hubris) potentially overweening:

> So the king of England advanced in pomp with his forces with an abundance of supplies for them. He arranged also for the collection of herds of cattle, and flocks of sheep and of pigs beyond number, corn and barley with portable mills for supplying the army, and wine in large jars and casks. Gold and silver, golden and silver vessels and every kind of precious furnishings he took from the king's treasury. He himself set out with his attendants, his vehicles and wagons, carts and horsemen, slingers and archers, crossbowmen and men-at-arms, with their ingenious pieces of equipment for besieging castles such as petraries and mattocks, trebuchets and mangonels, ladders and engines, pavilions and awnings, slings and cannons, and other engines of war, while trumpets and horns rang out so that every district which they reached became fearful with frightened dread. So like locusts they covered the surface of the entire land until they reached Bannockburn.[15]

After arranging to have the English hordes reconnoitered, Bower's Bruce, like Baston's, has his men dig camouflaged pits in the ground with sharp stakes fixed in them – an effective tactic against warriors on horseback. Yet the monk Bower directs more attention to King Robert's piety than to his tactics. Passing over Bruce's excommunication by the Pope several years before for murdering John Comyn, Bower shapes his narrative so as to highlight the advice that Bruce at Bannockburn gives his men before battle 'to make confession and hear masses devoutly, and that they should all take communion in the sacrament of the body of Christ, and put their trust in God alone'. At this pious point Bower intensifies his narrative by supplying his most extended quotation from the Latin poetry of 'the said Abbot Bernard', who writes of how, at first light, masses were celebrated on the advice of the king, who then addressed his troops. Where Baston avoided mentioning 'liberty', in all Scottish accounts of Bannockburn it is freedom that is the writers' predominant theme. So, here, in Bernard's poem Robert Bruce orates benignly to his men 'pro libertatis honore', for the honour of liberty:

> O leaders, my people, true lovers
> Of liberty – for which the royalty
> Of Scotland has suffered, and offered
> Its sufferings to God – we have had,
> Here, eight arduous years,
> Fighting, remember, for our right
> To the kingdom, for integrity, for liberty.[16]

Abbot Bernard's Bruce speaks in verse of a foe who has commanded the extinction of Scotland, and 'does not believe we can offer resistance'. Yet, calling upon 'the Lord', Bruce emphasises that the first day of battle is the birthday of John the Baptist. As well as St Andrew, he invokes St Thomas Becket of Canterbury (dedicatee of Bernard's abbey at Arbroath) and 'the saints of Scotland' – all of whom the Scottish king sees as fighting 'today for the honour of the people, with Christ in the vanguard'. His rhetoric rouses wholehearted commitment.[17]

It is highly unlikely that the king on the battlefield, maintaining God was on his side, addressed his troops in elaborate Latin verse. Yet the *Scotichronicon*'s use of poetry attributed to Bernard of Arbroath and others brings us as close as we are likely to get to Bruce's military incitements. Like Baston's poem such verse marks the rhetoricisation of Bannockburn. It suggests, even before the battle is fought, that verbal artistry matters; and the *Scotichronicon* makes clear that, after the physical clash is over, victory too is bound up with oratory and poetry. Whatever else it may be, Bannockburn is a written triumph.

The *Scotichronicon* presents several Bannockburns: the prose account comes with three significant poems, each offering a different take. As well as Baston's verse and that attributed to Bernard of Arbroath, there is a further substantial poem in end-rhymed Latin couplets hymning God, praising Bruce and giving an account of the battle. This work, too, is very alert to the power of crafted language:

> Anglica, que plenis promebas cantica venis,
> sume sub hiis plenis Jeremie consona trenis.

> England, who used to sing full-blooded songs,
> Smitten, your Jeremiads will be sung.[18]

Other Latin verses from Wales and Ireland festoon Bower's narrative. There are so many poems that the chronicler seems to have been uncertain how to fit them all in. Bower relished poetry, knowing it could heighten his chronicle's rhetorical tone; earlier he also quotes two poems about William Wallace. But nowhere does so much verse crowd his narrative as when he deals with Bannockburn. His chronicle establishes the 1314 victory as spiritedly literary.

The Declaration of Arbroath

The earliest Bannockburn writings belong to the same rhetorical climate that powers the 1320 document now most commonly known by its post-medieval title, the Declaration of Arbroath. Itself included in the *Scotichronicon* and addressed in the names of the Scottish nobility, this formal plea was sent to Pope John XXIII not long after he had excommunicated Bruce for recapturing the town of Berwick from the English. Like some of the *Scotichronicon*'s Bannockburn verse, the Declaration of Arbroath has been attributed to Bruce's chancellor, Bernard of Arbroath. To this day it remains the most famous piece of Scottish political rhetoric, its ringing sentiments a consequence of the writing of Bannockburn.

For all that the letter is dated from the north-east Scottish coastal town of Arbroath on 6 April 1320, it may have been authored earlier and elsewhere. Nonetheless, its tone, tenor and detailed phrasing would need to have been officially sanctioned. That alone signals why it is so fully consonant with the poetry attributed to Bernard in the *Scotichronicon*. Its most famous passage, like the speech of Bruce in Bernard's poem, exalts the cause of liberty in the face of English imperialism, stating with regard to the victor of Bannockburn:

> Quem si ab inceptis desisteret, Regi Anglorum aut Anglicis nos aut Regnum nostrum volens subicere, tanquam Inimicum nostrum et sui nostrique Juris subuersorem statim expellere niteremur et alium Regem nostrum qui ad defensionem nostram sufficeret faceremus. Quia quamdiu Centum ex nobis viui remanserint, nuncquam Anglorum dominio aliquatenus volumes subiugari. Non enim propter gloriam, diuicias aut honores pugnamus sed propter libertatem solummodo qum Nemo bonus nisi simul cum vita amittit.

> Yet if he should give up what he has begun, and agree to make us or our kingdom subject to the king of England or the English, we should exert ourselves at once to drive him out as an enemy and a subverter of his own rights and ours, and make some other man who was well able to defend us our king; for, as long as but a hundred of us remain alive, never will we on any conditions be brought under English rule. It is in truth not for glory, nor riches, nor honours that we are fighting, but for freedom – for that alone, which no honest man gives up but with life itself.[19]

Striking for rhetorical power and constitutional resolution, these sentences show that the letter's signatories, the Scottish barons, were willing to depose Bruce if he did not defend Scottish liberty. Some commentators detect here 'a nationalist theory of popular sovereignty', but R. James Goldstein argues 'that the king would hardly have accepted a republican form of government able to depose him at the will of the community of the realm'.[20] Goldstein also indicates how unstable was baronial support. Five of the many barons whose seals were attached to the letter were charged with treason just months after it was sent. Yet it is easy to understand how, encouraged by the course of Scottish politics and literature, the Declaration of Arbroath came to be interpreted as a proto-democratic manifesto. Its suggestion of an elected leader can be read as anticipating aspects of the Renaissance political thought of George Buchanan. Writing of Scottish rules of kingship, Buchanan would manifest some republican sympathies, and his work would be reprinted in America in the years leading up to the American Revolution. However, the Arbroath petition in 1320 was a campaigning document emanating from an unstable society, and its author or authors could not be sure if they would be on the winning side.

One indication of this may lie in the way the Declaration's rhetoric is boosted by phrasing from the ancient historian Sallust's *Bellum Catilinae*, an account of a first-century BC rebellion against the rule of Rome.[21] In his narrative of Catiline's rebellious conspiracy against the Roman authorities, Sallust includes a declaration of the ideals for which the rebels fight: 'None of us has been allowed, in accordance with the usage of our forefathers, to enjoy the protection of the law and retain our personal liberty.' The example is cited of 'the commons themselves' ('ipsa plebes') who have in the past 'taken up arms and seceded from the patricians': this does have a certain popular revolutionary ring to it, and, in the much later context of 1320 Scotland, prompts the thought that Sallustian language of republicanism does indeed become part of this iconic literary representation of Scottish freedom. Sallust writes,

> At nos non imperium neque divitias petimus, quarum rerum causa bella atque certamina omnia inter mortalis sunt, sed libertatem, quam nemo bonus nisi cum anima simul amittit.

> But we ask neither for power nor for riches, the usual causes of war and strife among mortals, but only for freedom, which no true man gives up except with his life.[22]

The phrasing of 1320 is very close to this, though the medieval writer, surely aware he is addressing the Pope, has substituted 'vita' (life) for 'anima' (the soul) in suggesting what a true man is willing to forfeit for freedom. Strikingly, the Sallustian context is that of a rebellion which eventually ends in terrible failure. The medieval Scottish writer's echo may be intended as deliberate allusion, implying he accepts that the apparently high ideals of Bruce's cause, too, could end disastrously. If the passage is simply an opportunistic echo, it is still revealing that the author of the Arbroath Declaration, shaping his phrases in the midst of a struggle whose outcome was far from clear, was attracted to this particular Classical passage for his most ringing rhetorical effect.

Seemingly picking up on Bruce's emphasis in his Bannockburn speech as versified by Bernard of Arbroath, the Declaration, issued just six years later, draws on Sallust to continue the same resonant theme. Its emphasis is very much on 'Regnum nostrum' (our kingdom), on rights, and on fighting 'propter libertatem' (for freedom). Attuned to the rhetoric of Bannockburn, the Declaration of Arbroath resonates, also, alongside the greatest of all the medieval poems that popularised such ideals in the vernacular. Becoming the central source for many generations of historians' accounts of the battle, *The Bruce* continued the writing of Bannockburn and further mythologised King Robert Bruce as an emblem of Scottish independence.

Barbour's *Bruce*

Walter Bower knew the monumental poem *The Bruce*, but it was far too long to include in his *Scotichronicon*. He pays tribute to King Robert's 'cheerful and indomitable spirit' and his 'victories and battles', but does not enumerate these 'because Master John Barbour archdeacon of Aberdeen has made the case adequately in our mother tongue about his several deeds with eloquence and brilliance, and with elegance too'.[23] Bower implies that Barbour's verse account of Bruce is familiar. Rather than giving a very detailed account of the battle of Bannockburn itself, he writes simply, 'For an account of the marvellous fashion and glorious form of the victory in that battle see the book about the said lord King Robert which the archdeacon of Aberdeen composed in the mother tongue.'[24]

The 'mother tongue' was the Scots vernacular. Yet the book-length poem by John Barbour (c. 1325–1395) is only one among many which sang Bruce's praises in the fourteenth century; and not all were written in Scots. A Latin epitaph, composed sometime after Bruce's burial at Dunfermline Abbey in 1329, praises

King Robert's verbal eloquence, and presents a long litany of comparators fit for a king:

> Begotten of Priam, like Achilles the leader of the Greeks,
> Praiseworthy as Ajax, many-talented like Ulysses,
> Beloved as the Macedonian, like Arthur a jewel among men,
> A leader of the peoples, a Maccabeus for intelligence.

This last comparison was often used of Bruce, a king of cleverness as well as of killing. His flowing Latin epitaph looks not just to his greatest victory, but also towards songs about it:

> In good order the king of Scots brings his standard forth,
> Fighting mightily he bears it through a thick-packed host.
> To boundless praise he triumphs mightily over the foe,
> And sent him homewards, the English king, as our new lyric goes.[25]

Though in translation those words 'sent him homewards' sound disconcertingly like a quotation from the twentieth-century anthem 'Flower of Scotland', the medieval 'new lyric' mentioned here is long lost to us. So are other works glorifying Bruce, including one mentioned by the French chronicler Jean de Bel, who makes reference to an 'hystoire faitte par le dit roy Robert' about the Scottish king's deeds.[26] Historians may lament these vanished sources. From the standpoint of literary imagination they simply confirm a medieval cornucopia of Bannockburns, the greatest and most lasting of which is that of Barbour's *Bruce*.

Eventually divided into twenty books, with Bannockburn at its centre, Barbour's huge poem seems to have been composed with the encouragement of Bruce's grandson, King Robert II. It glorifies that king's heroic ancestor by fusing truthful historiography ('suthfastnes') with the 'romanys' genre and exalting 'chevalry'. Barbour wrote when eye-witnesses to Bannockburn were still alive. Yet he relished, too, heroic medieval romances about Alexander the Great and figures from the Arthurian cycle. Protesting the truthfulness of his matter, while hinting at his taste for fiction, his opening lines show him operating on a borderline between textual poetry and oral tradition. He likes verse that will appeal not just to readers but to hearers.

Storys to rede ar delatibill	*enjoyable*
Suppos that thai be nocht bot fabill,	*nothing but fables*
Than suld storys that suthfast wer	*should; true*
And thai war said on gud maner	
Have doubill plesance in heryng.	*hearing*
The first plesance is the carpyng,	*recitation*
And the tother the suthfastnes	
That schawys the thing rycht as it wes,	*shows*
And suth thyngis that ar likand	*appealing*
Till mannys heryng ar plesand.[27]	*man's*

Bonding the textual to the acoustic, Barbour also grants himself a certain licence in presenting his heroes, Robert the Bruce and his friend Sir James Douglas – 'Off thaim I think this buk to ma[ke]'; in so doing, this 'makar' (poet) alerts us to the artistic 'making' necessary to any piece of good writing.

Where the Latin epitaph named Bruce alongside Classical heroes, Barbour, though focused on the Scottish Wars of Independence, sets the Scottish king in the milieu of medieval courtly romance. Several times the makar claims both the structural elasticity and the conventional allure of the romance genre: 'Lordingis, quha likes [who like] for till her [hear], / The romanys now begynnys her[e].'[28] Periodic invocation of romance as an undergirding genre heightens the vividness of Barbour's historical account. When Bruce stabs Comyn, his rival for the Scottish crown, in church, the narrative voice censures the hero, but also alludes to conventions 'in romanys'.[29] Asides referring to quite elaborate details about 'Duk[e] Betys' and 'Gaudifer' in the French *Roman d'Alixandre* suggest Barbour has in mind a sophisticated audience, perhaps that of Robert II's court. Elsewhere he interpolates a passage mentioning a 'Nygramansour' (a worker of black magic) from Guillaume le Breton's French Latin chronicle.[30] Sections such as the opening of Book Five of the poem, with its set-piece about spring blossoms on trees, and the 'syngyng' of 'byrdis' heralding a voyage made by 'the nobill king', are drawn from the standard lexicon of medieval courtly verse.[31] Often historians treat Barbour's *Bruce* as if it were a chronicle. Freighted with history, it is also a product of literary imagination.

Barbour's King Robert has his own taste for romances. While

being rowed across Loch Lomond, he entertains his companions by recounting the 'Romanys off worthi Ferambrace'– a tale from stories of resolute 'chevalry' associated with the French monarch Charlemagne.[32] On another occasion Barbour weaves into his Bruceian narrative 'Suth' (truth) about the Classical hero Tydeus as retold in the French *Roman de Thèbes*.[33] Skilfully weaving together historiography and poetic priorities, *The Bruce* draws on several genres including romance, chronicle and the ancient tradition of 'advice to princes'. Sally Mapstone has shown that this last genre underpins a great deal of the Older Scots literary corpus.[34] It presents uplifting examples of conduct for monarchs. Robert Bruce, though on occasion fallible, emerges as a paragon of chivalric kingship. In an age riven with aristocratic plots and counter-plots, his robust, courtly friendship with Sir James Douglas serves as a model of military loyalty.

However imaginative, Barbour's large-scale, romance-inflected account does develop themes important to surviving official documents. Its most famous passage, often presented as a free-standing extract 'In praise of Freedom', picks up on that Sallustian 'libertas' which marked the rhetorical high-point of the Declaration of Arbroath. Such continuities confirm Roger Mason's argument that 'the Latin *libertas* and its vernacular equivalents *liberty* and *freedom* were keywords in the political vocabulary of late medieval Scots [. . .] it was the value of freedom – and freedom as a value – that the Scottish *mythomoteur* served above all else to extol and underwrite'.[35]

Yet Barbour's universalising praise of liberty opens with a wistfully exclaimed monosyllabic 'A!', suggesting that freedom may be exhaustingly elusive. This imaginatively crafted aspect of the poet's libertarian paean gives it its peculiar, lasting resonance. It also led to its being written up as a 'permanent text' on the blackboard of an Edinburgh school during the years of the Second World War. The teacher of the young Archie Duncan (who went on to become a friend of the modern *Scotichronicon* editor, D. E. R. Watt, and then to edit Barbour's *Bruce*) asked his class to memorise these lines in the early 1940s.[36]

A! Fredome is a noble thing
Fredome mays man to haiff liking.   *allows; contentment*
Fredome all solace to man giffis,
He levys at es that freely levys.   *ease; lives*
A noble hart may haiff nane es
Na ellys nocht that may him ples
Gyff fredome failyhe, for fre liking   *without freedom*
Is yharnyt our all other thing.   *desired; over*
Na he that ay has levyt fre
May nocht knaw weill the propyrte
The angyr na the wrechyt dome   *condition*
That is couplyt to foule thyrldome,   *thralldom*
Bot gyff he had assayit it.   *But if*
Than all perquer he suld it wyt,   *perfectly; know*
And suld think fredome mar to prys   *more; prize*
Than all the gold in warld that is.[37]

During the Second World War this was not anachronistic, but inspiring. In the immediate medieval context of Barbour's poem, terms in the passage just quoted are picked up on by Bruce addressing his forces before Bannockburn. His pre-battle oratory invokes 'our fredome' and 'our land', repeating the word 'fredome' several times as well as outlining the dangerous possibility of 'threldome'.[38] Yet it is the poem's earlier paean, beginning 'A! Fredome' and articulated not by Bruce but by the overall narrative voice, that has caught the imagination of generations of readers. It has served both as a great articulation of the ideal of Scottish independence and, globally, an idealisation of freedom all the keener for its insistent sense of being menaced.

These famous lines early in *The Bruce* set up not just Bannockburn, but Bruce's whole career as indissoluble from liberty. Across the centuries Barbour's words and ideology have continued to resonate. James Goldstein sees *The Bruce* as 'arguably the most impressive work of national ideology produced in Scotland before the novels of Sir Walter Scott'.[39] Today the core narrative of Barbour's poem, that of Bannockburn, is better known than the plot of any of Scott's novels. If there is a canon of battles, Barbour more than anyone else makes the Scots' victory at Bannockburn, perceived as a great national assertion of freedom, utterly canonical. He does for this 1314 victory what Shakespeare would do later for the English triumph at Agincourt.

Throughout hundreds of lines of verse Barbour sets out the battle in great detail. He shows at early-morning mass men 'That thocht to dey [die] in that melle / Or than to mak thar contre fre'; he explains troop movements and Bruce's strategic cleverness.[40] Readers see the Scottish king attacked at full tilt by English knight Henry de Bohun. Bruce avoids de Bohun's blow. Standing upright in his stirrups, he strikes so vigorously with his 'ax [. . .] hard and gud' that he cleaves through de Bohun's helmet and skull: a gift to later illustrators.[41] Military historians have pored over just what happened where and when; Barbour portrays England's 'drownyt hors and men' – and the rabble of Scots youths who 'slew thaim doun foroutyn [without] mercy'. Throughout, he shows Bruce to be an inspirational leader able to converse with 'Bath mar and les commonaly' – both highborn and low together. Without downplaying the carnage, Barbour humanises Bruce even as he renders him heroic.

This process continues throughout the poem. So, for instance, Bruce holds up the progress of his entire army so that a laundrywoman can give birth. In a poem where freedom seems to belong exclusively to men, and to noblemen at that, this short, female-accented passage is all the more striking. It speaks volumes for Bruce as a king that he is ready to attend to the needs of the humblest of his followers, simply because he 'has hard [heard] a woman cry'. After relating how the monarch waits with his army until this laundrywoman's child is born, Barbour emphasises the episode's significance.

This wes a full gret curtasy	*great courtesy*
That swilk a king and sa mychty	*such; so mighty*
Gert his men dwell on this maner	*made*
Bot for a pouer lauender.[42]	*poor laundrywoman*

This passage has the effect of a folktale, or an incident from a romance. If Bruce's praise of valour in Book Six or his urging on his troops in the cause of freedom in Book Twelve confirms his kingly virtue, then so does this story about the laundress from Book Sixteen. Escapologist, fighter, friend and considerate leader, Bruce becomes, too, an incarnation of Scotland's unquenchable desire for liberty.

Barbour's Bruce is heroic not least in his friendship with Sir James Douglas, termed 'the Black Douglas' for his swarthy complexion. Towards the end of the poem, Barbour tells how after Bruce's death it is Douglas who carries the king's heart inside a silver container onto the battlefield on a crusade. Much earlier, when the two friends are reunited after each has feared the other has been killed, there is great mutual weeping. The makar goes out of his way to explain that this is a particular kind of manly crying – not the sort of weeping sometimes indulged in by 'wemen, that can wet / Thair chekys quhenever thaim list with teris [whenever they like with tears]'.[43] Tender, but not effeminate, then, Barbour's valorous Bruce is never the 'semivir' (half-man) reproached by the famous William Wallace elsewhere in the *Scotichronicon*.[44]

Yet, as Goldstein and others have emphasised, Barbour's victor of Bannockburn is very much an artistically crafted figure. The poet simply avoids discussing why the younger Bruce had supported England's King Edward I, the notorious 'Hammer of the Scots'. In completely omitting Wallace, *The Bruce* may have been designed to counter the allure of that hero. If so, it failed. Already acclaimed, Wallace's story would come to be so bound up with that of Bruce that the nature of Bruceian symbolism and even the meaning of Bannockburn would be recast.

Blind Hary's *Wallace*

Something of the way the victor of Bannockburn was redefined can be sensed in an influential passage (perhaps 'a traditional tale') inserted into Walter Bower's *Scotichronicon*.[45] Bower presents an encounter between Bruce and Wallace, the earliest account of whom (in the mid-fourteenth-century *Gesta Annalia* II) links Wallace with 'all who were in bitterness of spirit and weighed down [. . .] under the unbearable domination of English despotism'.[46] Bower's Bruce and Wallace meet just after Wallace's defeat at the 1298 battle of Falkirk. This meeting is probably a work of literary imagination, but does encapsulate dramatically struggles within the Scottish leadership. In the longer term, it helped establish a *topos* attuned to that facet of the Declaration of Arbroath which later interpreters, rightly or wrongly, saw as gesturing towards aspects of popular sovereignty.

The Bruce in Bower's post-Falkirk encounter is not the fighter for Scottish independence at Bannockburn but a Scot still loyal to England's king. This earlier, pro-English Bruce is glossed over by Barbour. In Bower's text, however, after Falkirk, Bruce calls across a steep glen to Wallace, 'asking him who it was that drove him to such arrogance as to seek to fight in opposition to the exalted power of the king of England and of the more powerful section of Scotland'. Wallace's reply, eloquent alike in Latin and English, is a reproach to a Bruce seen as having betrayed the cause of Scottish liberty:

> 'Robert, Robert, it is your inactivity and womanish cowardice that spur me to set authority free in your native land. But it is an effeminate man even now, ready as he is to advance from bed to battle, from the shadow into the sunlight, with a pampered body accustomed to a soft life feebly taking up the weight of battle for the liberation of his own country, the burden of the breastplate – it is he who has made me so presumptuous perhaps even foolish, and has compelled me to attempt or seize these tasks.'[47]

With its opening exasperated repetition (in Latin 'O Roberte, Roberte'), this speech portrays a king lacking in virility and needing to be incited by his subject Wallace to lead the struggle for Scotland's freedom. The encounter was soon amplified by later writers, including the author of the mid-fifteenth-century *Liber Pluscardensis*.[48] Bower's equation of manliness with a strong sense of national liberty will characterise much future nationalist discourse, running, sometimes problematically, as far as nineteenth-century fiction and even *Braveheart*; but it is surprising to see Bruce in this early fifteenth-century narrative being taunted as a 'semivir' lacking masculine commitment.

Here Wallace, the acclaimed head of a popular move-ment, emerges as the power behind the throne. He is the 'dux Scotorum' (leader – or sometimes 'guardian' – of the Scots), as he is first introduced in the *Scotichronicon*.[49] Without Wallace's efforts, this narrative implies, the victory at Bannockburn would have been impossible. As in influential later literary reimaginings, Wallace converts Bruce to the cause of Scottish independence. He does not dispute Bruce's right to kingship, but highlights the way Bruce has abused that.

Dead almost a decade before Bannockburn, Wallace had been praised in popular poems and songs ('carmina' Bower calls them) from at least the early fourteenth century.[50] The minor poet Andrew of Wyntoun (c. 1355–1422) wrote about Wallace in his late-fourteenth-century *Orygynale Cronykil of Scotland*:

Off his guid deidis and his manheid	*Of his good deeds*
Gret gestis and sangis ar maid;	*Great gestes and songs*
Bot yit sa mony, I trow nocht,	*do not believe*
As he in his dais wrocht.	

Wyntoun goes on to speculate that

Quha his worschip all wald write,	*Who*
He suld a mekle buke endite;	*long book write*
And all his deidis to write in heire	
Thareto I want wit and laysere.[51]	*leisure*

Almost as if spurred by these words, the sophisticated poet nicknamed 'Blind Hary' composed a Wallace poem around the 1470s, splicing older, popular materials together into one extended heroic narrative to counterbalance Barbour's *Bruce*.[52] Tellingly, the sole manuscript copy of Hary's poem ('Advocates MS 19.2.2') survives inscribed in single columns on 124 vellum leaves transcribed by John Ramsay in 1488 and now in the National Library of Scotland. Formerly it was bound together with Ramsay's 1489 manuscript transcription of Barbour's *Bruce*. The bonding of these poems and their heroes was emblematic. Not only Bruce but also Wallace came to be seen as foundational to the writing of Bannockburn.

Anne McKim, its twenty-first-century editor, points out that Hary's *Wallace* is designed in part 'to incite hatred of the English in his readers'.[53] A fanatical, no-holds-barred defence of independence, *The Wallace*, like the work of Bower, Barbour and other Scottish writers of the period, deals 'not just with the lives of rulers and their narrow circle of supporters but the collective life of the Scottish nation'.[54] Authored after many decades of warfare, Hary's poem was made to quicken the cause of Scottish freedom in a period when some, including Scotland's King James III, may have been inclined, out of pragmatism and relative weakness, to accept English overlordship. Probably the poem, whose sole surviving manuscript witness dates from just after King James IV's accession to the throne, succeeded in its aim: James IV went on to resist the determination of England's Henry VIII to crush Scotland. Yet, disastrously for Scottish independence, James's resistance was put to the test at the 1513 battle of Flodden where the Scottish monarch and many of his nobility perished.

In such circumstances of loss, Hary's bloodily patriotic, metrically resourceful work grew increasingly popular. Sophisticatedly, its author claims to follow a Latin biography of his hero by the surely fictitious John Blair. Clearly Hary knows not only Chaucer's *Troilus and Criseyde* and *Canterbury Tales* but also Barbour's *Bruce*. He alludes, too, to medieval authorities including the philosopher Boethius and the heroic French romances of Charlemagne, Arthur and Alexander. The Scottish poet has absorbed chronicles by Wyntoun, Bower and Froissart. Yet from its opening lines his *Wallace* trumpets its unflinching political slant: 'Our ald Ennemys cummyn of Saxonys blud, / That neuyr yeit to Scotland wald do gud.'[55]

The poem's interminable preoccupation with 'blud' involves, James Goldstein argues, 'a discourse of hatred of the Other'.[56] Nicola Royan admits that 'It is possible to read the *Wallace* as a racist text, for it dehumanizes the English as "Sotheron"'; yet the poem 'offers acute perspectives on Scottish nationhood, sharper than those of the more diffuse historiographers'.[57] Arguably the medieval epic character of the poem may make the modern terminology of racism somewhat anachronistic, but Hary's *Wallace* certainly mixes love of liberty with violent anti-Englishness. His Wallace seems 'a man divinely ordained to free Scotland from English oppression'.[58] Indeed, in a dream vision he is hailed by St Andrew, Scotland's patron saint, who gives the hero a special sword: an emblematic weapon in the iconography of Wallace until *Braveheart* and beyond. The dreaming Wallace then beholds a female visitant who tells him 'his destiny is to free Scotland from English oppression and to martyr himself for the nation'. Writing in 2011, Kylie Murray argues that this dream vision 'replaces the kingly genealogy so central to Scotland's independence, with a spiritual one, reflecting once more Wallace's role, which is powerful yet distinct from kingship'.[59]

Revealing his learning, Hary refers to Scottish royal genealogical myths and to 'Scwne' (Scone), where 'kingis was cround viii hundyr yer and mar'.[60] Yet his warring Wallace has a cartoon-hero quality, seeming as much the avenging superhero of a dark graphic novel as a figure of courtly romance. Not royal, but (despite his noble title) a man of the people, Wallace soon decides that there is less point in killing ordinary members – 'commounis' – of the occupying force than in going after 'thair Chiftanis'.[61] Linked to the Ayrshire of 'Cunyngayme and Kille [Kyle]', Wallace, scorned by his enemies as a mere 'king off Kyll', extends his campaigning to much of Scotland and northern England; at one point he even threatens London.[62]

While sometimes accurate, Hary's poem often reimagines history. It postpones, for instance, the battle of Falkirk by five years, and links Wallace to a battle at Loudon Hill in Ayrshire that was fought instead by Bruce. Hary's Wallace traverses Scotland, inflicting losses on English occupying forces. Historians might be tempted to credit these successes to other, now forgotten local resistance fighters, but in the poem they enhance Wallace's emblematic ruthlessness. So, in the seventh book of what post-medieval editors divide into a twelve-book poem, readers follow Wallace and his men as they slay English occupying forces and their collaborators. In the north of Scotland at 'Dwnottar' (Dunnottar) Wallace's fighters spill huge amounts of 'Sotheroun blud'.

Wallace in fyr gert set all haistely,	*[set all on fire]*
Bryn twp the kyrk, and all that was tharin.	*Burned up; therein*
Atour the roch the laiff ran with gret dyn.	*Around the rock the*
	rest
Sum hang on craggis rycht dulfully to de,	*crags; miserably*
Sum lap, sum fell, sum floteryt in the se.	*leapt; floundered*
Na Sotheroun on lyff was lewyt in that	*[was allowed to live];*
hauld,	*refuge*

And thaim with in thai brynt in powdir   *ashes*
cauld.[63]

Hary's vehemently Anglocidal hero may be merciless, but he
saves Scotland when even Bruce sides with the English 'contrar
his natiff men'.[64] In the poem's eighth book Wallace is invited to
take the crown; later we are told that he did so, but only for one
token day. This fundamentally unkingly aspect of Wallace is a
powerful source of his popular appeal. As the poet Alan Riach
puts it, 'He was common. He was / of the people.'[65] Hary's
Wallace may have obtained the power to 'gowern all Scotland',
but he acts only as guardian until her rightful king returns.[66]
Wallace's campaigning both upholds and serves as a stinging
reproach to the Scottish monarchy. Towards the end of Hary's
eighth book, Wallace even parleys with the English queen, who
seems attracted towards him. A skilled leader, he is capable of
sophistication and, invoking 'Sanct Androw', even, at times, of
piety.[67]

From one perspective this Wallace is every inch heroic. With
his 'Cler aspre Eyn [superlative eyes] lik dyamondis brycht'
he might have stepped straight from the pages of romance.[68]
Yet Hary's Wallace is no mere poetic ornament. He is an ideological force. As Hary daringly surpasses the barer outline in
the *Scotichronicon*, Wallace's absolute resolution leads him to
upbraid his king in steadfast terms. Hary's Wallace meets Bruce
'wpon Caroun syd' – on the banks of the River Carron – after
the pair have fought at Falkirk. In one of two encounters, which
the great scholar Sir William Craigie called 'perhaps the most
dramatic scenes in the whole of old Scots literature', Wallace
straightforwardly accuses Bruce of 'tresson':

In cursyt tym thow was for Scotland born.
Schamys thow nocht that thow neuir yeit   *Are you not ashamed*
    did gud,
Thow renygat deuorar off thi blud?[69]   *renegade devourer of*

Bruce tries to laugh off Wallace's 'ernystfulnas' (earnestness).
Soon, though, after battling on behalf of King Edward against
the Scots, Bruce omits to wash his bloody hands before eating,
and is taunted by a 'Sotheroun' lord: 'Behald, yon Scot ettis

[eats] his awn blud.' At this point Wallace's 'wordis' come back to Bruce with a vengeance, leading him to recommit himself to the Scottish cause and fight no more 'contrar Scots'.[70] Scotland remains 'in hard perplexite'. Yet readers and hearers of the poem can be confident Wallace has brought back to Scotland's defence the man whom he later calls 'worthi Bruce'.[71] Independence has been preserved.

Showing that Wallace remains true both to Bruce and to Scotland right to the end, Hary omits Wallace's torture at his London trial and execution; the poet invokes 'Master Barbour' in his final book, and his martyr-like hero makes possible future Scottish victory.[72] For all that the battle is never once mentioned, Blind Hary's implied future is manifestly Bannockburn. Wallace's sacrifice makes that victory possible.

Cartoonily ruthless, Blind Hary's *Wallace* also has an idealistic side. Though not a democratic work in any modern sense, its clear sympathy with Wallace produces a poem markedly inclined towards the popular, rather than simply the kingly, cause of freedom. This popular aspect of Hary's text helped make it much loved in a Scotland whose later monarchs seemed to have priorities very different from Scottish independence. *The Wallace* came to embody a spirit of popular resistance: a longing for the possibility of Bannockburn.

Renaissance legacies of Bruce and Wallace

For all its vitriolic Anglophobia and bloodiness, Blind Hary's *Wallace* is still capable of inspiring idealism. The American critic Elizabeth Walsh argued in 1984 that 'Wallace's struggle for freedom symbolizes not only Scotland's desire for political liberation, but every man's struggle to free himself from the tyranny of others.'[73] Throughout the very different times of the early sixteenth century, even those who thought in the wake of Flodden that Scotland might be wise to accept union with England could admire aspects of Hary's work. In 1521 the logician John Mair published his punningly titled *Historia majoris Britanniae tam Angliae quam Scotiae*: the title can mean 'History of Greater Britain, England and Scotland' or 'Mair's

History of Britain, England and Scotland'. Mair is the dry patron saint of the ideology of modern Britishness. His work seems angled to discourage Scottish independence, but its audience was small compared with that of Hary's poem, and today Mair is seldom remembered. Even he clearly regarded Hary as 'peritus' (skilled) in his use of folk materials. It was simply that this Glasgow professor, 'an unashamed advocate of union with England', did not believe them all.[74] The poet and his hero were unignorable, however. Mair and fellow Scottish historian Hector Boece apparently made use of aspects of Hary's Wallace in their accounts of that heroic leader. Mair likens Wallace to Hannibal or Ulysses, while John Bellenden, reworking Boece's work in 1536, styles Wallace a 'campion' (champion) of 'inuincible curage'.[75]

By Bellenden's time, printing had come to Scotland. Though only fragments survive in Glasgow and Cambridge, we know that Hary's *Wallace* was one of the first books printed with the types of Walter Chepman and Andrew Myllar in Edinburgh around 1509: a sure sign of the poem's marketability. The pioneering printers seem to have used a manuscript now lost: their version divides Hary's poem into eleven books, rather than the twelve in Ramsay's 1488 transcription. Chepman and Myllar's printing of the *Wallace* was part of a project of cultural nationalism. They also brought into print Scots poetry by Robert Henryson and by William Dunbar who lamented how death 'has Blind Hary and Sandy Traill / Slane with his schour of mortall haill'.[76] If Flodden curtailed aspects of the literary Renaissance in Scotland, preventing for many years the publication of Gavin Douglas's great pioneering translation of Virgil's *Aeneid* (completed in 1513), nonetheless the 1549 *Complaynt of Scotland* includes shepherds who recount stories about Wallace and Bruce.[77] Moreover, the Renaissance poet and historian George Buchanan continued to sing the praises of those heroes and the ideals of Scottish independence even as a 'British unionist ideology' was gathering pace, inviting Scots to accept 'dependent status within a redefined British imperial framework'.[78]

Republished for centuries in Latin and in English translation throughout Scotland, England and beyond, Buchanan's history of Scotland would be a standard school text for generations of Enlightenment Scots. From its sixteenth-century publication onwards it helped cement the image of Wallace not so much as an aristocrat but, with all his daring military 'Pranks', as a man of the people: a hero from 'an ancient and noble family, but one that have lived poorly and meanly, as having little or no Estate'.[79] Buchanan's interest in Wallace was of a piece with his concern with political theory. In *De Iure Regni apud Scotos Dialogus* (A Dialogue on the Law of Kingship among the Scots) as in his biblical drama *Baptistes* (The Baptist), Buchanan was fascinated by resistance to tyranny. Roger Mason indicates how Boece in his 1527 *Scotorum Historia* highlighted the Scots' 'restraint and overthrow of errant monarchs'; Buchanan followed his teacher John Mair in showing how Edward I's favourite for the Scottish kingship, John Balliol, was 'deposed by the nobility' of Scotland and replaced by Bruce. Buchanan insisted that, 'When our kings are publicly inaugurated, they give a solemn promise to the entire people that they will observe the laws, customs and ancient practices of our ancestors, and that they will adhere to that law which they have received from them.'[80] He went so far as to argue that Scottish kingship had been elective from its origins.

Buchanan's Protestant radical thinking was detested by his Scottish pupil, the future monarch of Britain, King James VI and I, who maintained in a sonnet that

> God giues not Kings the style of *Gods* in vaine,
> For on his throne his Scepter do they swey [. . .] [81]

Appalled by the Scottish Reformation's 'populaire tumulte and rebellion', which had led 'sum of our fyrie ministers [. . .] to fantasie to thame selfis a democratike forme of gouuernement', James warned against 'sicc infamouse inuectiues as buchananis or knokisis [Knox's] croniclis'.[82] He banned Buchanan's *History*, and it was the posthumous fate of the learned admirer of Wallace and Bruce to have his works proscribed or even burned on more than one occasion.

In England James's most famous subject, the dramatist associated with those actors known as the King's Men, authored a play whose wild, violent Scots' readiness to commit regicide results in shockingly bloody chaos: only the defeat of the wicked Macbeth who seeks to 'scour these English hence' from Scotland can restore order.[83] This drama about medieval Scottish murder clearly relates to the politics of the 1603 Union of the Crowns; *Macbeth* also comments more obliquely on Jacobean politics than did *The Tragedy of Gowrie*, which dealt with the attempted assassination of King James VI in Scotland in 1600 and was performed by Shakespeare's company in 1604 but banned almost immediately for its portrayal of the living monarch on the stage.[84] As John Kerrigan puts it in *Archipelagic English*, 'if Macbeth represents in some measure the forces in Scotland (and, indirectly, England) that were hostile to British union, Malcolme is an Anglicizer'.[85] While Kerrigan contends that '*Macbeth* helped pave the way for British colonialism in Ireland', thespians are not wrong to term this work 'the Scottish play'.[86] Shakespeare's complex, politically propagandistic drama recasts the historical Macbeth (who seems to have been a good king) in order to present Scotland as desperately needing English support: 'Gracious England' offers refuge and 'ten thousand men' to provide military backing for Malcolm as he quells the monstrous Scottish usurper.[87] The answer to MacDuff's famous question, 'Stands Scotland where it did?' is 'Alas, poor country! / Almost afraid to know itself!'[88] Confused, bloody and riven, *Macbeth*'s Scotland can be saved only through English-backed military intervention. *Macbeth* unwrites or over-writes Bannockburn, imposing a vision of a broken, treacherous kingdom crying out for English oversight. A theatrical triumph, it is also the most effective piece of literary propaganda directed against notions of Scottish independence.

Shakespeare's Scottish patron, the poet-king James, spent almost all of his life after 1603 in England. Pronouncing himself 'Kinge of Great Brittaine, France & Ireland', he advised against 'deuiding [. . .] Kingdomes'; Shakespeare's political message in *King Lear* is similar: better together.[89] For this dramatist of genius, English overlordship in Britain seems paramount: as generations of English kings had done before him, his Richard II even equates the whole 'sceptred isle' with 'England'.[90] Nothing could be further from the Scottish political ideology of Barbour's *Bruce* or Blind Hary's *Wallace*.

In his *History of Scotland*, Buchanan had again presented the Scottish kingship, including the rule of the victor at Bannockburn, as dependent on the will of the community. Bruce was admirable, not least, in having been guided by Wallace. Though loyal to the Scots king, Buchanan's '*Wallace* was proclaimed *Regent* by the tumultuous Band that followed him, and so he managed things as a lawful Magistrate, and the Substitute of *Baliol* [the king who preceded Bruce]. He accepted of this Name; not out of any Ambition or Desire to rule, but because it was a Title given him by his Countrymen out of pure Love and Good-will.'[91] Drawing on Bower, and aware of Blind Hary, Buchanan gives the encounter between Wallace and Bruce on the banks of the River Carron after the battle of Falkirk a classic and dramatic formulation:

> They two alone stood over against one another, where the River hath the narrowest Channel, and the highest Banks: And first *Bruce* began, and told *Wallace, He wondred what was in his Mind, that, being hurried on by the uncertain Favour of the Vulgar, he should expose himself to such assiduous and imminent Danger against a King, the most potent of that Time, and who was also assisted by a great Number of the* Scots; *and that to no purpose neither, for if he overcome* Edward, *the* Scots *would never grant him the Kingdom; and if himself were overcome, he had no Refuge but in the Mercy of his Enemy.* To whom *Wallace* reply'd, *I never proposed any such End of my Labours, as to obtain the Kingdom, of which my Fortune is not capable, neither doth my Mind aspire so high: But when I saw my Countrymen, by your Slothfulness (to whom the Kingdom doth rightfully appertain) destitute of Governors, and exposed not to the Slavery only, but even to the Butchery of a cruel Enemy, I had pity on them, and undertook the Cause which you deserted; neither will I forsake the Liberty, Good, and Safety of my Countrymen, till Life forsake me: You, who had rather chuse base Servitude with Security, than honest Liberty with Hazard, follow, and hug the Fortune which you so highly esteem: As for me, I will die free in my Country, which I have often defended; and my Love to it shall remain, as long as my Life continues.* Thus the Conference was broken off, and each of them retired to their forces.[92]

Buchanan presents this encounter between Wallace and Bruce with deft literary skill, using their meeting to further his ideal of a monarchy governed by the people. A passionate advocate of religious reformation, this great European poet of Renaissance

Scotland gives Wallace a potent eloquence. Though later he chronicles Bannockburn and writes of how 'The Fame of this Victory being divulged all over *Britain*, did not only abate the Fierceness of the *English*, but raised up the *Scots* even from an Extremity of Despair', it is through Wallace's 'conference' with Bruce that the determined spirit of Bannockburn is most forcefully expressed in Buchanan's prose.[93]

In Latin verse, though he did not write directly of Wallace and Bruce, Buchanan celebrated in a splendid epithalamium (here quoted in my English version) the virtue of Scottish independence.

> Though Roman clearances made others exiles
> Or slaves, Rome needed northern frontier walls
> To keep the Scots' axe-wielding warriors back.
> Stopped in its tracks, Rome faltered. Terminus,
> The Roman god, marks where Rome turned away
> Beside the River Carron [. . .][94]

Buchanan knew the Carron had been the location of a supposed encounter between Wallace and Bruce, as well as the site of a Roman temple to the deity Terminus. Yet he was keen also that Scotland should be regarded as part of Europe. His epithalamium for the marriage of Mary Queen of Scots to the French Dauphin refers to the traditional agreement between Scotland and France, often called the Auld Alliance, and hopes France and Scotland will go on to share a common government.[95] Building on an older tradition of Francophilia, Buchanan furthered a sense of Scotland's being pro-European, a political stance still invoked to this day.

After Buchanan's death, 1603 brought not a Franco-Scottish union but one between the Scottish and English thrones when James VI of Scotland became also James I of England. This British monarch, son of a famous Scottish Catholic queen, had grown up in a Scotland where Wallace and Bruce remained potent symbols throughout the decade following the Protestant reformation. The year 1570 had seen a new, Edinburgh-published edition of Hary's *Wallace*, celebrating 'The actis and deidis of the illuster and vailzeand campioun' who had, an added quatrain emphasises, 'fre[e]d this land' from 'thraldome'.[96] Printed by 'Robert Lekpreuik at the expensis of Henry Charteris', this 'Protestantised' text came from a partnership which would publish the first known printed version of Barbour's *Bruce* in 1571. Lekpreuik emended Hary's original so that in Book Seven the line, 'Pater Noster, Ave he said and Creed' becomes 'Pater Noster, he said, and als ane creid'; similarly, 'Our Lady' is changed to 'ane Lady', while the line, 'Modyr of Hym that all this warld has wrocht' is expunged.[97] Here was a publication fit to carry Wallace's assertion of Scottish independence forward among Reformation Protestants. Generally, this text usurped the Catholic original. Editions of the *Wallace* and the *Bruce* over the following 150 years saw the poets' names vanish from the title page, so these works appeared anonymous narratives from Scottish history. This reinforced a sense they conveyed the historical record, confirming their classic standing.

That status was boosted by Henry Charteris's Edinburgh-printed *Wallace* of 1594. Charteris had bankrolled Lekpreuik's edition. His own production has assured rhetorical flourish, its decorated title page boasting three Latin epigraphs from Cicero and one from Ovid. Listing ancient heroes from the biblical Samson and Jephthes (subject of a play by Buchanan) to Julius Caesar, Hannibal and Robert the Bruce, Charteris's introduction maintains that 'in vailzeantnes' Wallace is 'posteriour to nane'. During 1590s speculation about the future of the monarchy in England and Scotland, Charteris sets out the 'intricate questioun' of the medieval Scottish succession during the era of Bruce and Wallace. He indicates that the young Bruce refused Edward I's overlordship, but also states that Bruce later joined Edward as an 'enemie' to Scotland: before he matured into the victor of Bannockburn, Bruce had become 'mair cruel agains his awin, yan euer was Marcus Coriolanus against his natiue town of Rome'. Then he gives an account of Wallace, asserting that Wallace had learned 'this auld verse' from a priest,

Dico tibi verum, libertas optima rerum:
Nunquam servili sub nexu vivito fili.   That is
Libertie of all thingis best is, to the[e] I schaw,
My sons from servitude se thou the ay withdraw.

So Charteris links Wallace not just to liberty, but to poetry. His wise Wallace strives to sustain 'this [Scottish] commounwealth' among contending noblemen. A 'vailzeand Chiftane [. . .] tratourlie betrayit', Wallace must be defended against the 'schameful leis [lies] of Caxtoun' and other English historians who term him 'ane Tratour', despite his fighting to defeat 'Tyrannie'. Denouncing English accounts of Wallace ('The like has neuer bene hard sen [heard since] the beginning of the warlde'), Charteris ends by seeing him as sent by God to deliver his 'oppressed countrie'; the Renaissance printer is confident that if Scotland keeps faith with God and Wallace, then God who 'disponis Empyres [. . .] distributes kingdomis' and 'remuifis Natiounis' shall still 'not only rais vp ane Wallace, but mony'.[98] Scholarly, idealistic and writing just seven years after the execution of Mary Queen of Scots as well as at a time when there was growing speculation about what might lie in store for the constitutional future of Scotland and England, Charteris republishes in Edinburgh a work which speaks as much as any other about Scottish liberty. Charteris's successor, Robert Charteris, republished the poem in 1601, just two years before the union of the Scottish and English crowns.

After 1603, narratives about Wallace and Bruce grew even more popular, with a flurry of Scottish patriotic publishing. Still, George Brunsden astutely points out that in successive editions of the *Wallace* and 'the majority of editions of the *Bruce*' it is 'noticeable that the language gradually takes on a more English character': Scotland's language was no longer Middle Scots, and printers tried to take account of that while still sounding patriotic notes.[99] Andro Hart's 1611 Edinburgh edition of the *Wallace* follows Charteris in appending to its title page an epigraph from Cicero about giving one's life 'pro Republica', and in describing Wallace as 'Maintainer of the Libertie of SCOTLAND'. Such touches indicate less modern republicanism than a continuing wish to uphold the ancient freedom of the Scottish state even as Scotland's monarch had moved south to London. In England the poet Samuel Daniel might welcome 'Union', hymning 'Great Britain', and hoping there would be 'No Scot, no English now, nor no debate', while fellow poet Michael Drayton maintained 'That Scotch and English without difference be'; Ben Jonson, however, having praised the Union in a masque, went on to collaborate on the play *Eastward Ho* which clearly mocked the Scots.[100]

Keith Brown has shown how in the decades after 1603 'Britain gradually was subsumed into an English view of monarchy', despite the Stuart dynasty's Scottishness.[101] Hart's 1611 *Wallace* counterbalances this by upholding an older, non-monarchical, Scottish hero. According Wallace classic status, the Protestant version of Hary's poem now comes prefaced by Latin verses memorialising 'William Wallace, the most distinguished leader' ('Clarissimi Ducis Gulielmi Wallace').[102] Soon poet Patrick Gordon (claiming access to manuscript sources about Bruce now lost) presents King Robert as himself a poet with his own mantra of freedom who

> in his manie sorowfull discourses wold always repeat these verses following.
>
> Ni me Scotorum Libertas moveret
> Non mala tot paterer orbis ob Imperium.
> *Robertus Brusius*

With his own verses meaning 'Unless the Liberty of the Scots impelled me, / I could not endure so many evils at the hands of Empire', Bruce is presented as still very much part of Scottish culture: 'Theis verses written and subscribed with his owin hand in his Manuall book which he always careed about with him was extent within thes feew years.' Yet Gordon also regrets that older accounts containing 'owtworne barborous speichis' are now hard to comprehend. An admirer of the French poet Du Bartas, he seeks to add 'poetik floures' to his narrative.[103] Licensed for publication at St Andrews in late 1613, it was not published until 1615. Probably Gordon's *Famous Historie of the Renouned and Valiant Prince Robert surnamed the Bruce* was composed to celebrate the 300th anniversary of the 'wondrous straunge and dreadfull fight' at the place Gordon terms 'Bannochburne'. The battle narrative forms his volume's climax.

In rewriting Bannockburn, Gordon incorporates historical details; his Scots dig battlefield pits to wrong-foot the English cavalry. Yet, moving the conflict in the direction of romance, he uses the stanza form of Spenser's *Faerie Queen* as he praises the 'wise Lord' Bruce's wisdom and sets forth the drama of the clash in a poetic form perhaps more acceptable to English ears than the Scots-tongued couplets of Hary.[104] Conscious that, so soon after the 1603 Union, his poem might be read as hostile to the Scots' southern neighbours, Gordon argues that

> nether doe I therein wrong the *English* but rather to my power extolle their valour and with more mildness modifie that which our writers most sharplie haue wretin Thereby to extinguish (if it be posibill) the euil opinion that hath bein so long ingrestid in the hearts of manie by reading of those old historeis hoping yat this my work may haply mak thois that tretith of the sam mater to be forgotin by tyme being onlie desirous to steir vp euerie manes mind to the following of glorious actions.

So, perhaps a little unconvincingly, Gordon presents his verse Bannockburn not as a straightforward celebration of a victory against English imperialism, but as offering a pattern of glorious conduct and countering the anti-Englishness of earlier Scottish historians. Thinking of 'the number of the Kings discendit from the *Bruce*', he sees a lineage in which Bruce is 'the first and prince *Charles* the last'.[105] In this way he connects the victor of Bannockburn with Charles I, Britain's future monarch.

Bannockburn for Gordon becomes a battle that may offer later British royalty an exemplary chivalric pattern. Reprinted in 1718 and 1753, his knightly poem is quickened by battlefield bloodshed. As in Sir Philip Sidney's *Arcadia* there is a relishing of tableaux of slaughter. Gordon's Bannockburn has a mannered choreography, a baroque geometry of the fallen:

> Long foght the knights but neither side wold yield
> Equall their hope and equall was their feare
> Spears helms & swords were stroud through all the field
> Heads arms and legs by headless bodies wer:
> Some dieing look to heauin leans on their shield
> In deaths pane some blood from their wounds forth tear
> These ranks to marche reteir or chairge that minds
> Trods on the bodies of their slaughtered friends [. . .][106]

While Gordon's title page proclaims that he is presenting a 'Famovs Historie', several of the testimonial poems by other poets in the book suggest this work matters because it allows

'*forgottin* Bruce *obscurd so longe [. . .] to ryise againe victorious*'.[107] Certainly in Scotland there was renewed interest in
Bannockburn's hero. The year 1616 brought the Edinburgh publication by Andro Hart (also the publisher of Hary's *Wallace*) of
*The Actes and Life of the Most Victoriovs Conqverovr, Robert
Brvce, King of Scotland*. '*Newly corrected, and conferred
with the best* and most ancient Manuscripts', this was a text
in gothic type of Barbour's *Bruce*, presented as 'antique' and
therefore 'venerable', setting forth 'worthie actions' linked to
'our Antecestours in this Islle'. Such terminology in the printer's
preface again gives the work a British rather than a purely
Scottish orientation. Its Barbour belongs with 'ancient Poets
the *Bardes*, who wrote in verse the deedes of their most valiant
men'. Hart refers knowledgably to medieval sources including
the *Scotichronicon*; his Bruce is 'a man of Heroik spirit, [who]
refused absolutely to subject a free Realme to the seruitude of
any forraine Prince whomsoeuer' at a time when the Scots acted
'in esperance of liberty'.[108]

Presenting Barbour's poem as 'this Historie', Hart aligns
Bruce with heroes including Scipio and Charlemagne: '*Scotland*
will not forget this Prince, for she cannot.' Some may censure
the republished *Bruce* as 'hurtful, as embers of consumed
discord', but for Hart 'it is not the publishing of the simplicitie
of our predecessours that can diuide vs, or cause any discord,
but rather our owne too great subteltie, ambition & auarice'.
Hart sees the reading of Tacitus and 'of Secretar *Machiauell*'
as more likely than the *Bruce* to provoke 'ague in our state'.
Instead, he protests,

> I am perswaded that all men of sound minds wil rather abhorre
> discord in reading of these bookes, seeing what the miseries & hor-
> rible calamities these warres bring forth & what great occasion we
> of both Nations haue to magnifie Gods goodness, that in our daies
> since the Gospell hath bene in sinceritie published amongst vs, hath
> turned all these bloodie broyles into a peaceable Calme, especially
> now in the person of our dread Soueraigne.

The *Bruce*, then, exemplifies what the more recent 'paines taken
[. . .] by the wisest of both Nations, to knit this vnion' have
successfully overcome.[109] In an era when *Macbeth* and *The*

Tragedy of Gowrie staged the murderous Scottish past and *King Lear* showed the folly of a kingdom divided, even Barbour's Bannockburn could be subjected to Unionist spin.

If Hart's introductory prose seems rather at odds with the verse that follows, there is another revealing discrepancy between preface and poem: though Barbour's *Bruce* nowhere even mentions Wallace, Hart devotes a considerable part of his introductory remarks to chronicling this hero 'of Noble and ancient Familie', who acted not out 'of desire to Empire, but onelie (like another SAMSON) vpon compassion and loue of his Countrie-people'. Then, in a passage that surely owes as much to Buchanan as Buchanan owes to the *Scotichronicon*, Hart (who also published some of Buchanan's work), recounts the meeting between Bruce and Wallace beside the Carron. Addressing Wallace, Hart's Bruce

> first said, he wondred at him, that being carried with the facile fauour of the people, would hazard himselfe in so many perils against a King most puissant of that age, athsted also with great support of Scots, & that without any hope of recompence of his paines: for albeit he vanquished *Edward*, the Scots would neuer allowe of him to be King, & if hee were ouerthrowen, hee had no refuge, but in the mercie of his enemie. To whom *Wallace* answered, I (said hee) neuer tooke these paines to purchase to my selfe a Kingdome, for that is vnagreable with my condition, and my minde couets it not, but seeing my Countriemen through your cowardice to whom the Realm of right appertaineth, destitute of Rulers, and hereby casten into their most cruel enemies hands, not onely in bondage & slauerie, but euen to the shambles, I pitied their cace, and haue enterprised the defence of their cause, forsaken by you, whose libertie I shall not forsake, before my life forsake me, & so the conference ended, either of both returning to their owne.[110]

At a time when James VI and I vehemently espoused the theory of the divine right of kings, this encounter between subject and monarch when the subject is so manifestly more noble and right than the king was all the more striking. Later Hart gives an account of Wallace's execution by the English king, remarking that

> This was the end of this most worthy mans life, who for high spirit in interprising dangers, for fortitude in execution comparable in

deede to the most famous Chiftanes amongst the Ancients, for loue to his natiue Countrie, second to none Hee only free, the rest slaues, could neither bee bought with benefits, nor compelled by force, to leaue the publike cause which he once profest.[111]

Hart's eulogy to Wallace, prefacing Barbour's Wallace-less poem, shows just how strongly the figures of Wallace and Bruce were now bonded. If Barbour's tale of Bruce was still regarded as the pre-eminent Bannockburn poem, then the kingly victor and the heroic subject are carried forward into the High Renaissance era as indissolubly united.

Demand led Hart to reprint his *Bruce* edition just four years later. Before he did so he brought back into print in 1618 a companion work: *The Life and Acts of the Most Famous & Valiant Champion, Syr William Wallace, Knight of Ellerslie: Maintainer of the Libertie of Scotland*. In terms of linguistic colouration, the text of these volumes became something of a standard for later editions.[112] Addressing readers at the start of his *Wallace*, Hart maintains that 'This Historie of *Sir William Wallace*, is so linked to that of King *Robert the Bruce*, that the one followeth jumpe vpon the other.' He proceeds to explain that when he published the *Bruce* 'to cleare the whole Historie, I was forced to set downe (briefelie) the summe of the Historie of *William Wallace* collected word by word out of our best and approued *Historiographers*, in the Preface of *Bruces* Booke'. Hart cites Bower to demonstrate the truth of the material in Hary's poem, which shows that Wallace spent time in France – another popular manifestation of the strength of the Auld Alliance. Wallace for Hart was literally heaven-sent: 'GOD stirred vp this valiant Champion, *William Wallace*.'[113] Following closely passages from the introduction to his *Bruce* volume, the Edinburgh printer reproduces word for word in the preface to *Wallace* the full account of the conversation between king and subject on the banks of the Carron about the 'liberty' of the Scottish people. Much of the material in Hart's two prefaces is identical – a sign, perhaps, of haste and publishing opportunism. Yet this shared material also shows how much these two poems, like their two heroes, were for Hart parts of one whole. In 1620, the year when he reprinted his edition of the *Bruce*, Hart made available alongside it a reprint of his *Wallace*.

As the seventeenth century progressed, the *Bruce* continued to be published, often in compact forms shorn of any preface. Editions came from Edinburgh's presses in 1648 and 1670, for instance, and from Glasgow's in 1672. Two of these were produced by university printers, suggesting that the *Bruce* may have appealed particularly to a learned audience ready to come to terms with antique language reproduced in a gothic typeface. The 1672 Glasgow *Bruce* concludes with more modern lines: 'Here ends the Book of the noblest King / That ever in Scotland yet did reign'; however, strikingly, as the century advances, the popularity of the *Wallace* (as measured by its frequent republication) outdistances that of the *Bruce*. There were just twelve popular editions of Barbour's poem between 1571 and 1914, but perhaps three times as many of Hary's *Wallace*.[114]

Seventeenth-century editions of Hary's work include one produced in Aberdeen by Edward Raban for David Melvill in 1630. This reprints Hart's 1618 preface and is followed by Edinburgh editions of 1640, 1648, 1661, 1666 and 1673, and Glasgow editions of 1665, 1685 and 1699.[115] Graeme Morton points out that 'Harry first appeared [in print] as the named author of the *Wallace* in the 1645 edition published by Robert Bryson.'[116] The Edinburgh editions of the seventeenth century reproduce the Latin poem on Wallace from Hart's 1611 edition, retitling it 'Epitaphivm Gilielmi Wallace', and most often reprint a preface that differs from Hart's. From its opening words, this later preface continues to link the poems and 'Historie of sir *William Wallace*, with the other of the valiant king *Robert Bruce*'. Together the *Wallace* and the *Bruce* contain

> the relation of the most famous war that ever fell out in the Ile of *Britaine*, foughten most valiantly for the space of 40 yeares, betwixt the two Realms of *Scotland* and *England*, the one unjustly pursuing, the other constantly defending the liberties of this Countrey; During which broiles, there happened great alterations, both in the generall state of this Kingdome, and in the overthrow and advancement of particular Families, the one for betraying, the other for maintaining their countries freedom and wilfare.[117]

So, during and after the English Civil War and the Covenanting times in Scotland when factional fighting convulsed the country, readers might be prompted to reflect on an earlier period of strife within 'the Ile of *Britaine*'. Yet such readers were encouraged to see things from a particularly Scottish perspective – that of 'this Countrey' as the Scots printer puts it. His phrasing shows how the *Wallace* was regarded as a poem of British significance, yet also as one clearly most treasured in Scotland. Wallace's nigh Classical status is evident from the 1633 Latin poem *Valliados*. He enjoyed, too, some persisting recognition south of the Scottish border, as witnessed by the 1637 publication in London of a drama, *The Valiant Scot*, authored by one 'J. W. Gent.', which draws on Hary for its plot and even for occasional lines.[118] However, Hary's poem seems never to have been published in England. Its vehement patriotic resonance led to frequent republication in Scotland where it was arguably the clearest literary transmitter of the ideal of independence in the decades leading up to the signing of the 1707 Act of Union between the Scottish and English parliaments. Even as Scotland's aristocratic politicians headed towards Union, popular educated taste continued to relish *The Wallace*. That poem's hero never fought at Bannockburn. Yet for many Scots he was a vital part of the writing of that potently emblematic battle. Bannockburn's Robert Baston was generally forgotten; instead, more than any other medieval imaginative writers, it was John Barbour and Blind Hary who would carry forward to later ages the steadfast assertion of Scottish independence.

Chapter 2

Burns and Bannockburns

Bannockburns

Bannockburn lasted. More than anything else, the rewriting of it, and poetic reworkings of Bruce and Wallace, kept ideals of Scottish political freedom alive during the eighteenth and nineteenth centuries. Even after the 1707 parliamentary Act of Union, the narrative of Scottish independence continued to hold appeal. Britishness was important to many Enlightenment and Romantic-era Scottish writers including the biographer James Boswell, novelists Tobias Smollett and Walter Scott, and poet James Thomson, but it failed to fire the imaginations of English-born creative writers.[1] In England Thomson penned 'Rule, Britannia'; in Scotland Robert Burns made rather different political songs.

At the heart of the present chapter are the work of Scotland's greatest poet and the verse of an early eighteenth-century Scottish author whom Burns admired hugely. As in every era, minor writers as well as major ones kept the independence story alive. William Hamilton of Gilbertfield and Robert Burns operated largely beyond the confines of the eighteenth-century Scottish academic system where teaching of rhetoric and belles lettres encouraged Anglocentric values.[2] Neither poet devoted himself exclusively to imaginative articulation of Scottish independence. Yet both relished the opportunity. A host of other writers from the pro-Union Daniel Defoe and the anti-Union William Forbes to dramatist Gabriel Nisbet (author of *Caledon's Tears: or, Wallace. A Tragedy* (1733)) and Jacobite

William Hamilton of Bangour contributed to debates about Scotland, England and Britain. Some did so crudely, if robustly. As part of a pamphleteering flurry around the time of the Union of Parliaments, Forbes in *A Pil for Pork-Eaters: or, a Scots Lancet for an English Swelling* (1705) reproaches England for seeking 'to abuse a free and neighbouring State!'

> Let *England* Bully, but let *Scotland* Fight:
> And let another *Bannockburn* redress,
> Too long endur'd Affronts and Grievances [. . .]³

Blessed at times with a deliciously vivid imagination, the Scottish physician John Arbuthnot, who became a close friend of Alexander Pope, invented perhaps the most famous of all icons of Englishness. Collected in 1712 as *The History of John Bull*, Arbuthnot's series of pamphlets set his 'plump [. . .] Darling' John beside 'Peg', the 'pale and wan', under-resourced 'Miss' who represents Scotland.⁴ Soon pro-Union Arbuthnot's John Bull acquired a Union-Jack waistcoat and became a globally recognised emblem. His Scottish sister Peg was left to pine. Elizabeth Wardlaw's 1719 'Hardyknute' sets a medieval King of Scots against a domineering foreign invader, and rejoices in the clash of arms, yet its battle is not Bannockburn but the 1263 Battle of Largs and its invaders are Norwegians. For pro-Union eighteenth-century readers this may have been a more politically correct way to present traditional Scottish independence, rather than involving the 'auld enemy', England. Nevertheless, independence, Bannockburn-style, was blazoned in *The Bruciad* by 'John Harvey, M. A.', while classic ballads like 'Sir William Wallace' still circulated alongside awkward new balladeering: 'They boldly fought for liberty, for honour and applause, / And defy'd the power of England's king to alter their laws.'⁵ At St Andrews University the young Robert Fergusson, whom Burns would describe as 'Heaven-taught', is said to have planned a tragedy dealing with the death of Wallace.⁶ Apparently entertaining anti-Union as well as Jacobite sympathies (the two often went together), in his published *Poems* of 1773 Fergusson writes about sailing along the Forth:

On thy green banks sits Liberty enthron'd,
But not that shadow which the English youth
So eagerly pursue; but freedom bought,
When Caledonia's triumphant sword
Taught the proud sons of Anglia to bemoan
Their fate at *Bannockburn*, where thousands came
Never to tread their native soil again.[7]

There was no shortage of literary Bannockburns. Admirers of the Ossianic Fingal rediscovered even Robert Baston's battle-field verses.[8] As David Hume put it in his bestselling *History of England*, that conflict had not only 'secured the independency of Scotland'; it might also 'be deemed the greatest overthrow, which the English monarchy, since the conquest, has ever received'.[9]

William Hamilton and his legacy

Yet while many eighteenth-century writers engaged with the notion of Scottish independence, and antiquarians dryly investigated it, William Hamilton of Gilbertfield and his eager reader Robert Burns did most to give it life. Daringly, Burns fused the treasured struggles of Bruce and Wallace with the fervour of modern democratic aspiration. This was risky. At the very least in a Scotland where he had no vote and where, latterly, he earned his keep as a salaried official of the British crown, his political radicalism got Burns into trouble. More than once he was obliged to protest his loyalty in prose and in verse in order to protect the livelihood on which he and his family depended. Often he did so slyly. This exciseman poet was under no obligation to voice dissident sentiments – quite the reverse; so his repeated and excited articulation of them is much more revealing than any of his dutiful retractions. For every modern-day Unionist who takes at face value Burns's little-known verses 'The Dumfries Volunteers' (which protest loyal Britishness), there are thousands of other readers who treasure the very different sentiments of the more justly celebrated song beginning, 'Scots, wha hae'.

Blind Hary's *Wallace* continued to be reprinted throughout

the eighteenth century. Apparently it had attracted academic attention around 1730. In that year, just months after the poem had been reissued in Glasgow, the scholarly, English-born and patriotically Scottish Jacobite printer Robert Freebairn in Edinburgh typeset an edition which seems to have involved a transcriber named Tait going back to the manuscript in the Advocates' Library and to some extent modernising the spelling. It has been claimed that this work was done as early as 1714, but the outbreak of the 1715 Jacobite rebellion caused publication to be suspended. Freebairn's text, whose title page proclaims erroneously that the poem was 'Written by Blind Harry in the year 1361', did not appear for sale until 1758.[10] Long before then, however, the poem had been reinvented for the modern world not by a scholar or a printer but by a retired soldier.

The bloodily military character of Hary's *Wallace* readily appealed to a Scottish battlefront veteran. Named after his father, who had been killed in action fighting the French, William Hamilton was born near Kilwinning in Ayrshire around 1665. He had fought on several European battlefields as a lieutenant. Retiring on half pay, Hamilton set up home in a traditional Scottish tower-house (which survives to this day as a picturesque ruin) at rural Gilbertfield, situated by Dechmont Hill between the eighteenth-century villages of Cambuslang and East Kilbride, south-east of Glasgow. Ensconced at Gilbertfield, the old soldier turned to literature. His poem, 'The Last Dying Words of Bonnie Heck', a dramatic monologue placed in the mouth of 'A Famous Greyhound in the Shire of Fife', tells of a dog celebrated in his youth for 'doughty deed'; Hamilton's lyric 'Willie Was a Wanton Wag' is about a man who enjoys sex and dancing, yet is also a veteran of 'the weapon-shaw' (military mustering).[11] This poet seems to have liked poems into which he could put something of himself.

As far as is known, Hamilton studied at no university. Instead, he shared a penchant for vigorous autodidacticism and conviviality with his friend the Edinburgh poet Allan Ramsay. These two bon viveurs corresponded in rhyme, using the verse form called 'Standard Habbie' – a term Ramsay coined. Several times in 1719 the Edinburgh writer addressed Hamilton as a

'Sodger' (soldier) who has *'ventur'd bauld'* (adventured boldly), but has now retired to a rural Lanarkshire 'Bog'. Jauntily, the correspondents discussed older Scottish poetry such as the work of Scots Latinist Gavin Douglas: Ramsay thought 'Our Country then a Tale cou'd tell.' Hamilton on his side of the correspondence reveals a familiarity with work by Jonson, Dryden and Aristotle.[12] Operating outside academia, but well read, these friends shared a preoccupation with older Scottish verse.

That interest was bound up with a wider, post-1707 reassertion of the dignity of native Scottish cultural traditions, as exemplified by the patriotic printer James Watson's three-volume *Choice Collection of Comic and Serious Scots Poems Both Ancient and Modern* (1706, 1709, 1711). This anthologised Hamilton's 'Bonny Heck' and 'Ancient' materials including the energetic 'Christis Kirk on the Green' from the sixteenth-century Bannatyne Manuscript. Watson declared his anthology *'the first of its Nature which has been publish'd in our Native* Scots *Dialect'*.[13] Like Hamilton and Ramsay, he had a taste for the ancient confidently bonded to the modern.

By 1718 Ramsay was drawing on works of late medieval Scottish literature such as 'Christis Kirk on the Green', and in 1724 he published his *Collection of Scots Poems, Wrote by the Ingenious before 1600*, purposefully entitled *The Ever Green*. At the same time as Ramsay was recuperating older Scottish texts, his friend Hamilton was modernising Blind Hary's *Wallace*. These men's labours can be seen as a concerted project to carry forward into the public sphere of early Enlightenment modernity highlights of medieval Scottish tradition, passing on the literary heritage of an independent Scotland. Such work had an energising effect on Fergusson, Burns and their successors.

Hamilton's version of Hary's *Wallace* was published in Glasgow by William Duncan in 1722: *A New Edition of the Life and Heroick Actions of the Renoun'd Sir William Wallace, General and Governour of Scotland*. Neither Hamilton's name nor Hary's appears alongside its title whose wording was designed to appeal to the traditional patriotic constituency. This 'new edition', far 'more Intelligible', could be read 'without the help of a Glossary'.[14] Though Hart's early seventeenth-century text had to an extent modernised and Anglicised Hary's language, Hamilton's heroic couplets suited audiences in the Augustan age of Alexander Pope. Sheer readability gave this new *Wallace* currency. The soldier-poet did not so much translate Hary's William Wallace; he reinvented him.

Though it went on being republished, Hary's original, often printed in a Gothic font, had become hard to comprehend. Many editions used substantially corrupt texts, their spelling modernised in piecemeal fashion. Here, for instance, are the opening lines of the poem in a 1648 Edinburgh edition (I have not reproduced the gothic font):

> Owr Antecessours whom wee should of read,
> And hold in minde their fame and worthy deed:
> We let over-slide, through very slothfulnesse
> And cast us ever to other businesse.[15]

This is fairly straightforward, but it soon gets much more difficult: a demanding 400–page read. Anachronistically, at its start it has been reworked awkwardly from a Unionist point of view, which leads to mention of the 'great kindnesse' shown to the Scots 'of late' by their southern 'next neighbours'.[16] Nothing could be further from the spirit of Hary's original. For the sake of comparison, here are the opening lines of that original from the fullest and most scholarly modern edition, edited by Matthew P. McDiarmid for the Scottish Text Society in 1968:

> OUR antecessowris that we suld of reide
> And hald in mynde, thar nobille worthi deid
> We lat ourslide throw werray sleuthfulnes,
> And castis ws eu*ir* till vthir besynes.

Getting back to the earliest surviving manuscript of Hary's text, this version removes the later Unionist apology, restoring a sense of resolute resistance to 'Our ald Ennemys'. It is also hard to read. Hamilton neither re-presented the awkwardly corrupted text nor reproduced the exhumed original. Instead, he deployed his hard-won poetic voice. English in diction, sometimes gauche in rhyme, and spiced with an occasional tang of Scots, this fused with his own patriotic martial vigour. The early eighteenth-century ex-soldier produced not a masterpiece of high art, but a work of effectively purposeful, accessible verse. He opens forthrightly by invoking images

OF OUR ANCESTORS, brave true ancient Scots,
Whose glorious scutcheons know no bars nor blots [. . .][17]

Hamilton moves in his first sixteen lines from 'ancient Scots' to 'modern'; his second line signals this is popular verse, not high-flown poetry. With its manifest desire to 'maintain our rights' in the face of 'haughty neighbours', Hamilton's recreated *Wallace* sounded notes that would ensure its popularity (particularly, I suspect, among men and boys) in Scotland. User-friendly, while still book-length, it was, too, considerably shorter than its extended medieval exemplar. Cutting material, the modern poet also 'adapted the work to suit early eighteenth-century Presbyterian sensibilities'.[18] Often Hamilton followed Lekpreuik's 'Protestantizing' edition of 1570. In an extended visionary episode the Blessed Virgin Mary is replaced by Dame Fortune. Elsewhere, an 'Ave Maria' vanishes, though in the 'kirk' Wallace does say 'a Pater noster and a Creed'.[19]

For most modern readers Hamilton's version has a kick of life, whereas Hary's original is necessarily sedated under a dense cloud of glossarial annotation. This retelling was straightforward and exciting to read. Revealingly, with all its Scottish popularity, Hamilton's *Wallace* does not seem to have been published in eighteenth-century England. A Scottish cultural nationalist, Hamilton kept alive in the decades after the Union of Parliaments a detailed and engaging sense of the heroic fight for Scottish independence. Sometimes crudely sensational, his poem captured many imaginations.

On a small-scale and at a macroscopic level, Hamilton's creative artistry is clear. Picking up on words used by Hary, he too writes of 'English thraldom'; early on, though, he jettisons much of Hary's back-story, yet adds direct political propaganda: 'Shall ancient Scotland hold of England? No.'[20] Writing of Scotland's 'independent crown', the eighteenth-century poet presents it as subject to the authority of the Scottish Parliament. With regard to Bruce and Baliol, each of whom sought to be king, Hamilton again makes it clear that 'Neither could be, without the firm assent / Of the estates of Scottish parliament.'[21] Invoking a theory of popular sovereignty, Hamilton implies that pre-Union Scotland once enjoyed a measure of democratic control over its monarch. This and his work's sometimes spiky vernacular energy speak up loudly for Scottish independence.

Consciously, Hamilton writes of a time when 'Scotland was almost lost'.[22] Published just fifteen years after the controversial Union of Parliaments, such words had a special resonance for Scottish readers. Full of places they knew, the poem offered heroic emblems that were inspiring but also unsettling in their potency. While the young Wallace is in 'the New Town of Ayr', a prophecy of 'Thomas the Rhymer' predicts that 'When Wallace' actions we to light produce, / We'll find him not inferior to Bruce.' The royalty of Robert Bruce, Earl of Carrick, is acknowledged in Hamilton's poem; but Wallace, 'come of gentle blood' yet no monarch, is the poet's popular protagonist.[23] After fighting at Ayrshire's Loudon Hill, and having 'broke the prison in the town of Ayr', Wallace, aged just eighteen, is knighted by 'good King Robert' – 'For in the Bruce's wars his trusty arm / On Englishmen had oft wrought meikle harm.'[24] Burns, a youthful reader of this poem, who shared his first name with the victor of Bannockburn, could call such images to mind as he strolled past Ayr's celebrated Wallace Tower.

Maintaining Hary's anti-English rhetoric, Hamilton begins with extended accounts of adventures set in the Ayrshire landscape of his own infancy where Wallace moves between 'Richartoun' (Riccarton), 'Mauchline Moor', 'Loudon hill' and Ayr in conflicts that 'dyed the field that day with South'ron blood' before he 'rode / For better safety to the Lagland wood'.[25]

> But in his mind remain'd another thing;
> Nor could he rest him, though he were a king;
> Till he his friends, and native land might see,
> From thraldom, and proud English lowns set free.[26]   *men*

Though this Wallace does fall in love, Hamilton warns that 'hazard is in trusting womankind'; such a note of misogyny is perhaps only hinted at by Blind Hary at the end of his poem's fourth book.[27] In Hamilton's rather stereotypically masculine work, as in Hary's, the murder of Wallace's patriotic wife focuses the hero's thoughts more intensely on Scottish independence, leading to 'fatal blows'.[28] An eighteenth-century poet's Indiana Jones, Wallace fights his way to freedom. He battles a headless 'hellish spright' who advances 'Holding his bloody head in his right hand'; the soldierly hero lives rough, sleeping outdoors as he dodges his enemies: 'The shrubs his pillow, and the grass his bed'. Eager to avenge 'My country's wrongs' he fights alongside 'dauntless Scots' determinedly 'resolv'd to win or die'.[29]

Divided like the 1570 edition of Hary's *Wallace* into twelve books, Hamilton's poem also offers separate chapters with subtitles such as '*How the Queen of England Came to Speak with Wallace*'. Some of the eighteenth-century poet's books even come with prose summaries. In an era when fiction was growing rapidly in popularity, this *Wallace* could be read almost like a novel. Purposefully, and perhaps with aggrieved irony, it focuses on a past whose hero is forever looking forward 'Till circling time bring back the happy day, / When Scotland shall be free from English sway'.[30] Hamilton's Wallace addresses his men, 'Inflaming ev'ry breast with love of liberty'.[31]

Hamilton follows Hary in cross-referencing his poem to 'the history of Bruce'. While encouraging everyone 'the Bruce's book [i.e., John Barbour's *Bruce*] to read', he reshapes the narrative, adding strikingly cartoony elements of his own: 'Now Scotland's free, lives in great peace and ease, / And South'rons are fled home to toast their cheese.'[32] Nothing so cheesy crops up in the poetry of Hary, but such modern populist touches garnished the resonant political message. Repeating that he will not be 'such a rogue as to usurp the crown', Hamilton's Wallace spurs on his men using phraseology that would be picked up later by Robert Burns: 'Then let us to it, either do or die' – 'wyn or de' (used earlier in his poem by Hamilton) is Hary's less alliteratively zingy equivalent.[33] Though further detailed research needs to be done on the earlier eighteenth-century reception of this work, Hamilton's repeated invocation of the power of a 'Scots parliament' (not mentioned at all by Blind Hary at comparable points in his original) must surely have encouraged the reflection that such an institution no longer existed.[34] Repeatedly, in subtle and not so subtle ways, Hamilton's poem stimulated popular thoughts about Scottish independence, seeing it both as blood-thirsty heroic adventure and as a vulnerable, principled ideal.

In Hamilton's text, when England's King Edward fails to cow Wallace, the English queen makes a softer attempt. Wallace recounts to her the story of Bruce and England's puppet-king of Scotland, Baliol. He mentions, too, the killing of his own wife: 'The queen with Wallace so did sympathize, / The tears that moment blinded both her eyes.'[35] She even goes on to flirt with Wallace. Then she returns to London to speak well of him to her husband; but Wallace's demand for Edward to set free Bruce is refused. As in Hary's narrative, Wallace then proceeds to France where, fighting the English under the banner of the lion rampant – the 'Red Lion' – he becomes a favourite of the French king. Sophisticatedly European as well as forthrightly Scottish, Wallace chats with that monarch in Latin; and he is admired by the French 'Red Reiver', Tomas of Longoville, who ends up paying homage to the Scot as if the latter had been a 'king that wears the crown'.[36] Later, returning from the old ally France to Scotland – 'I'll free this land once more before I die' – Wallace campaigns with Sir William Douglas. Eventually, he fights against Bruce (still loyal to the English king) at Falkirk.[37]

There then follows one of the poem's set-piece scenes as Bruce and Wallace engage one other in close combat and, in Hamilton's version of a now long established literary *topos*, trade insults on the banks of the Carron. Wallace in particular reproaches Bruce:

> With that the tears came trickling from his eyes:
> 'Thou that should be our true and righteous king,
> Destroy'st thy own, a cruel, horrid thing;
> But 'gainst the South'ron, I must tell you sir,
> Come life, come death, I'll fight with all my bir.'   *force*
> 'But wilt thou do as I shall counsel give,'
> Said Bruce, 'and as a lord thou mayst live
> At thine own will, and enjoy ev'ry thing
> In peace, if thou wilt hold of Edward king?'
> 'No, no;' said Wallace, with disdain and scorn,
> 'I'd rather choose to be hang'd up on the morn;
> The great God knows, the wars I took in hand,
> Was to keep free, what thou dost now gainstand;
> In cursed time thou wast for Scotland born,

O renegado, faithless, and mansworn!
I vow to God, may I thy master be,
In any field thou shalt far rather die,
Than Turk or Pagan; this I shall keep good,
Thou grand devourer of thy native blood.'[38]

Though following Hary's text here, the later poet intensifies Wallace's moral heroism and military resolution. He also departs from Hary in inviting readers to lament over Wallace's fallen comrade Sir John the Graham, whose tombstone epitaph at Falkirk Hamilton quotes both in the original Latin and in translation.

So, in an eighteenth-century Scotland where Graham's tomb (as it still does) survives, the patriotic soldier-poet bonds the heroic independence struggle to present-day observable sites. Convincing Bruce to break free of King Edward, and sure that 'Once more I've set this ancient kingdom free,' Wallace resigns his office. He returns to France where the French king puts him in charge of the province of Guienne, hoping that the Scot who has cleared Scotland of English imperialists can help do the same on the continent.[39] Hamilton seems to relish the way Wallace is treated in France, with which 'ancient Scotland' had enjoyed 'so long / A kind alliance'.[40]

Celebrating the 'auld alliance' at a time when the Jacobite Stewart monarchy was exiled to the continent, Hamilton's poem may have appealed to Jacobite audiences. More generally, it won new readers to the story of this 'brave heroic Scot', emphatically reinscribing ideals of Scottish 'pristine freedom':

So long's my nostrils any breath retains,
Or Scottish blood does circle in my veins,
Like a true Scot, I'll fight and scorn to fly [. . .][41]

Maintaining to the end that he does not wish to be a 'martyr' but a victor, Hamilton's Wallace urges his men to 'bravely fight as long as we can stand, / For our old native country valiantly: / Come, let us to it, either do or die!' – again those last words (even to their exclamation mark) were to be picked up by Robert Burns.[42]

Yet eventually Wallace is, to use Hamilton's word, '*martyred*'.

'Carri'd south o'er Solway sands', he meets his end.[43] Hamilton's poem does not portray its hero's demise, but accelerates towards its conclusion, as Hary's had done, both commemorating Wallace and looking towards the narrative of Bruce's victory at Bannockburn as a sort of sequel. With regard to Sir James Douglas, he writes,

> A better chieftain, Bruce had never one,
> Save Wallace, who's without comparison,
> Yet of the Douglas' more good knights have been,
> Than in one house was e'er in Scotland seen;
> As Bruce's book doth plainly testify,
> By Mr Barbour written faithfully.[44]

Hamilton's work's status as verse rather than as poetry probably enhanced its appeal to Scottish popular taste; it went through at least twenty-three editions between its first publication and 1859, and spurred many (often inaccurate) reprints of Hary's *Wallace* with modernised spellings.[45] Frequently Hamilton's text was printed with a version of a much older introduction, which had appeared, for instance, in James Bryson's 1640 Edinburgh edition of Blind Hary. The effect was further to associate Hamilton's *Wallace* with Hary's original. Perhaps it was less a particular poem that purchasers sought than the inspiring story of Wallace himself. Title pages emphasised the sensational: *The Life, Surprising Adventures and Heroic Actions of Sir William Wallace, General and Governor of Scotland* is the title of the *New Edition* published at Crieff in 1774; by 1785 a Falkirk reprint has become *The Ancient and Renown'd History of the Surprising Life and Heroic Actions of Sir William Wallace, General and Governor of Scotland*. Like Wallace's own fame, the reputation of Hamilton's poem was far from confined to the major cities.

From at least 1770 several editions appended to Hamilton's *Wallace* a matching verse biography of Bruce in rhyming iambic pentameter couplets. In three books (later six), this work, with its substantial account of Bannockburn, was first entitled *The Life and Martial Achievements of that Valiant Hero, Robert Bruce, King of Scotland*. University-educated and reputedly a schoolmaster in Edinburgh with 'strong anti-Union sentiments', its author was John Hervey or Harvey.[46] His work lacks the populist zest of Hamilton's Wallace poem; its tone remains too proper: Harvey's Bruce, addressing his 'loyal bands' before 'Bannock-burn', delivers a versified history lesson, complete with scholarly footnotes. He prays fervently in advance of combat; and, having recounted the past glories of 'our Sires', manages to be both rousing and somewhat apologetic about his own prolixity:

> 'This glorious day shall ev'n eclipse their rage,
> And *Bannock-burn* roll redder in the page;
> A new, a nobler aera shall unfold,
> And *Scotia*'s sons shall stand in brighter gold.
> Pardon, my friends! That I the field delay,
> And stop with words the laurels of the day [. . .]

Denouncing 'tyranny', Bruce rouses his forces. Then, 'majestically great' as 'his piercing eye-balls glare', he leads them to victory.[47] For all its grandiosity, Harvey's work was deemed to merit reprinting. Interestingly, it seems to have been given a markedly Unionist epic makeover for an expanded, post-Ossian 1769 appearance in London as *The Bruciad* when its anonymous editor, apparently writing after the author's death, frowns at how Harvey 'confined his observations to the narrow boundaries and prejudices of the land of his nativity'; the poem's conclusion is incongruously retuned to celebrate 'Great Britain' and 'Union'.[48]

Works such as Harvey's did not stand the test of time. Yet they went through more than one edition, boosting Bruce and Bannockburn as literary topics. Barbour's *Bruce*, too, was reprinted in early and mid-eighteenth century Scotland, but infrequently. A 1737 Glasgow edition contains '*a* GLOSSARY, *explaining the difficult Words contained in this* BOOK *and that of* WALLACE' – phraseology that hints at why, though some still bought the reprinted, modified and sometimes garbled version of Hary's medieval *Wallace*, Barbour's *Bruce* found fewer readers.[49] No one did for Bruce what Hamilton had done for his heroic nationalist predecessor. A 1758 Edinburgh printing of Barbour's work is presented as 'Carefully corrected from the edition of Andro Hart in 1620', arguably signalling it was likely to appeal principally to antiquarians.[50]

Robert Burns

Thanks to Hamilton, however, Wallace in modern poetry had immediate appeal. So popular was the medieval freedom-fighter that Burns recalled how as a child in the 1760s one of the first books he read in private was 'the history of Sir William Wallace' and that 'the story of Wallace poured a Scottish prejudice in my veins which will boil along there till the flood-gates of life shut in eternal rest'.[51] Asserting what is 'Scottish [. . .] in my veins', Burns's phrasing may recall Hamilton's lines (spoken by Wallace) about being 'a true Scot' for 'So long's my nostrils any breath retains, / Or Scottish blood does circle in my veins'.[52] Burns's love of Hamilton's *Wallace* was both deep and lasting. In another letter, written in November 1786, not long after the appearance of the first edition of his *Poems, Chiefly in the Scottish Dialect*, remembering his childhood he recalled how,

> In those boyish days, I remember in particular, being much struck with that part of Wallace' [sic] history where these lines occur—
> 'Syne to the Leglen wood when it was late
> To make a silent and a safe retreat'—
> I chose a fine summer Sunday, the only day of the week in my power, and walked half a dozen miles to pay my respects to the 'Leglen wood', with as much devout enthusiasm as ever Pilgrim did to Loretto; and as I explored every den and dell where I could suppose my heroic Countryman to have sheltered, I recollect (for even then I was a Rhymer) that my heart glowed with a wish to be able to make a Song on him equal to his merits.[53]

Burns's slight misquotion of Hamilton's lines – 'Then to Laigland wood, when it grew late, / To make a silent and a soft retreat' – is surely an indication that he is summoning from memory a passage that had stayed with him since boyhood. These lines occur in Hamilton's poem just before a mention of 'the pleasant ancient town of Ayr', one of many allusions to the young Burns's nearest substantial community and to Ayrshire places familiar to him.[54]

If some of Burns's earliest youthful song-making was bound up with dreams of Wallace, such impulses continued when he began to write with a view to publication. In May 1785, in a verse letter written (like those of Hamilton of Gilbertfield and

Allan Ramsay) in Standard Habbie, he sets forth his hopes to develop as a writer. His aim is to climb 'Wi *Allan*, or wi' *Gilbertfield*, / The braes o' fame'. Classicising the local place-name 'Kyle' by Latinising it as 'Coila', Burns writes to his friend William Simson of how

> We'll sing auld COILA's plains an' fells,
> Her moors red-brown wi' heather bells,
> Her banks an' braes, her dens an' dells,
>   Where glorious WALLACE
> Aft bure the gree, as story tells,   *[came off best]*
>   Frae Suthron billies.
>
> At WALLACE' name, what Scottish blood,
> But boils up in a spring-tide flood!
> Oft have our fearless fathers strode
>   By WALLACE' side,
> Still pressing onward, red-wat-shod,   *shod with red blood*
>   Or glorious dy'd!*55*

The word 'Suthron' here is very much a term from Hamilton's version of Blind Hary. Those lines about 'Scottish blood' that 'boils up' recall both Hamilton's phrase 'Scottish blood' quoted above, and Burns's own prose statement about a 'Scottish prejudice in my veins which will boil along there'. Bloodiness – 'red-wat-shod, / Or glorious dy'd' – is one of the characteristics of Hamilton's Wallace that most impressed his most famous reader. It was not, however, the only one. If in his prose letter Burns linked Wallace to 'every den and dell', here again, in his verse epistle to Simson, Wallace is bonded to 'dens an' dells' but also to plains, moors, fells and Ayrshire 'banks an' braes' such as those Burns knew from his infancy beside Ayrshire's River Doon.

Infusing the landscape with a spirit of freedom, the Ayrshire-born Hamilton of Gilbertfield seems a tutelary spirit of Burns's native county as well as of his native country. That this was so for the younger poet is confirmed by an entry in his 'First Commonplace Book', a sort of writer's journal that he kept in his mid-twenties. There he put on record his wish to write of

> my dear native country, the ancient Bailieries of Carrick, Kyle, and Cunningham, famous both in ancient and modern times for a

gallant, and warlike race of inhabitants; a country where civil, and
particularly religious Liberty have ever found their first support,
and their last asylum; a country, the birth place of many famous
Philosophers, Soldiers, and Statesmen, and the scene of many important events recorded in Scottish History, particularly a great many
of the actions of the GLORIOUS WALLACE, the SAVIOUR of his
Country.[56]

Such associations would be repeated in 'The Vision', the verse
manifesto that Burns wrote around the same time. Again, alert
to Wallace and his Ayrshire connections, it reveals a sense of
'*Scottish Story*' and '*Heroes*'. Footnoting 'The Vision', Burns
identifies the 'Race heroic' he invokes as 'The Wallaces', and
'His COUNTRY's SAVIOUR' as Wallace himself. He writes,
too, of 'Adam Wallace of Richardton, cousin to the immortal
Preserver of Scottish Independence'.[57] Adam of 'Richartoun'
features also in Hamilton's *Wallace* where he is knighted by
Robert the Bruce. 'The Vision' mixes '*Arts*' and '*Arms*', while
Burns's muse Coila recognises him as '*mine own* inspired
Bard'.[58] Appearing to her poet in a dream to inspire his fidelity
to his native land, Coila is similar in some ways to 'The bright
and shining queen' who descends from on high to present a
vision of his destiny to Hamilton's Wallace when that hero rests
after a celebrated incident in the poem, the burning of the Barns
of Ayr.[59] Burns's rather less celestial female visitor is seen in
an Ayrshire celebrated for beauty, present-day distinction and
(following Hamilton) ancient associations with Wallace and
Scottish independence.

    Another of Burns's famous early poems, 'The Cotter's
Saturday Night', exalts 'scenes' ancient and modern from which
'old SCOTIA'S grandeur springs'. Here Burns's second-last
stanza begins by hymning 'SCOTIA! my dear, my native soil!'
Full of praise for frugal, Presbyterian-accented virtues, his
penultimate stanza seems to move from a particularly Scottish
to a respectably British patriotism with its mention of the 'ISLE'.
Yet the last stanza swings back decisively towards a distinctively
Scottish weighting. Characteristically associating Wallace with
blood, it confirms that Burns, shortly before he published his
first book, very much wanted to be seen as a poet of distinctly
Scottish-accented patriotism,

O THOU! Who pour'd the *patriotic tide*,
  That stream'd thro' great, unhappy WALLACE' heart;
Who dar'd to, nobly, stem tyrannic pride,
  Or *nobly die*, the second glorious part:
(The Patriot's GOD, peculiarly thou art,
  His *friend, inspirer, guardian* and *reward*!)
O never, never SCOTIA'S realm desert,
  But still the *Patriot*, and the *Patriot-bard*,
In bright succession raise, her *Ornament* and *Guard*![60]

Burns here mixes a volatile cocktail of religion and nationalism. Modern readers may be wary of his excitedly protesting,
exclamatory rhetoric. 'The Cotter's Saturday Night' emerges
from the century that also produced the rather different nationalistic British jingoism of 'Rule, Britannia'. In linking his
aspirations to those of Wallace, however, Burns sounds a culminating patriotic note very distinct from his fellow Scot James
Thomson's Britannic anthem. He announces himself as owing
allegiance to a markedly Scottish line in which, as in earlier
poetry – most notably Hamilton's – the story of the 'guardian'
Wallace and the call of the patriotic poet were fused.

As well as growing up with Wallace poetry, Burns had come
to love Wallace landmarks. Ayr's '*Wallace Tow'r*' is one of 'The
two steeples' mentioned in his 1786 poem 'The Brigs of Ayr'.[61]
So it was not mere sycophancy that led him to write to one of his
principal Ayrshire patrons, Mrs Frances Dunlop (who claimed
descent from William Wallace), quoting a line from Thomson's
Autumn, and telling her that,

Had you been thoroughly acquainted with me, Madam, you could
not have touched my darling heart-chord more sweetly, than by
noticing my attempts to celebrate your illustrious Ancestor, the
SAVIOUR OF HIS COUNTRY,

'Great Patriot hero! Ill-requited Chief!'[62]

James Thomson's celebrated passage about a 'Muse' who 'Sees
Caledonia, in romantic view' goes on to suggest that emigration
and more recent imperial opportunities gave the no longer independent Scots a future 'O'er every land'.[63] His lines indicate how
even Wallace might be subsumed into an ideology of imperial
Britishness. For Burns, though, Wallace remained manifestly an

emblem of Scottish independence. In Edinburgh in the winter of 1786–7 Burns was being toasted as 'Caledonia's Bard', and was discussing Wallace.[64] Writing on 15 January 1787, he disputes Mrs Dunlop's criticism of what she regarded as an inappropriate adjective – 'unhappy' – to describe Wallace in 'The Cotter's Saturday Night'. Countering Frances Dunlop's argument that Thomson's epithet *'unhappy* [. . .] When applied to Wallace [. . .] seems to me unsuited to the *patriot Hero* or the *patriot Bard'*, Burns explained to her that the word meant simply 'unsuccessful'; some years later, though, in the 1793 edition of his *Poems* he changed 'great, unhappy WALLACE' heart' to 'Wallace's undaunted heart' in the second line of the last stanza of 'The Cotter's Saturday Night'.[65] In 1787 he went out of his way to protest his undimmed enthusiasm for Wallace, successful or not, insisting that he was using no 'improper epithet', and that 'My heart glows with a wish to do justice with the merits of the *Saviour of his Country*, which, sooner or later, I shall at least attempt.' Enjoying 'the patronage of the descendant of the immortal Wallace', Burns was not simply keeping Mrs Dunlop sweet.[66] His fascination with Wallace was enduring. He knew, too, that his native Ayrshire terrain was associated with the victor of Bannockburn, also known as the Earl of Carrick. Calling Bruce 'the great Deliverer of his country', Burns had written earlier in the 1780s in 'Halloween' about the River Doon 'Where BRUCE ance rul'd the martial ranks, / An' shook his *Carrick* spear'.[67]

When the twenty-eight-year-old Burns published the second edition of his *Poems, Chiefly in the Scottish Dialect* in Enlightenment Edinburgh in 1787 there was no shortage of interest in Bruce, Wallace and ancient Scottish patriotism. Edinburgh bookseller William Creech, soon to secure the right to publish Burns's *Poems*, had recently published John Pinkerton's edition of *Ancient Scotish Poems* with a prefatory essay that went back as far as 'The Caledonians of Tacitus'.[68] At the start of February 1787 the eccentric and vain but by no means imperceptive Wallace enthusiast, the Earl of Buchan, advised Burns to tour classic sites of Scottish lore. Burns was anxious about the financial outlay involved, but not averse to the idea. Probably he had Wallace and Bruce in mind when he replied to the Earl, using wording reminiscent of his letter to Mrs Dunlop a few weeks earlier,

> Your Lordship touches the darling chord of my heart when you advise me to fire my Muse at Scottish story and Scottish scenes.—I wish for nothing more than to make a leisurely Pilgrimage through my native country; to sit and muse on those once hard-contented fields where Caledonia, rejoicing, saw her bloody lion borne through broken ranks to victory and fame; and catching the inspiration, to pour the deathless Names in Song.[69]

Given Burns's phrasing, it is a reasonable assumption that the Earl had encouraged him to visit Bannockburn. That year, with the support of Edinburgh's Faculty of Advocates (who made available the 1489 manuscript of Barbour's *Bruce*), Buchan oversaw a fresh transcription of Barbour's poem, apparently by the scholar John Pinkerton. On 27 September 1787, Buchan signed and dated a statement that

> I David Steuart, Earl of Buchan, have compared this transcript of the MS. dated 1489, in the Lawyers' Library at Edinburgh, with the original, and find it to be a true copy, having corrected such errors as I have been able to observe, in the course of a very minute investigation and comparison.[70]

While this work was going on, Burns had indeed set out for Bannockburn and other historic sites. On 26 August 1787 he wrote excitedly to his friend Robert Muir,

> —I left auld Reekie yesterday morning, and have passt, besides by excursions, Linlithgow, Borrowstouness, Falkirk & her[e] am I undoubtedly.—This morning I kneel'd at the tomb of Sir John the Graham, the gallant friend of the immortal WALLACE; and two hours ago, I said a fervent prayer for old Caledonia over the hole in a blue whin-stane where Robert de Bruce fixed his royal Standard on the banks of Bannockburn [. . .][71]

The site at Bannockburn where Burns prayed is still marked. His enthusiasm for the location is clear, and this first deliberate song-collecting trip was bound up with his strong sense of Scottish patriotism. Gathering and reshaping songs became for Burns a patriotic endeavour, a way of fusing his voice with the voices of Scotland's people. Yet neither at Bannockburn nor at those other Stirlingshire sites did Burns produce verse about Bruce or Wallace. That took some time to gestate.

Further evidence of Burns's bardic enthusiasm for Bruce in 1787 comes from James Adair who later that year accompanied the poet on another tour to Stirling, then through Clackmannan to Dunfermline. Adair recalled how Burns's meeting with an elderly Mrs Bruce 'interested his feelings powerfully'. She claimed to be related to the victor of Bannockburn.

> She was in possession of the hero's helmet and two-handed sword, with which she conferred on Burns and myself the honour of knighthood, remarking that she had a better right to confer that title than *some people*. You will of course conclude that the old lady's political tenets were as Jacobitical as the poet's [. . .] She gave us her first toast after dinner, 'Awa Uncos', or Away the Strangers! Who these strangers were, you will readily understand.[72]

Ultimately the exiled Stewart dynasty to whom the Jacobites remained loyal was descended from Marjorie Bruce, daughter of King Robert. So to be a Jacobite (opposed to the Hanoverian 'strangers' who now occupied the British throne) and to be an admirer of Robert the Bruce made perfect political sense. Taking their leave of Mrs Bruce, Burns and Adair progressed to another Bruce-related site: the ruined Dunfermline Abbey where Burns in high spirits delivered to Adair from the pulpit a mock-sermon reproaching him for sexual wickedness. In addition the poet performed with a flourish a more solemn act of devotion:

> In the church, two broad flag-stones marked the grave of Robert Bruce for whose memory Burns had more than common veneration. He knelt and kissed with sacred fervour, and heartily (*suus ut mos erat*) execrated the worse than Gothic neglect of the first of Scottish heroes.[73]

For Burns, Bruce was not simply the champion of Bannockburn from the medieval Wars of Independence, but also, in spite of 'Gothic neglect', a significant continuing presence.

Another Stewart monarch of an independent Scotland who functioned in a similar way for Burns was Mary Queen of

Scots. In Edinburgh in May 1787 he sent verses to the historian William Tytler of Woodhouselee, whom Burns in the heading of his poem designated 'Author of a Defence of Mary Queen of Scots'. Knowing his poem was politically 'rather heretical', in his covering letter the poet urged Tytler to 'Burn the above verses when you have read them'.[74] He probably suspected Tytler would not burn the manuscript, but knew he could trust the recipient's discretion. Though the poem is neither Burns's best nor his best-known, it indicates how ready this bard could be to reveal what he saw as not just his own but his familial loyalty to the Stewart cause that was bound up with opposition to the 1707 Union and the Hanoverian monarchy.

Such Jacobitism may have been in part sentimental; it was also abiding, and would lead Burns to more poetically potent, outspoken songs in the future. In 1787, this Protestant poet so readily sympathetic towards Catholic worship wrote about the Catholic Mary Stuart, the last queen of an independent Scotland, and addressed Tytler as

> Revered Defender of beauteous Stuart,
> Of Stuart! – a Name once respected,
> A Name which to love was the mark of a true heart,
> But now 'tis despised and neglected!

If, according to Adair, Burns in 1787 saw 'the first of Scottish heroes', Robert the Bruce, as a victim of 'Gothic neglect', then in the same year he saw Mary as a Stuart heroine similarly 'despised and neglected'. 'Let no man misdeem me disloyal' protests Burns, shedding a poetic tear in his next verse. At first sight, this might appear a protestation of fidelity to the modern British state. In fact, though, it is a declaration of loyalty to the Stuart monarchy. He sees his own heritage as bound up with heroic struggles from the national past:

> My Fathers that *name* have rever'd on a throne,
> My fathers have died to right it;
> Those Fathers would spurn their degenerate Son
> That NAME should he scoffingly slight it.

These verses continue by paying lip-service to King George, descendant of the Elector of Hanover – part of what Burns calls 'th' Electoral Stem' – but the scornful tone makes clear that this is lip-service only.[75] Before it silences its own potentially dangerous political protestations, the poem addressed to Tytler has done quite enough to make clear Burns's true, if often self-protectively concealed, allegiance to a Scottish Stuart tradition at odds with that of the modern Hanoverian British state. The poet who in May 1787 wrote these lines is the same man who, a few months later, prayed at the neglected tomb of Robert the Bruce.

Burns's politics could be seen as dangerous, and were clearly known in the Scottish capital. The Ayrshire-domiciled Edinburgh University philosopher Dugald Stewart recalled that 'In his political principles' Burns 'was then a Jacobite'.[76] At the end of December 1787, laid up with an injured leg and in the midst of his intense epistolary exchange with the beguiling 'Clarinda', Burns wrote about the 'false [Hanoverian] Usurper' who now 'commands the towers and lands, / The royal right of ALBANIE'. Though the title of his 'Scots Ballad' implies that it is a traditional piece, and some of the phraseology and spellings suggest antiquity, it is very much Burns's own. Allusively contemporary, it clearly refers to Charlotte, daughter of the exiled Charles Edward Stuart, who took the title Duchess of Albany on 6 December 1787.[77] Even more vehemently Jacobite is a poem he wrote soon afterwards for a Jacobite gathering in Edinburgh, celebrating Charles Edward's birthday.

In its title, 'A Birth-day Ode. December 31st 1787', this work echoes the official 'birthday odes' written for King George III by his Poet Laureate – productions Burns satirised elsewhere. Some of the language of the Scottish poet's 'Birth-day Ode' images the exiled Charles Edward Stuart as Christ-like, his nativity linked to a 'shed'. Burns acknowledges that the Jacobite cause seems hopeless (Prince Charles Edward died a month after the poem was written), but there is no mistaking the poet's outspoken commitment as he recalls the 'honor'd mighty Dead / Who nobly perish'd in the glorious cause', and remembers men such as 'bold Balmerino', a Jacobite earl executed in London after Culloden, whose 'old Highland durk' Burns later claimed to possess.[78] After apocalyptic imagery of an avalanche, the 1787 'Birth-day Ode' concludes with denunciatory oratorical anger. Mocking the Duke of Brunswick, brother-in-law to the Hanoverian George III, the poem envisions Hanoverians in hell. These damned 'Apostates' are condemned as 'Rebels', just as they once condemned the Jacobites.[79] This rhetorically super-charged poem is politically vehement, seeking poetic justice for the exiled ancient Scottish monarchy. Burns is moved by a cause at once hopeless and true.

Though their number could be exaggerated, many songs Burns collected in his tours of Scotland from 1787 onwards had Jacobite resonances. Some may be surprising. The scholar James Kinsley noted that 'Editors have turned up a number of political songs, against the Union and the Hanoverians, which make use of the sentiments of "auld lang syne".' In 1788 when Burns sent that poem to Mrs Dunlop he wrote of how it was 'an old song and tune which has often thrill'd thro' my soul'; later he claimed, 'I took it down from an old man's singing'.[80] The song, with its fidelity to the past on the part of those between whom 'seas [. . .] braid hae roar'd', may well have a Jacobite tinge, as may other well known Burns lyrics including 'My Heart's in the Highlands'.[81] Sometimes the poet seems to have come across a tune and quickly matched words to it, as perhaps with 'Awa Whigs Awa', the Jacobite song he shaped in 1790, around the same time as 'My Heart's in the Highlands'. It denounces 'a pack o' traitor louns'. [82] Other songs, including 'Johnie Cope', 'The White Cockade' and 'Killiecrankie', show Burns revelling in his Jacobitism at the same time as presenting it as part of a general, popular tradition bound to love of the Stuart monarchy and the distinctive Scottish past.

Some tunes from that treasured past he carried in his head without finding ideal words for them. One was 'Hey Tuti Tatey'. Tradition maintained that this melody had entertained Bruce's men en route to the battlefield at Bannockburn. In 1788 Burns set a drinking song to it, including the words, 'God bless the king'.[83] He does not, however, specify whether he means King Robert the Bruce or an exiled Jacobite monarch or the ruling British Hanoverian. To anyone who knew him, it would have seemed unlikely that he intended King George. A few years later, still carrying this tune in his head, Burns would set to it much more arresting words, producing not only the most famous poem about Bannockburn but also one of his finest full-throated political lyrics. As such it would circulate around the globe sounding (as it still does) determined notes of Scottish independence.

Even before moving south from Edinburgh to Ellisland farm in 1788, he had his eye on securing paid employment with the British Excise service. Collecting Jacobite songs hardly accorded ideally with that, but it served as a way of remaining true to his political make-up even as he sought to enter the employ of the Hanoverian state. To the end of his life he maintained an ideal of personal independence, which, he hoped, would include financial self-sufficiency bolstered by an exciseman's salary. He wrote to Mrs Dunlop in 1789, that it was ideal 'to stand on the legs of INDEPENDENCE and hold up the face of AN HONEST MAN'. Yet Burns was also aware of living, literally as well as metaphorically, in territory where the word independence resonated beyond the merely personal. In the same letter he writes of nearby 'Lochmaben a small town once the private residence of Robt BRUCE and romantically situated among six or seven little lakes'.[84] It seems to have been here, during his exciseman's rounds, that he later transcribed the ballad 'Gude Wallace' in which the Scottish hero longs for 'my ain king [. . .] / The rightful king o' fair Scotland' and, after outwitting and vanquishing his English foes, sits down with 'his merry men a'' to 'dine in Lochmaben town'.[85] This ballad was just the sort of oral culture Burns relished. With an undiminished sense of ancient Scottish patriotism, he wrote in verse during 1789, that year of the French Revolution, about 'brave Caledonia' as 'bold, independent, unconquer'd and free', mentioning 'Camelon', a place near Falkirk believed to be 'the ancient metropolis of the Picts'.[86] Burns had passed through Camelon in 1787 on his way to Bannockburn.

As often happened, this poet's Jacobitism progressed in tandem with enthusiasm for the Scotland of Bruce and Wallace. A poem on Wallace had been among those offered to Bonnie Prince Charlie when he and his forces had entered Edinburgh in 1745; to link the nation of Wallace, whose rightful king was long exiled, with the Scotland of more modern times was not difficult.[87] In 1790, around the period when Burns gave classic form to such Jacobite songs as 'The White Cockade', 'The Battle of Sherra-Moor', 'Killiecrankie' and 'The Campbells are Comin'', he also penned for the theatre in Dumfries a 'Scots Prologue'. He had 'some thoughts of the Drama' and seems to have had in mind writing a work for a distinctly 'Scottish Audience' that might correspond with their 'native growth'.[88] Conscious that the prologue he was authoring contained 'a dark stroke of Politics', he sent it to a magistrate acquaintance, acting 'like a faithful loyal Subject' in case, as Burns jokily put it, the 'Poem be found to contain any Treason, or words of treasonable construction [so (*deleted*)] or any Fama clamosa or Scandalum magnatum, against our Sovereign lord the King'. Assuring his correspondent that, if this were so, 'the said Prologue may not see the light', the bard was covering his back.[89] It is hard to read the piece without getting a clear sense of where his true loyalties lay.

> Is there no daring Bard will rise and tell
> How glorious Wallace stood, how hapless fell?
> Where are the Muses fled, that should produce
> A *drama* worthy of the name of Bruce?
> How on *this* spot he first unsheath'd the sword
> 'Gainst mighty England and her guilty Lord,
> And after many a bloody, deathless doing,
> Wrench'd his dear country from the jaws of Ruin![90]

In this hearty prologue, written to be spoken by Mrs Sutherland, wife of the manager of the theatre company, Burns also expresses a wish for a drama that would 'paint the lovely hapless' Mary Queen of Scots. Though he did not compose 'A *drama* worthy of the name of Bruce', or a play about Mary Stuart, he did write a lyrical monologue in the form of a 'Lament of Mary Queen of Scots on the Approach of Spring'. Very movingly set to music by the composer James MacMillan in the twenty-first century, this song, like several of Burns's Jacobite lyrics, laments the lost Stuart cause. It also feminises what elsewhere in the poet's oeuvre can be a markedly masculine Jacobite tone.

> I was the Queen o' bonie France.
>   Where happy I hae been;

Fu' lightly rase I on the morn,
    As blithe lay down at e'en:
And I'm the sovereign of Scotland,
    And mony a traitor there;
Yet here I lie in foreign bands,
    And never ending care.[91]

Characteristic of Burns's poetry at this period is his use of the word 'traitor' not to refer to someone who resists the Hanoverian monarchy – a Jacobite – but to describe those who resist the royal house of Stuart. The poet at this time thought about a lot more than Jacobitism and the politics of Scottish independence; 1790 was the year in which he wrote his mock-heroic masterpiece of teasing masculinity, 'Tam o' Shanter'. Yet it is clear he remained preoccupied with aspects of Scottish history that for him remained vividly alive.

Burns presented 'Tam o' Shanter' to his English friend Francis Grose for the second volume of Grose's *Antiquities of Scotland*, published in the spring of 1791. Along with his antiquarian landlord, Robert Riddell, Grose and others, the poet discussed Scotland's heritage. Sometimes debates grew bibulously merry. The bard celebrated in verse a drinking contest at Riddell's house that involved competing for an ebony whistle said to have been brought to Scotland in the time of 'our James the Sixth'. Burns's poem speaks of a 'line, that have struggled for freedom with Bruce' and which, he maintains chimingly, 'Shall heroes and patriots ever produce'.[92] Drawing on his knowledge of topography and history, as well as on a network of local contacts, he supplied Grose not just with 'Tam o' Shanter' but also with 'an Itinerary thro' Ayr-shire', suggesting sites the Englishman should include in his book.[93] The places that Grose, whose travels were 'directed' by Burns, visited include such Bruce-connected locations as Crossraguel Abbey, Turnberry Castle (where Bruce went 'attacking the English'), Paisley Abbey, and 'St John the Baptist's Church, Ayr'.[94] This last landmark is still strikingly visible today, and Grose recorded that at the time of the Scottish Wars of Independence it had been 'the seat of a parliament, held in the time of Bruce and Baliol, and where a number of the nobility and gentry determined upon noble and free motives, for the former'.[95] Such an account surely accorded with the sentiments of Burns.

The poet's deepening interest in Scotland's literary past and in the history of Scottish independence is well attested during these years. When he came to add the epigraph to 'Tam o' Shanter', most likely he took it from the *Select Works of Gawin Douglass* published at Perth in 1787 as part of a series of 'Scotish Poets'. The publisher R. Morison republished Burns's admired Robert Fergusson in 1788. By 1790 Burns was enthusing to Mrs Dunlop about another work published by this same Perth entrepreneur with the encouragement of the Earl of Buchan: 'a fine copy of Blind Harry's history of Wallace printed at Perth, from a Manuscript of great antiquity in the Advocate's library; with an Engraving of him from a genuine picture in the possession of the Society of Antiquarians [. . .] the most elegant piece of work that ever came from any Printing-press in Great-britain'.[96] This *Wallace* was published by subscription. In its third volume the name of 'Mr Robert Burns, Ellisland' is listed among the hundred or so subscribers. Clearly he had taken an interest in the project from before its publication.

On its inner title page this three-volume edition of *The Metrical History of Sir William Wallace, Knight of Ellerslie, by Henry, commonly called Blind Harry* carried an epigraph,

> 'A! Fredome is a nobill thing!
> 'Fredome maks a man to have lykinge,
> 'Fredome all solace to man gives,
> 'He lives at ese that freely lives!
>   BARBOUR'S BRUS

The work bears a fulsome dedication to the Earl of Buchan. Paying tribute to his 'exertions in promoting Literature, and Public Spirit, [which] claim the Gratitude of every well-wisher to his Country', it thanks him for his support for 'our plan of publishing the SCOTISH POETS'. Buchan is praised, too, for having procured a copy of the manuscript and made possible the publication of a portrait of Wallace.[97] Burns may well have heard of this patriotic publishing project from the Earl himself. Certainly the way the publication was presented quickened his enthusiasm. For all that they politely changed 'Hary' to 'Henry', the publishers knew how to make the most of their material.

> No book has been more popular in any country, than Henry's Life
> of William Wallace was in Scotland for some hundred years. It was
> read by persons of high rank, who were taught to admire the valour
> of Wallace. It was thought a fit book to be put into the hands of the
> common people: Some now living can remember how the stories
> it contains were fondly received, and frequently rehearsed by the
> vulgar [. . .] there is no doubt that Henry's Book contributed in no
> small degree, in after times, to maintain among the Scots a Spirit of
> Independence.[98]

Delving into Hary's background, and attempting to present a
text much closer to that of the manuscript, this scholarly edition
maintained that 'we learn from Major [i.e., John Mair], that
Henry was a kind of traveling Bard' – just the sort of thing
that was likely to appeal to the self-proclaimed 'Patriot Bard'
Burns. Indeed Burns's own success with his 'Scottish Dialect'
poems may well have encouraged this republication of Hary's
older Scots original. The introduction goes on to cite the
seventeenth-century Scottish polymath Thomas Dempster as
someone who had maintained that Hary 'was indeed another
Homer', though the eighteenth-century editor considered this
'rather ridiculous'.[99]

Arguing that nowadays English people too could take pride
in Wallace's story, the Enlightenment editor tried a little
awkwardly to reconcile this bloodthirstily anti-English poem
with the modern Union between Scotland and England. He
hoped traditional 'animosities [. . .] have for ever subsided'.[100]
However, it is hard to believe that Burns, when he wrote about
this edition so enthusiastically, did so out of any enthusiasm
for Unionism; at the same time he also recommended to Mrs
Dunlop 'Barbour's life of Robert Bruce, done from an old
Manuscript in the Advocate's library'.[101]

This was John Pinkerton's 1790 *The Bruce; or the History
of Robert I, King of Scotland, written in Scottish Verse by
John Barbour* which advertises itself on its title page as *The
First Genuine Edition, Published from a MS. Dated 1489; with
Notes and a Glossary*. Pinkerton's substantial introduction sets
the republication of the *Bruce* in an international context, and
mentions that there had been 'about twenty editions' of the
poem published in Scotland since 1616, though all had been

inaccurate. Championing the *Bruce* as 'the most ancient production of the Scotish muse extant', Pinkerton stresses that his edition, also supported by the Earl of Buchan, depends on close attention to the manuscript. For this reason, while for readability he has subdivided his printed text into twenty 'books', his work carries a special authenticity. An exaggerated national pride accompanies Pinkerton's endeavours: 'Perhaps the editor may be accused of nationality, when he says that, taking the total merits of this work together, he prefers it to the early exertions of even the Italian muse, to the melancholy sublimity of Dante, and the amorous quaintness of Petrarca [. . .]'. Pinkerton boosts his *Bruce* as fit to be 'opposed to those of any other early poet of the present nations of Europe'.[102] Setting the matter of Scotland in the context of Europe, rather than simply comparing it with the matter of England, was a continuing strategy.

The controversial Pinkerton, a man later denounced for racist assumptions and a pathological dislike of Highlanders, did not hold back in praising the poem and his own editorial work. Perusing it, Burns would have encountered many familiar places, such as Ayrshire's '*Lowdoun hill*' and '*Galstoun*', not to mention '*Kylmarnok* and *Kilwynnyne*' (Kilwinning).[103] On occasion Pinkerton compares Barbour's language with that of 'Gawin Douglas', but he seems to have little time for the claims of Blind Hary or, as he calls him, 'Henry the Minstrel'. That poet was, according to Pinkerton, 'no authority, his work being an absurd romance'.[104] This label 'Henry the Minstrel' would become so fashionable that it still persists on paper and online in some twenty-first-century library catalogues, sounding so much more inauthentically respectable than plain 'Blind Hary'. When the king in Pinkerton's edition of *The Wallace* orates about fighting 'for owr fredome, and for our land', the editor calls attention to Bruce's 'long speech' before Bannockburn as being 'far from void of martial eloquence, and peculiarly adapted to the time, and to the hearers'.[105] Burns may not have agreed with all of Pinkerton's comments – indeed he may not have read them – but the simultaneous appearance of these new texts of both the *Bruce* and the *Wallace* clearly impressed him at a time when he was also reading works such as Tobias Smollett's 'Ode to Independence' and was, as he often seemed to be, much preoccupied with the meanings of independence both personal and political.

The word 'independence' features several times in songs he collected in the 1790s, as well as in his personal correspondence. Some readers take his use of the term to refer simply to individual independence: 'The man of independent mind, / He looks and laughs at a' that.'[106] But the idea of independence in Burns's work is frequently politically loaded. Though it was dangerous to do so in the years of political suspicion that followed the French Revolution, at times he merges his Jacobitism with Jacobinism, making clear a wish for Scottish political independence. This may be most nakedly evident in a letter to Mrs Dunlop written in April 1790. Remarking that, while he enjoys reading periodicals such as the *Spectator*, *Adventurer* and *Rambler* (the last edited by the famously Scotophobic Samuel Johnson), Burns says he does so 'still with a certain regret that they were so thoroughly and entirely English!' Then he remarks to his correspondent, 'You know my National Prejudices', continuing,

> Alas! Have I often said to myself, what are all the boasted advantages which my Country reaps from a certain Union, that can counterbalance the annihilation of her Independence, & even her very Name.[107]

In the same 1790 correspondence Burns goes on to misquote slightly the Irish poet Oliver Goldsmith. In 'The Deserted Village' Goldsmith maintains (as Burns puts it) that 'States of native liberty possest, / Tho' very poor, may yet be very blest.'[108] In misquoting Goldsmith, Burns substitutes for Goldsmith's word 'strength' the word 'liberty' – a significant alteration to make in the year after the French Revolution when 'liberté' was so much in the air.

It is clear in Burns's letter that he laments a specifically Scottish liberty, an independence lost with the 1707 Union of Parliaments which, for Burns, has produced a British House of Commons that is still widely regarded as if it belonged to England. Mocking an upper-class English accent ('Embassador'), he thinks that modern British culture and politics have meant simply England's dominance.

Nothing can reconcile me to the common terms, 'English Embassador, English Court, &c.['] And I am out of all patience to see that [e]quivocal Character, Hastings, empeached by 'the Commons of England'.—Tell me, my Friend, is this weak prejudice? I believe in my conscience such ideas as 'my Country; her independence; her honor; the illustrious Names that mark the history of my Native Land;' &c. I believe these, among your *Men of the world*, men who in fact guide [& *(deleted)*)] for the most part & govern our world, *they* look on such ways of thinking as just so many modifications of wrongheadedness.—They know the use of bawling out these terms to rouse or lead The Rabble; but for their own private use, with almost all the *able Statesmen* that ever existed or now exist, when they talk of Right & Wrong, they only mean Proper & Improper; & their measure of conduct is, not what they OUGHT, but what they DARE.[109]

Here Burns gives vent in his correspondence to a disgust with politicians who have colluded with an English eclipse of Britishness. That topic preoccupied many Scottish authors of the period. The Wallace-loving poet regrets the way the Union has wiped out Scottish independence. Just such sentiments, combined with his longstanding and recently rekindled fascination with Wallace, Bruce and the role of the 'Patriot Bard', underpin Burns's most effectively outspoken political songs on this topic.

In the early 1790s when Burns added to his oeuvre further Jacobite lyrics such as 'Ye Jacobites by Name', there was no shortage of anti-Union songs, often associated with Jacobitism.[110] Lyrics including 'The Union', 'The Thistle and the Rose' and 'The Curses' would be collected by James Hogg in his 1819 *Jacobite Relics of Scotland*. So would 'The Awkward Squad' in which the supporters of the 1707 parliamentary union propose 'to enhance to themselves all our treasure', and, as James Kinsley points out, the singer laments,

> Shame fa' my een,   *eyes*
> If e'er I have seen
> Such a parcel of rogues in a nation![111]

The song that Burns made on this theme draws on just such sentiments and wording. Rhyming 'sold' with 'English gold', it picks up, too, on an identical rhyme in Hamilton's *Wallace*. In that poem the English King Edward I is advised by one of his 'traitor' counsellors that Wallace 'must be betrayed' by being 'sold' by some of his 'bon companions' with a 'liking to the English gold'.[112] Burns's song 'Such a Parcel of Rogues in a Nation' also contrasts 'traitors' with 'loyal WALLACE' as its speaker looks back on the Scottish past from the perspective of the aftermath of the eighteenth-century Union.

Referring to the widely known circumstances that had seen Scottish parliamentarians bribed from south of the Border to vote for political union, Burns's poem makes a 'declaration'. The American Declaration of Independence had been the most remarkable document published in the newspapers of the poet's youth, and very probably he had read it.[113] In 'Such a Parcel of Rogues in a Nation' Burns's own 'declaration' is one of lost independence as the voice of the song pledges to go on denouncing the 1707 Union.

> FAREWEEL to a' our Scottish fame,
>   Fareweel our ancient glory;
> Fareweel even to the Scottish name,
>   So fam'd in martial story!
> Now Sark rins o'er the Solway sands,
>   And Tweed rins to the ocean,
> To mark where England's province stands,
>   Such a parcel of rogues in a nation!
>
> What force or guile could not subdue,
>   Thro' many warlike ages,
> Is wrought now by a coward few,
>   For hireling traitors' wages.
> The English steel we could disdain,
>   Secure in valor's station;
> But English gold has been our bane,
>   Such a parcel of rogues in a nation!
>
> O would, or I had see the day
>   That treason thus could sell us,
> My auld grey head had lien in clay,
>   Wi' BRUCE and loyal WALLACE!
> But pith and power, till my last hour,
>   I'll mak this declaration;
> We're bought and sold for English gold,
>   Such a parcel of rogues in a nation![114]

Burns was thirty-three when he penned these verses. He did not have an 'auld grey head'. This political lyric is produced by a literary imagination, and one may conjecture that its speaker is imagined as having actually 'seen the day' in 1707 when the Union came into being. Yet though the song involves politicised imaginative licence on Burns's part, it does come close to the thoughts on 'a certain Union' and the 'annihilation' of Scottish 'Independence' that the poet had expressed in his correspondence with Mrs Dunlop two years earlier. The song's most stinging word is that noun 'province': the Union is seen as having reduced an independent Scottish nation of 'ancient glory' to the modern condition of being merely 'England's province'; the equivalent in twenty-first-century British politics might be the term 'region'. In his internationalism – voiced most memorably in 'A Man's a Man' – as in his nationalism and collection of traditional Scots songs, Burns sought to counter Unionist provincialising by asserting what it might mean for Scotland to have the culture and politics not of a 'province' or a region, but of 'a nation'.

For all its spirit, though, this political song's 'Fareweel' is bound up with pastness. Spoken in a voice that invokes old age, it is resolute. Yet it implies a day may come when the speaker is no longer there to voice such sentiments, and so denunciation of the Union may come to an end. There is no indication that Burns wishes this to happen. Indeed the very success of the song means that such denunciation continues whenever it is sung. The lyric, then, is at once endlessly resolute and forever bonded to a past political betrayal. This was the problem, too, which Jacobite songs embodied, and it was one that risked being trapped in the political as well as cultural impasse of nostalgia. Burns's political imagination is remarkable not simply because he gave classic formulation to such sentiments, allowing them to last as long as the language; but also because, without betraying his or his implied audience's loyalty to the Scottish past, he found a way in perhaps his greatest political song to hint that such energies might escape mere nostalgia and connect the past of an independent Scotland with a potentially democratic future.

It is worth repeating that this poet did not live in a democracy in the modern sense; only a hundred or so privileged menfolk in his native Ayrshire were enfranchised. Yet, as I have argued in my biography of Burns, *The Bard*, he can be recognised as the master poet of democracy, not least because of the way he managed to fuse his own voice with the voices of the people he came from. He does this nowhere more arrestingly than in his songs of love, place and politics; and among these last he does so especially in a poem which, if one may judge from his own remarks on it and from the number of times he copied it out to send to friends, was a personal favourite. One title he gave to this song was 'Bruce's Speech to his Troops'; he mentioned in 1793 that he had written it around the same time as 'reading the history of the battle of Bannockburn, & figuring to myself the looks & feelings of the Scots Patriot Heroes on that eventful day, as they saw their hated but powerful Tyrants advance'.[115]

Given Burns's enthusiasm for Pinkerton's 1790 edition of Barbour's *Bruce*, where the king before Bannockburn is praised for his eloquence in addressing his mustered forces, it is likely that Barbour's was the 'history' he was reading. This assumption is reinforced by the fact that at the start of 1794 Burns sent a copy of his Bannockburn poem to the Earl of Buchan, who had been so instrumental in supporting the republication of Barbour and who had previously encouraged Burns to 'fire' his 'Muse at Scottish story'. The poet wrote to Buchan effusively, thanking him for his support and telling him in no uncertain terms that

> Independant of my enthusiasm as a Scotchman, I have rarely met with any thing in History which interests my feelings as a Man, equally with the story of Bannockburn.—
> On the one hand, a cruel but able Usurper, leading on the finest army in Europe, to extinguish the last spark of Freedom among a greatly-daring [but (*deleted*)] and greatly injured People; on the other hand, the desperate relics of a gallant Nation, devoting themselves to rescue their bleeding Country, or perish with her,—
> Liberty! Thou art a prize truly & indeed invaluable!—for never canst thou be too dearly bought![116]

'Usurper' is a word Burns uses elsewhere with regard to the Hanoverian monarchy. His words may carry a trace of Jacobitism. However, given the state of affairs in continental Europe, it is probable too that even though, ostensibly, he is writing about a Scottish battle of 1314, he had the struggles in revolutionary France in mind. Buchan, as Burns would have known, was a Francophile republican sympathiser. That the poet had the French Revolution in his thoughts is confirmed by another account he gave of his song's composition when he sent a copy of it to the publisher George Thomson in 1793. Burns commented then that 'I had no idea of giving myself any trouble on the Subject, till the accidental recollection of that glorious struggle for Freedom, associated with the glowing ideas of some other struggles of the same nature, *not quite so ancient*, roused my rhyming Mania.'[117] Also in his mind, though, as he wrote the song, was Hamilton's *Wallace*. He says so explicitly in a further letter sent to Thomson just a few days afterwards,

> N.B. I have borrowed the last stanza from the common Stall edition of Wallace —
> 'A false usurper sinks in every foe,
> And liberty returns with every blow'—
> A couplet worthy of Homer.[118]

Burns was stimulated by the tune 'Hey Tuti Tatey' which he had long known and had heard of as '*Robert Bruce*'s march at the battle of *Bannockburn*'. The association of this tune with the battle was widespread, part of the popular oral cultural transmission of the ideals of Scottish independence. Though he thought it did not seem 'at all probable, that the Scots had any martial music in the time of this monarch', the late eighteenth-century English antiquary Joseph Ritson, who had been reading Barbour's *Bruce* and collecting for some time his two volumes of *Scotish Songs*, recorded that 'The tune of *Hey tutti taiti*, to which there is a song, with those words in its burthen, beginning, "Landlady, count the lawin", is said, by tradition, to have been king Robert the Bruce's march at the Battle of Bannockburn, in 1314.'[119] Stimulated by the old tune and its associations as well as by his reading of Barbour's recently re-edited *Bruce* and Hary's *Wallace* along with Hamilton's *Wallace*, Burns's 'Robert Bruce's March to Bannockburn' manages to conjure up simultaneously the politics of Scottish independence and contemporary struggles for democratic liberty in republican France.

Scots, wha hae wi' WALLACE bled,
Scots, wham BRUCE has aften led,
Welcome to your gory bed,—
    Or to victorie.—

Now's the day, and now's the hour;
See the front o' battle lour;
See approach proud EDWARD'S power,
    Chains and Slaverie.—

Wha will be a traitor-knave?
Wha can fill a coward's grave?
Wha sae base as be a Slave?
    —Let him turn and flie:—

Wha for SCOTLAND'S king and law,
Freedom's sword will strongly draw,
FREE-MAN stand, or FREE-MAN fa',
    Let him follow me.—

By Oppression's woes and pains!
By your Sons in servile chains!
We will drain our dearest veins,
    But they *shall* be free!

Lay the proud Usurpers low!
Tyrants fall in every foe!
LIBERTY'S in every blow!
    Let us DO — OR DIE!!![120]

Exclamatory and thoroughly committed, these excited and exciting lines make much of resisting slavery. This may seem odd on the part of a poet who had come close in 1786 to going to Jamaica as an assistant overseer on a slave plantation. However, at a time when (as Burns knew) opposition to slavery was strong, the song makes absolutely clear at least that any good Scot would fight against being enslaved, and the poem's overall trajectory drives, surely, towards universal liberty. In some ways the song's determination to fight for freedom accords both with the ongoing struggles in France and with the resolute commitment of Scotland's 1320 Declaration of Arbroath. Though that Declaration had been little known for centuries, it had been published in full in an English translation (not titled 'the Declaration of Arbroath' but termed, with striking modernity, 'a manifesto') by the poetry-loving anthologist Sir David Dalrymple, Lord Hailes, in his 1779 *Annals of Scotland*:

Non enim propter gloriam, divitias aut honores pugnamus, sed propter libertatem solummodo, quam nemo bonus nisi simul cum vita amittit.

(We fight not for the sake of glory, riches, or honours, but for the sake of liberty alone, which no good man relinquishes except with his life.)

In 1768 these famous words had appeared also as the epigraph to the book that first made the name of Ayrshireman James Boswell of Auchinleck famous – *An Account of Corsica*. [121] Burns had some interest in Boswell as well as in the Scottish Wars of Independence; it is not impossible that he had come across this martial protestation of ancient Scottish liberty. In any case, his reading about Bruce and Wallace had given him more than enough to go on.

Burns steals material from Hamilton of Gilbertfield. Yet in writing 'Scots, Wha Hae wi' Wallace Bled', he does not follow Hamilton's attempt to reconstruct a medieval original in a modern language. The younger, more innovative poet does not even try to be true to the spirit of an older text. He does, however, write what he conceives to be the spirit of Bannockburn. Burns links this to modern struggles for democratic liberty in France as well as in his own country. This poem, encoding French revolutionary sympathies, is written by the poet whom Liam McIlvanney styles 'Burns the Radical'.[122] It is at one with other late Burns lyrics such as the 'Song' which concludes,

For a' that, and a' that,
   Its comin' yet for a' that,
That Man to Man the warld o'er,
   Shall brothers be for a' that.—[123]

Marilyn Butler points out that this climactic verse is 'probably the closest rendering in English of the letter and spirit of the notorious Jacobin "Ça ira"', and she shows that 'As with "Scots Wha Hae", the climactic verse opens out on to a visionary scene, as spacious as futurity itself.'[124] Butler's point about 'futurity' is shrewd: it reminds readers how the conclusion of Burns's Bannockburn poem with its exaltation of 'LIBERTY' connects with the universal values of '*liberté*, *égalité, fraternité*', moving far away from medieval kingship. Though much scholarly attention is rightly paid to the great achievements of Unionists during the Scottish Enlightenment, Burns is usually regarded as awkward to fit into this picture. Instead, he represents an Enlightenment radicalism proudly wedded to older, popular Scottish traditions, some of them clearly anti-Unionist. To set his Enlightenment radicalism in a lineage that includes not just Tom Paine and the authors of the American Declaration of Independence, but also such Scottish cultural nationalists as Allan Ramsay, Hamilton of Gilbertfield and Robert Fergusson, is to challenge definitions of the Scottish Enlightenment that regard this phenomenon principally – and to Burns's disadvantage – in terms of ideological commitment to British Unionism.

Burns's politics can be seen as aligned to those of the 1790s Scottish 'Political Martyrs'. Poet and lawyer Thomas Muir's Francophile republicanism, as Burns knew, got him transported to Botany Bay where he became Australia's first political prisoner. Yet in stressing the contemporary and French Revolutionary aspect of Burns's great Bannockburn lyric, it would be a mistake to forget how vehemently the poem is rooted in the particular struggle for Scottish independence. This most vehement of political songs manages simultaneously to draw on bloody ancient history and on modern, also bloody, democratic aspirations. It is nationalist *and* internationalist. Its ability to see the cause of Scottish independence not only in the light of the 1314 Battle of Bannockburn but also, in quite different circumstances, as a continuing live issue makes the poem so ideologically resonant, cutting it loose from inhibiting nostalgia. Celebrating and transcending its occasion, it learns from, but kicks free of antiquarianism. It is as provocative today as it was in the 1790s.

'Robert Bruce's March to Bannockburn', Burns's still ringing poem of Scottish independence, was his most successful fusion of nationalist ideals with modern democratic struggles; but it was not his last attempt. Often, as when sending it to Thomson in 1793, Burns called his Bannockburn poem an 'Ode'; he saw it as commemorating a battle emblematic of liberty. After transcribing the poem for Thomson he wrote below, 'So may God ever defend the cause of TRUTH and Liberty, as he did that day!—Amen!'[125] The following year he produced another 'Ode'. This one was intended not for William Wallace or Robert the Bruce but for the birthday of George Washington. It aligns the American War of Independence with the medieval Scottish Wars of Independence in which Wallace had fought, and again implies wider links with democratic struggles *'not quite so ancient'*.

In his triangulation of Wallace, Washington and French Revolutionary republican sympathies, Burns is once more following the example of the Earl of Buchan. A few years earlier, as well as visiting revolutionary France, Buchan had sent Washington a box made from the famous Wallace's Oak in Torwood forest where the Scottish freedom-fighter was said to have hidden from Edward I.[126] This action was celebrated in the radical poet George Galloway's poem 'On the Earl of Buchan presenting General Washington (Jan. 3 1792) with a Box, made of the Oak Tree that hid Sir William Wallace, &c.', later collected in Galloway's Edinburgh-published collection *The Tears of Poland* (1795). For Galloway, an enthusiast for *'liberty'*, *'Bruce'* and 'Martyrs for Old Scotia', the Earl of Buchan's action is admirable at a time when

> Vile despots tremble while their subjects groan,
> Since *Wallace* is reviv'd in *Washington*.[127]

Burns's more substantial Washington poem also sounds 'Liberty's bold note', not against England's medieval King Edward but against the Hanoverian King George III, portrayed as 'the Despot of Columbia's race': 'Columbia' was a word often used of America by those who championed its independence. Imagery of slavery – a 'broken chain' dashed 'in a tyrant's face' – and invocation of 'Liberty' connect this poem with Burns's Bannockburn ode of the previous year. There is also a link to the political ideology of the 'Song – For a' that and a' that' which exalts 'Man to Man the warld o'er', though Burns's elaborately Pindaric Washington poem is decked out in high-flown, formal English diction,

But come, ye sons of Liberty,
Columbia's offspring, brave as free,
In danger's hour still flaming in the van:
Ye know, and dare maintain, The Royalty of Man.[128]

This American 'Ode', which hymns 'that hallowed turf where WALLACE lies', is not one of Burns's greatest poems; read aloud, however, it possesses surprising oratorical force.[129] It longs for an England and a Scotland that it can sing in terms of independence and liberty. Yet it censures them as wanting. Mentioning 'heaven-taught song', Burns uses the compound adjective that Henry Mackenzie had once used of the poet when he first came to Edinburgh, and was hailed by that man of letters as a 'Heaven-taught ploughman'.[130] The erstwhile ploughman poet seems to include himself as one of the famous singers of Scotland; but his is a nation, unlike Washington's America, from which 'Freedom [has] fled'.

Towards the end of his life (he died in 1796, aged thirty-seven) Burns styled himself a 'Bard' whose 'heresies in Church and State / Might well award him Muir and Palmer's fate' – that is, he saw himself as facing the same sort of harsh criminal prosecution as other Scottish democratic radicals such as Thomas Muir and William Palmer who were then being tried and sentenced to transportation.[131] Realising that his Scotland is a very different society from those of continental France or transatlantic America, he turns to writing, to rewriting – both directly and indirectly – Bannockburn. Linking that clash to contemporary democratic struggles, he performs the greatest service both to the ideals of modern democracy and to the cause of Scottish independence. But Bannockburn was, as Burns knew, long in the past. It would be many decades before Scottish political institutions evolved to make such a vision of independence even remotely possible through democratic means.

Chapter 3

Beyond Scotland

England's Bruce and Wallace

Scottish poets jostled in Burns's wake. Several gave their books suspiciously derivative titles. *Poems, Epistles and Songs, Chiefly in the Scottish Dialect* by Robert Galloway, for instance, displays Stirling Castle

> In Wallace wars, thrice lost and won,
>   While stern contention fill'd the land,
> Till Bannockburn was o'er and done
>   And Bruce, the brave, was near at hand.[1]

For Galloway and his countrymen, Wallace and Bruce remained dust-free national treasures. Other writers beyond Scotland's borders saw them that way too, sensing potentially widespread appeal in material connected with Bannockburn. Since the 1790s Scotland's medieval warriors have charged across eroticised melodramas or starred in gung-ho fictions that set the freedom-fighter Wallace, despite his having slaughtered countless 'Southrons', beside quintessential English imperialists like Sir Francis Drake – joining a pantheon of mythologised figures merrily co-opted by the British Empire. At times it has seemed that Scottish independence might be recast wholly out of existence; or might survive only as bilious nostalgia.

The most striking sign that the popular stars of Caledonian liberty could be admired beyond Scotland in the late eighteenth century lies less in the rapidly disseminated *Poems* of Burns (published in London in 1787 and soon afterwards in Belfast,

Dublin, Philadelphia and New York) than in the work of a precocious English public schoolboy. In 1791 Henry Siddons, a seventeen-year-old pupil at Charterhouse, published his first novel, *William Wallace: or, The Highland Hero*. Despite the inauthentic, Ossianic subtitle, this schoolboy novelist maintained that his was *A Tale, Founded on Historical Facts*, and dedicated it to Thomas Erskine. Related to the Earl of Buchan, Thomas was younger brother to another of Burns's supporters, radical Scottish lawyer Henry Erskine, who would soon offer to act for Thomas Muir and that other notorious democrat Tom Paine. Routinely during the treason trials of the 1790s, in the years following the French Revolution, prominent British supporters of democracy were given harsh sentences. In such an ideological climate Bruce and Wallace could be regarded in London as radical emblems, ancient defenders of threatened liberty. When democrats Thomas Hardy (defended by Thomas Erskine) and John Horne Tooke were tried for high treason at the Old Bailey in 1794 evidence was read from *An Address to the British Nation*, which argued for 'Equality of Rights' not just in England but also 'for you, PEOPLE OF SCOTLAND'.

> The banks of the Forth, the fields of Bannockburn and Culloden, and that Tribunal of Edinburgh, which has disgraced your capital, shall yet bear testimony to the cause for which FLETCHER wrote, and WALLACE bled.[2]

As well as referring to the writings of Andrew Fletcher of Saltoun who had opposed the terms of the 1707 Union, the *Address* surely alludes to Burns's 'Scots, wha hae wi' WALLACE bled'. All this post-dated Siddons's 1791 'little history' *William Wallace*, but his hero's protesting 'he never yet deserved the name of rebel' before an accuser who denounces him as a '"Traitor!"' would have had unsettling political resonances.[3] Siddons adds romantic interest to his strictly two-dimensional melodrama, and his Wallace is, like Thomas Erskine, an inspiring orator for liberty. He urges Scots troops to 'follow me to death or victory'.[4]

In this heady romance complete with 'wandering Savoyard singing', Bruce marries Wallace's daughter Isabella, while Bruce and Wallace grow ideologically aligned. Eventually, with a misquotation from *Hamlet*, Wallace walks 'to the scaffold with a calm dignity of the noble mind', having 'to look upon death as a "Consummation devoutly to be wish'd for"'.[5] Siddons asserts that Bruce's 'fame can never be forgot by his countrymen, while their annals record the memorable victory of Bannock Burne'.[6] That pronoun, 'their', indicates that while the English public schoolboy author admires the Scottish hero, he stands at a distance from the tradition that Bruce represents. Perhaps surprisingly, his novel concludes by saying of Wallace's execution,

> Such was the fate of this brave man, who so long opposed tyranny, and kept his country free from the cruel stroke of oppression.
>
> Edward here stained all his former glories; for he should have considered, that mercy and compassion for unfortunate merit are the true insignia of
>
> A BRITISH HEART.
> FINIS[7]

Aligning his novel with Britain, this Charterhouse teenager was no Scottish nationalist. But his *William Wallace* clearly indicates how a Scottish nationalist hero could emblematise liberty in a Britain where, particularly to some like Thomas Erskine (who not long afterwards made an enthusiastic visit to revolutionary France), freedom seemed under state-sponsored, anti-democratic threat.

Siddons was not alone. In *The Ruined Cottage* Wordsworth's Pedlar was given a background 'steeped in "Scotch songs [. . .] Scotch poetry, old ballads, & old tales / Love-Gregory, William Wallace & Rob Roy"'.[8] In *The Prelude*, a work begun in the 1790s and expanded in 1805, Wordsworth reveals he had considered dealing with

> How Wallace fought for Scotland; left the name
> Of Wallace to be found, like a wild flower,
> All over his dear Country; left the deeds
> Of Wallace, like a family of Ghosts,
> To people the steep rocks and river banks,
> Her natural sanctuaries, with a local soul
> Of independence and stern liberty.[9]

Written after the Cumbrian poet had toured Scotland, as well as after his time in revolutionary France, this passage testifies to the remarkable ubiquity of Wallace place-names north of the Border: further evidence of how thoroughly Wallace remained part of Scottish popular culture.[10] Valuing resolution and independence, Wordsworth could admire Wallace as exemplifying liberty. So, more predictably, could minor Scottish poets such as John Finlay, whose *Wallace* (1802) has the figure of 'Genius' tell the infant leader a time will come when 'Freedom's touch' will 'restore / To injur'd Scotia's arm the sword of might'.[11]

Beyond Scotland, though they wrote relatively little about him, Wallace was an exemplary reference-point for other English Romantic poets. In 1798 twenty-four-year-old Robert Southey, then a radical Jacobin, wrote 'The Death of William Wallace'. Wearing a 'laurel wreath of scorn', Southey's Wallace is surrounded by a crowd who were once terrified by his very name, but now throng to see him as he is taken from his treason trial to his place of execution. Unlike many later nineteenth-century writers, Southey presents the full horror of Wallace's death: 'the hangman's hand' grasps a 'heaving heart' inside the hero's 'living breast'.[12] In a very different, chatty but heartfelt 1815 verse letter, John Keats relished writing

> Of him whose name to every heart's a solace,
> High-minded and unbending William Wallace.

Understandably, when he thinks of England's northern neighbour, Keats links Wallace to 'Burns', seeing both as noble.[13] The young Southey's poem celebrates Wallace as Scottish political martyr; the older Southey, Poet Laureate and author of *Lives of the British Admirals*, was no longer radical. His career indicates, however, how one might slip from enthusiasm for Wallace to support for modern British military campaigns.

For most people Britain's state and empire were now so securely established that Scottish independence was not a live political issue. Particularly in post-Culloden Scotland there was an anxious wish to demonstrate loyalty to the Hanoverian British state. As the Industrial Revolution accelerated, many Lowlanders grew rich from the spread of British imperialism. Such folk spoke up for the Union. Yet self-conscious articulation of Britishness as distinct from Englishness held no imaginative interest for major English writers. Instead, it became a key project for several of Scotland's most successful novelists from Tobias Smollett in the eighteenth century through Walter Scott in the nineteenth to the imperial soldier and colonial administrator John Buchan in the early twentieth.[14] In Scottish universities the official tones of academia could be intensely political. As Edinburgh University's Professor Alexander Fraser Tytler put it in the published version of his history lectures which the young Scott attended, 'William Wallace' had been 'one of the greatest heroes whom history records'. However, there had been a clear need to outgrow 'mutual prejudices of the two nations'; the present-day 'admirable fabric of the British constitution' represented an ideal culmination. '*Esto perpetua!*' (Let it last forever!) added Tytler with a committedly Unionist rhetorical flourish.[15]

Fascinated by feudalism, Scott became the greatest proponent of Britishness in imaginative literature, much of it with a Scottish focus. He published *Waverley*, his first historical novel, in 1814, the year when 15,000 people flocked to Bannockburn to celebrate the 500th anniversary of that victory.[16] Yet the Scottish battles that preoccupied Scott were the later defeats at Flodden and Culloden which had led to the development of the British state and Empire. *Waverley*'s focus on Scottish cultural difference encouraged nationalist explorations of identity in Italy, France, Spain, America, Germany, Japan and elsewhere. In a Scotland that lacked nationalist leadership and craved access to an empire's opportunities, the hugely influential Scott was seen as advocating Scotland's full participation in the British imperial state. When, after over a century during which no British monarch had set foot in the Scottish capital, King George IV visited Edinburgh in 1822, the choreographer of his visit was his most loyal knightly subject, Sir Walter.

Scott's literary breakthrough, his 1805 novella-length narrative poem *The Lay of the Last Minstrel*, celebrated patriotism. Its 'Canto Sixth' opens,

Breathes there the man, with soul so dead,
Who never to himself hath said,
This is my own, my native land!

Scott blazons Scotland,

> O Caledonia! Stern and wild,
> Meet nurse for a poetic child!
> Land of brown heath and shaggy wood,
> Land of the mountain and the flood [. . .][17]

Often quoted, these lines praise Scottish distinctiveness and even independence; but in a poem sung by an ancient 'Bard' soon to 'draw his parting groan', they help consign Scottish independence to the past.[18] Based partly on the Border ballad 'Gilpin Horner', Scott's poem is on the whole a medievalising concoction set in an Ossianic zone of lastness, fading and death. In Scott's era Wallace and Bruce might emblematise lost causes. After the 1790s treason trials, Paisley weaver poet Robert Tannahill, hymning 'dark winding Carron' and 'Freedom', cast Wallace as a doomed outsider: 'But I, a poor outcast, in exile must wander, / Perhaps, like a traitor, ignobly must die.'[19]

Minor poets such as the anonymous author of *The Shade of Wallace* (a Glasgow pamphlet of 1807) could have Wallace's ghost promising that with Bruce would come 'freedom on each hill and heath'.[20] Yet when Walter Scott discussed writing on Wallace in a February 1810 letter to Joanna Baillie, he argued somewhat unconvincingly. During the year when English novelist Jane Porter published *The Scottish Chiefs*, Scott maintained that a modern treatment of Wallace 'will not please Scotch folks' since 'Wallace is one of those historical characters that get beyond the reach of poetry'; later, James Hogg, who wrote his own 'Wallace' and so may have had an axe to grind, claimed that Scott had said of Porter's novel that he 'could not bear to see the character of Wallace frittered away to that of a fine gentleman'.[21] Perhaps stung by a popular vision of Wallace from beyond Scotland, Scott (as reported by Hogg) argued that 'Her [Porter's] Wallace' was not 'our Wallace'.[22] True, Scott's rather weak late novel *Castle Dangerous* (1832) draws on Barbour's *Bruce*, but his much better medievalising *Ivanhoe* (1820) commends 'the traditions and manners of old England', contending in its game-playing 'Dedicatory Epistle' 'that the patriots of England deserve no less renown in our modern circles, than the Bruces and Wallaces of Caledonia'.[23] Bruce features, too, in Scott's 1815 poem *The Lord of the Isles*, but by that time Sir Walter's poetic energies were waning. Neither Wallace nor Bruce even shows up in the indexes to recent studies of Scott's global impact.[24] *Waverley*, his archetypal Scottish fiction, takes its title from its protagonist's surname – that of an invented Englishman unknown to history; in Porter's novel, by contrast, Wallace and Bruce, those great medieval celebrities, *are* the eponymous *Scottish Chiefs*.

In *Marmion, A Tale of Flodden Field* (1808) Scott writes about a very different battle for Scottish independence. The first person named in his verse introduction is England's Admiral Horatio Nelson; the second is British Prime Minister William Pitt. Scott makes his allegiance crystal clear: 'Deep graved in every British heart, / O never let these names depart'. He celebrates the Briton as 'conqueror', and especially as victor over the French.[25] Prefatory verses also mention the Scot Sir Ralph Abercrombie, victor of colonial fighting in Egypt, and namecheck 'Wallace wight'.[26] Yet this is the merest cursory glance. *Marmion* is not about Wallace and Bruce. Instead, on 'Flodden's fatal field' the Scottish 'Royal Standard flies, / And round it toils, and bleeds, and dies, / Our Caledonian pride!'[27] For Scott, a frustrated soldier, the heroes of independence, if mentioned at all, are largely the stuff of footnotes or antiquarian curiosity. *Waverley*'s backward-looking Baron Bradwardine with his 'auld stiff limbs' reads 'Barbour's Bruce, and Blind Harry's Wallace'. Alluding to 'our ain valiant Sir William Wallace', he quotes the proverbial remark associated with the loss of the old Scottish Parliament in 1707, 'and there's the end of an auld sang'.[28] Caledonian independence belongs entirely to the past.

As a child Scott had been taken to see sites associated with Wallace at Falkirk. Almost half a century passed before he really brought his formidable literary imagination to bear on Wallace and Bruce in his late work, *Tales of a Grandfather* (1828). Its opening paragraphs present England as in important ways superior to Scotland. The author makes the point that

as these two nations live in the different ends of the same island, and are separated by large and stormy seas from all other parts of the world, it seems natural that they should have been friendly to each other, as one people under the same government.

Having opened his tome under the normalising sign of Unionism, Scott can then mention the 'many long, cruel, and bloody wars, between the two nations', implying that Scottish independence, while fascinating, is in modern terms aberrant.[29]

In writing of Wallace, 'one of the strongest and bravest men that ever lived', Scott draws on Blind Hary.[30] Yet Scott's Wallace is leader of 'a ferocious and barbarous people'. Though he knew the story, the staunch Tory royalist omits the by now almost obligatory encounter between Wallace and Bruce on the banks of the Carron.[31] Instead, for Scott, Wallace is at his best showing 'calm resolution'. Wallace's execution, with its 'cruel and unjust manner', led other 'patriots [. . .] to assert the cause of Scottish liberty'.[32] When Sir Walter goes on to deal with Bannockburn, he is accurate but relatively brief. The set-piece that his readers relished most was not Bannockburn but the account of Bruce deliberating while 'on his wretched bed' and 'looking upward to the roof of the cabin in which he lay' when 'his eye was attracted by a spider'.[33] This folk-tale in which Bruce learns perseverance from the spider was one that Scott brought into historiography for the first time. It features neither in earlier histories nor in the classic account of Barbour's *Bruce*. Yet more than anything else about King Robert it captured Scott's imagination and that of his global audience. He makes Bruce less an emblem of Scottish independence than one of tenacity, a virtue Sir Walter knew first-hand. Novelising Bruce for a moment, he showed in this late work what he might have done with the victor of Bannockburn elsewhere in his best 'story books', but which, though his inferior, posthumously published novel *Castle Dangerous* (1832) is set during the wars of Bruce, he had clearly chosen not to do.[34]

Today for every person who knows the Unionist narrative of *Waverley* there are many more people familiar with the story of Bruce and the spider. Not long after Scott wrote down that tale, English poet Bernard Barton thought it an ideal moral emblem for children; so did Eliza Cook, whose 'Try Again' is a highlight of her *Rhymes for Young Readers*. The other story to which Scott gave fresh life tells how, as Bruce wished, his heart, after his death, was carried on to a Crusading battlefield by his faithful friend Sir James Douglas. In America, Linda Howard

Sigourney in her 1834 *Poems* took from *Tales of a Grandfather* her epigraph for 'The Heart of King Robert Bruce'. So Scott, though he did not write substantial works of fact or fiction about Bruce and Wallace, assisted in their becoming icons beyond Scotland.

Sir Walter's loss was English writers' gain. Ironically, Scott's popularity led authors south of the Border to view the champions of Scottish independence opportunistically in a literary marketplace eager for Caledonian material. English radical poet Leigh Hunt, interested in 'the agitations' of Wallace's 'noble mind', and mentioning 'Harry the Minstrel', was inspired 'by one of the notes to the *Lay of the Last Minstrel*' to write his ballad 'Wallace and Fawdon' which pays more attention to Wallace than Scott does in his verse.[35] Other English poets followed: sixteen-year-old Horatio Waddington's *Wallace, A Poem*, celebrating 'the great, the brave, the patriot' as a hero of 'Liberty' from the 'Land of the Minstrel', was published in Cambridge in 1815.[36] Earlier, however, England had seen the composition of a much longer, book-length poem on Wallace. Its Cheshire author had read Burns, Blind Hary and George Buchanan. Stylistically, however, she was manifestly an imitator of Scott.

First published anonymously a year after *Marmion*, Margaret Holford's *Wallace; Or the Fight of Falkirk; A Metrical Romance* (1809) was written around the time its author posted to the poet of *Marmion* her 'Lines Occasioned by Reading the Poetical Works of Walter Scott'.[37] Holford's *Wallace* opens with a dedication to a female friend. Sounding somewhat defensive, it trumpets the author's nationality: 'Yes! [. . .] mine eyes first open'd on the day / In England! . . . / England! among the nations singly bless'd!' Loudly declaring absolute loyalty to the British monarch – 'George the Good!' – these verses lead to a prose preface which again seeks to protest Englishness, while arguing that 'It is of little consequence to the reader whether or not the author of Wallace loves England and England's constitution and king'.[38] Holford goes on to align Scott with the soldier 'Abercrombie', modern Scottish military champion of 'the battle of Alexandria'. She then presents 229 pages of verse about 'old Scotland's wrongs' and (alert, like so many others, to the bloodiness of the Wallace narrative) plentiful 'Southron gore'.[39]

Holford's Wallace boasts 'the calm of a noble mind', but fights to remove 'the invader from our land' and make 'Scotland free'. Featuring a hermit, battle scenes and a claymore-carrying Wallace who has lived rough in the wild Scottish landscape as well as sleeping behind a waterfall ('My curtain, the white foam of the linn'), the poem was designed to appeal to readers of Scott's romances.[40] Holford's 'Wallace [is] like his own mountains, bold and free'.[41] He also has competing love interests: his murdered lover Marion and his wife Agnes who dies 'with bursting heart' when she beholds her husband in fetters.[42] Strategic cross-dressing sees Agnes disguise herself as 'David', Wallace's page, so she can stay close to him in his military role. Soon cross-dressing would return in the nineteenth century's most influential Wallace fiction, that of Jane Porter, but it was already a feature of the traditional Scots ballad 'Sir William Wallace' where Sir William seeks help from 'his ladye' so that he can turn himself into what others perceive as a 'lusty dame' and so escape right under the noses of his 'Southron' foes.[43]

Holford's addition of more substantial female interest gets beyond those hints of misogyny present in Hary's and Hamilton's accounts. Judith Bailey Slagle points out that it 'connects the poem to a female audience'; moreover, Wallace's love life involves him in 'a conflict between the private and the public – a conflict with which women readers would empathize'.[44] Holford avoids presenting Wallace's actual execution. Maintaining that his name 'lives still, cherish'd and shrin'd / In every Scottish patriot's mind', this poem does not tend to deploy such terms as 'liberty' and 'freedom'; often it views events from the perspective of the English side.[45] Wallace's cause is hardly hidden: nor is its nature blazoned. While Holford's poem (which Slagle calls a 'pervasively Anglicized retelling') is a work about Scotland's ancient struggle for independence, that word is never used.[46] This is independence lite.

The Scottish chiefs abroad

Still, the Wars of Independence could attract English writers keen to trumpet the cause of Scottish freedom. Internationally,

by far the most successful of these was Jane Porter. Though
not discussed by Ina Ferris and Katie Trumpener in their skilful
studies of how Scott regendered earlier kinds of 'national tale'
and historical fiction, both in Britain and in North America
Porter's work was widely read throughout the nineteenth
century and well into the twentieth.[47] Resoundingly the most
important historical novel set in Scotland before Scott published
Waverley, *The Scottish Chiefs* (1810) was translated into several
languages, including French, German and, later, Greek and Irish
Gaelic. The 1814 French translation, *Les Chefs écossais: roman
historique*, was regarded as so dangerous by Napoleon that its
publication was proscribed; it appeared in Paris immediately
on the recall of the Bourbons.[48] Porter's work had an immediate impact in Scotland where the first Wallace monument (at
Wallacestone near Falkirk) was erected in August 1810; and
after her novel was translated into German she was proud to
be awarded 'the Cross of the Lady of the Teutonic Order of St
Joachim'.[49] Hers was the most important nineteenth-century
fictional treatment of the struggle for Scottish independence.
Surely prompting Charles Maturin's novel of Irish nationalism,
The Milesian Chief (1812), it spurred the development of that
genre called 'the national tale'.

Particularly in North America, several recent critics have
argued 'that Porter's significance in the development of the historical novel and national tale has been seriously undervalued'.[50]
Thomas McLean shows that her earlier novel *Thaddeus of
Warsaw* (1803) anticipates narrative devices used in *Waverley*.
To progress from writing fiction featuring Polish nationalism
to a novel involving struggles for Scottish independence made
sense at a time when, as one Scottish writer put it in 1795, 'The
situation of Poland since 1769, is somewhat similar to Scotland,
during the fatal contest between Baliol and Bruce in 1297,
when the all-grasping tyranny of Edward I of England over-ran
the country.'[51] Recently Devoney Looser has pointed out that,
while its meaning may have shifted over the decades, the term
'historical novel' was being used in the subtitles of English-
language books from 1725 onwards. Sympathetic to Porter's
'strong claims to having successfully popularized the blending of
true history and romance', Looser supplies evidence that in the

year when *The Scottish Chiefs* was published a contemporary commentator, noting Porter's 'many imitators', saw *Thaddeus* as 'a new species of composition, an harmonious union between the heroic matter of ancient romance, and the domestic interest of a modern novel'.[52] This description of Porter's tale of Polish nationalism is at least as applicable to her account of Wallace's fight for Scottish independence.

Emanating from beyond Scotland, much loved in North America and often abridged, Porter's lengthy novel went through at least seventy-five nineteenth-century reprints.[53] Continuing to find audiences in the twentieth century, when a substantial 1924 New York-published version aimed at younger readers carried memorable colour plates by the celebrated American illustrator N. C. Wyeth, it remains in print, and new work by Graeme Morton has begun to view it in an international setting.[54] Its textual history is complex. Many authorial additions accrued – sometimes of notes and prefatory material – while there were later (often anonymous) abridgements. My argument in this chapter does not depend solely on the 1810 text, and most of my quotations are drawn from the 1895 New York 'Complete Edition'.

The Scottish Chiefs has been discussed relatively briefly in the context of Scottish writing.[55] Rather than assuming readers are familiar with it, I shall quote liberally, providing plot summary and context. Like her novelist sister Anna Maria, Jane Porter was born and lived most of her life in England. She wrote *The Scottish Chiefs* in Surrey, but was fascinated by foreign independence struggles. While *Thaddeus of Warsaw* (1803) had drawn on stories about Polish freedom-fighter General Kosciuszko, *The Scottish Chiefs* draws on aspects of its author's childhood, part of which had been spent in Edinburgh. An immediate spur to composition in 1809 may have been the success of Margaret Holford's *Wallace*, which also enjoyed an American edition in 1810.[56] Holford terms her Scottish leaders 'chiefs' and there seems to have been a commercial relationship between her work and Porter's: after Holford's *Wallace* first appeared from Cadell and Davies in London, it was republished in the following year by Longman, Hurst, Reece, and Orme – publishers, too, of the early London editions of *The Scottish Chiefs*.[57]

Wallace is at the heart of Porter's novel. Carrying an epigraph from Ossian, its title page appears elegiac: 'There comes a voice that awakes my soul. It is the voice of years that are gone! They roll before me with all their deeds.' Yet Porter's Wallace, 'one of the most complete heroes that ever filled the page of history', is no Ossianic ghost. Explaining that she has modified chronology, especially when her 'catastrophe' makes it seem that Bannockburn follows soon after Wallace's execution, Porter acknowledges 'Tradition [...] suggestions of my invaluable friend Mr Thomas Campbell [... and] the old poem by blind Harrie'.[58] Campbell's 1795 'Dirge of Wallace' had recounted how 'the lady of Elderslie wept for her lord' who had fought alongside 'the yellow-haired chiefs of his native land' before becoming 'a martyr slain'.[59] Wallace might have been made for the Romantic imagination.

As a child in Edinburgh, Porter had heard about Wallace from her schoolteacher and from 'several accomplished scholars' who visited her widowed English mother's home. Her early memories also confirm that stories of Scottish independence circulated widely among the urban as well as the rural lower classes in the early 1780s, just before Burns reached the Scottish capital.

> I was hardly six years of age when I first heard the names of William Wallace and Robert Bruce:— not from gentlemen and ladies, readers of history; but from the maids in the nursery, and the serving-man in the kitchen: the one had their songs of 'Wallace wight!' to lull my baby sister to sleep; and the other his tales of 'Bannockburn', and 'Cambus-Kenneth' to entertain my younger brother.[60]

Those 'songs of "Wallace wight"' ('strong Wallace') may be ballads collected in the early nineteenth century. Their hero successfully fights a group of Englishmen after encountering a young woman. One version begins, 'Wallace wight, upon a night / Came riding o'er the linn.'[61] This Wallace visits the house of his lover who says she has betrayed him; in several versions he escapes thanks to a ruse involving cross-dressing. For the young Jane Porter accounts of Wallace were mixed up with childhood lore about Jacobites. Excitingly, she remembered finding collapsed in Edinburgh's Royal Mile a very elderly Jacobite soldier who had given her a white Jacobite rose. Doctors discovered that 'the sufferer was a woman' whom Porter terms a 'Magdalen' – a prostitute.[62]

Though she presents her often pious *Scottish Chiefs* as conducive to virtue, Porter's account of this fallen woman dressed as a soldier does relate to her tale of Wallace. Henry Siddons, Margaret Holford, Scottish dramatist James Grahame and others had added female interest to their Wallace narratives.[63] Drawing on sensational Gothic conventions, Porter goes much further. Her novel has been discussed in terms of its 'sexually charged ferocity' by Ian Dennis, whose 1996 monograph *Nationalism and Desire in Early Historical Fiction* includes the fullest treatment to date.[64] *The Scottish Chiefs* attends not only to Wallace's relationship with his wife Marion, butchered by the English, but also to Joanna, Countess of Mar, and her beautiful step-daughter Helen. As Ian Dennis puts it, Porter's Wallace, 'Himself undesiring, in the sexual sense [. . .] is, to begin with, the object of intense, persistent and – given the fictional conventions of Porter's or, indeed, most eras – startlingly overt female desire.'[65] Porter's character Helen adores Wallace. Eventually, she marries him. More psychologically interesting is the older married Countess whose love for Wallace leads her to dress as a military man and visit him in the guise of 'The Knight of the Green Plume', exclaiming with signature melodrama, '"For you I have committed an outrage on my nature [. . .] you recognize her who has risked honor for you – with coldness and reproach!"'[66] Trying to treat the Countess decently, Wallace denies this; but, intensely jealous of her step-daughter, the Countess plays a part in his betrayal.

Sensationally plotted, *The Scottish Chiefs*, partly through cross-dressing, grants significant, if limited, agency to female characters in its account of Wallace's struggles. Ian Dennis argues that, 'Clearly, for Porter, patriotism does not so much sublimate as license overt sexual desire'; this Englishwoman's text 'brims with a purely Scottish nationalism'.[67] That Dennis, drawing on René Girard's anthropological theorising about violence and the sacred, can argue his case so strongly reveals much about Porter's work.

In the self-contained system of *The Scottish Chiefs* Wallace resembles a version of the figure Girard develops from anthropology and calls the sacrificial victim, or the primeval god. Almost infinitely plural, associated with sacred violence as well as with healing benevolence, his death enables the restoration of order and the supposedly profound moral differentiation represented by the political separation of Scotland and England.[68]

This reading sees Porter's Wallace as encouraging 'a proto-dictatorship, a cult of personality par excellence'.[69] Dennis's explication is understandable, but not wholly accurate. However wildly adulated, Porter's Wallace makes it clear more than once that he does not regard himself as Scotland's rightful ruler, let alone dictator: as in the poetry of Hary and Hamilton, his role is straightforwardly to restore independence and convince Bruce to reign as king of a free country. Porter's breathlessly articulated piety suppresses sexual desire to some extent, and occasionally she may gesture towards modern Britishness. Nevertheless, the imaginative fascination of her work sides with the champions of Scottish independence. She gives that ideal new life. Readers realise that beyond Wallace's death lies Bannockburn.

Surprisingly, perhaps, *The Scottish Chiefs* came to be viewed as ideal reading for children. Marinell Ash quotes the American folklorist J. F. Dobie recalling it as 1890s boyhood entertainment: 'I read it to myself, and at night as we sat by the fireplace my father read it aloud by the flickering light of a kerosene lamp. What heroes to emulate Wallace and Bruce were!'[70] Having read Hamilton's *Wallace* in his youth, and having supplemented this with *The Scottish Chiefs*, Andrew Munro of Brooklyn, New York, spent thirty-six years scripting a Wallace of his own, adorning his 1908 manuscript with charming watercolours of a tartan-scarfed hero on horseback, and a standing Sir William with sword, lion-rampant shield and plaid.[71] In Boston Public Library a 1920s edition was placed in the Young People's Room; in 1930s Scotland a London-published abridgement was given as a prize to a girl singing at a Gaelic festival; a graphic novel version was published in the 1950s 'Classics Illustrated' series; and as late as 1969 an American critic termed the novel 'a book read by or to innumerable children'.[72] In its blood-red or, sometimes in America, its tartan binding, Porter's tale was treasured as suitable as well as exciting. Recalling how she cherished it in Maine around 1870, American novelist Kate Douglas

Wiggin (author of *Rebecca of Sunnybrook Farm*) wrote of how 'The copy of "Scottish Chiefs" which was the companion of my early days [. . .] had been literally "read to death".' She remembered poring over Porter's novel despite her mother's calls to supper, pleading '"Oh! Only five minutes more, please! Wallace has just rescued Lady Helen and he's bearing her in his arms over the rushing torrent on a bridge of a single tree!"' Over forty years later Wiggin and her sister Nora would edit *The Scottish Chiefs* for Scribner's Illustrated Classics series, fascinated by its having been authored by a 'happy [. . .] carefully-sheltered young English spinster'; it was 'a masterpiece to be enjoyed by each succeeding generation'.[73]

From a twenty-first-century perspective it is easy to smirk at this. Stylistically mannered, *The Scottish Chiefs* bequeathed a legacy to Gabriel Alexander's 1850s fictions *Sir William Wallace: The Hero of Scotland, An Historical Romance* and *Robert Bruce, The Hero-King of Scotland*. But its paciness brings it surprisingly close to the Stevenson of *Kidnapped*, while, several years before Scott published *Waverley*, it established a wide readership for fiction featuring Scottish adventures. From its first printing in 1810 *The Scottish Chiefs* combined historical resonance with high ideals. Its first chapter, 'Scotland', begins,

> Bright was the summer of 1296. The war which had desolated Scotland was then at an end. Ambition seemed satiated; and the vanquished, after having passed under the yoke of their enemy, concluded they might wear their chains in peace. Such were the hopes of those Scottish noblemen who, early in the preceding spring, had signed the bond of submission to a ruthless conqueror, purchasing life at the price of all that makes life estimable, – liberty and honor.[74]

In this time and place 'the spirit of one man remained unsubdued [. . .] Too noble to bend his spirit to the usurper, too honest to affect submission, he resigned himself to the only way left of maintaining the independence of a true Scot.'[75] For Wallace this means living quietly with his wife Marion Braidfoot in their rural home at Ellerslie; but from page one the novel establishes an equivalence between 'independence' and being 'a true Scot'. Though the introduction to her first edition sets England's Nelson beside Scotland's Wallace, and praises the way 'destiny

[. . .] has [. . .] consolidated [. . .] rival nations into one', Porter thereafter pays no further attention to the British ideology of her time: the whole thrust of her story is to glorify the Scottish ideal of independence.[76]

Tartan-clad, wielding a claymore and boasting his own grey-haired harper, her Wallace is a Highlandised, Romantic-era version of the medieval Lowland Scottish hero, partly refracted through the Ossianic poems. Porter's Wallace is aware of the English King Edward's attempts to expunge or capture Scotland's political and cultural heritage – including the 'palladium' or Stone of Scone; but 'Scotland's history is in the memories of her sons' and her 'palladium is in their hearts'.[77] So, internalised, Scottish independence remains privately maintained in the face of a dominant state apparatus that tries to overcome it. Resistance is mounted not only by battling men. Wallace's wife speaks to English soldiery 'in a firm tone': she cannot understand on what authority they hunt down her husband.[78]

Unlike Hamilton of Gilbertfield, the Englishwoman Porter seems untroubled by mentions of medieval Catholicism. Her Lady Helen exclaims, '"Blessed Virgin, protect me!"'[79] Readers enter a monastery: such touches, redolent of Gothic fiction, heighten the atmosphere. Porter takes care not to present all English people as villains: early on, the English soldier Grimsby, though confessing himself 'a Southron', is so horrified by his fellow countrymen's brutality to the population of occupied Scotland that he joins Wallace's forces. Later, having won the Siege of Berwick, Wallace recognises the heroism of the English commander there, who in turn confirms Wallace a 'noble Scot'.[80] '"Preserving to my country its birthright independence"', Wallace recognises English perfidy, but honours English valour when he sees it.[81]

Porter's protagonist is associated with the deeply felt romanticism of his native landscape. In one chapter, 'Corie Lynn', he hides behind a waterfall. Turner had painted the Falls of Clyde at Cora Linn just a few years earlier; Wordsworth would soon include in his 'Memorials of a Tour in Scotland, 1814' lines 'Composed at Corra Linn, in Sight of Wallace's Tower', which quote his own earlier praise of Wallace, maintaining with regard to this Clyde waterfall that 'all who love their country, love / To look on thee', and evoking 'the Wallace Wight'.[82] A footnote to the first edition of *The Scottish Chiefs* states that the Cora Linn site is still revered as the cavern that sheltered Wallace. Porter presents her hero on a cliff-top, waving his sword that blazes in the northern lights; all her chapter titles are place-names, fusing Wallace with a sublime Scottish terrain of chasms, dark rivers, castles, glens, hermits and prisons.

This Gothic fiction comes with occasional history lessons. A hermit tells young Lady Helen about Bruce's lineage. Yet such instructional moments are relatively few in a narrative unburdened by Scott's antiquarian digressions. Still, Porter's novel draws on landscapes made fashionable by Scott's poetry, though not yet by his prose. Approaching Wallace's fastness at Craignacoheilg, his young supporters traverse quintessential 'mountain [. . .] tracts' of the Romantic imagination. 'Loch Venachoir' with 'mists [. . .] pouring torrents and gaping chasms' emblematises Scotland's independent spirit.

> The awful entrance to this sublime valley struck the whole party with a feeling that made them pause. It seemed as if to these sacred solitudes, hidden in the very bosom of Scotland, no hostile foot dared intrude. Murray looked at Ker, 'We go, my friend, to arouse the genius of our country! Here are the native fastnesses of Scotland; and from this pass, the spirit will issue, that is to bid her enslaved sons and daughters be free.'[83]

Though a 'Sir', Wallace denies that he wishes to be regarded as Scotland's monarch, and is adored by the common people. 'A hoary-headed shepherd' cries out to him, '"You free your country from tyrants, and the people's hearts will proclaim their deliverer their sovereign!"' Next, Wallace meets a woman carrying a baby: '"Look on my son!" cried she, with energy; "the first word he speaks shall be Wallace; the second, liberty."'[84] Ideologically, the text is wildly overdetermined. Yet precisely this quality ensures that it reinforces in unignorable ways links between Wallace, Scotland and political independence.

Its title's plural noun signals that *The Scottish Chiefs* is also in part about Robert Bruce; one theme is the relationship between Wallace and his king. Relatively early, it is suggested to Wallace that Bruce is betraying Scotland by apparently acknowledging Edward I's puppet-king John Balliol as monarch. Wallace counters with a somewhat mannered but ideologically purposeful retort: 'for fair Freedom's sake, my heart turns towards the Bruces with the most anxious hopes'.[85] Such determination counters the book's occasional Ossianic notes. Mention of 'Fingal' or of an ancient 'Morven chieftain' adds atmosphere, but where the Ossianic poems featured defeat, *The Scottish Chiefs* has a martyr hero who prefigures Bannockburn and victory.[86] A 'figure breathing youth and manhood', Wallace captures the obsessive attention of Mar's wife, Joanna. Her first reaction, when Wallace comes to rescue her imprisoned husband, is to

exclaim to herself, 'This is a wonder of man! This is the hero that is to humble Edward! – to bless, – whom!' was her thought. 'Oh, no woman! Let him be a creature enshrined and holy, for no female heart to dare to love!'[87]

Soon Joanna's 'traitress heart' determines to secure Wallace. She grows increasingly jealous of her step-daughter who also harbours a passion for this 'young Leonidas' – an allusion to the Spartan leader at Thermopylae, foreshadowing Wallace's absolute bravery and eventual sacrifice.[88] In an encounter which Scott will parody in *Waverley*, the Countess of Mar plays the lute for Wallace and seductively sings him an Ossianic song. Modern readers may snigger as she watches Wallace undressing: 'the heavy corslet unbuckled from his breast, disclosing the symmetry of his fine form, left its graceful movements to be displayed with advantage by the flexible folds of his simple tartan vest'.[89] Affording moments of voyeuristic pleasure, the text articulates female desire. Porter's Wallace is in part an alluring fantasy figure, though less psychologically developed than the later Mr Rochester or Heathcliff.

The book's women, too, act purposefully. Consumed by guilty lust, and bitter about 'the man she loved and the daughter she hated', Lady Mar ends up conspiring against her husband and step-daughter. Eventually, realising she cannot have him, she plots against Wallace too.[90] The younger Helen Mar, 'her bosom, heaving in the snowy whiteness of virgin purity', counters her wicked stepmother's fairytale guile and illicit desire.[91] There is no shortage of love interest. Porter preserves Wallace's military hypermasculinity, while feminising her narrative in a sensational way. To Helen, Wallace is both desirable and, it seems, unattainable. Her older companion, Lady Ruthven, speaking of Wallace's marriage to Marion, makes the widower sound similarly irresistible and unreachable: 'alas! [. . .] he is now for none on earth!'[92]

Porter's eroticisation of Wallace's story added to its magnetism: sexier than ever, the tale of Scottish independence remained brim-full of heroic valour and decorously filled with virtue. Helen's role is not just to adore Wallace; she must also save him from betrayal. Alone in the dark, Porter's young Scotswoman adventures across the stormy landscape, bringing word to her stepfather of a plot against the freedom-fighter, telling Wallace it is her 'duty' to 'regard you and my country as one'.[93] Shortly afterwards Porter presents her version of the meeting between Wallace and Bruce on the banks of the Carron: Wallace emerges as the true spirit of Scotland, able to guide his rightful ruler back to the path of independence. Repeated across the centuries, versions of this encounter at the Carron continue to add imaginative strength to the idea of Scottish popular sovereignty.

Arguing with Bruce, Wallace maintains resolutely that even though the ideal of Scottish independence seems hopeless, he will go on fighting for it.

> 'The cause is now probably lost for ever; and from whom are we to date its ruin, but from him to whom the nation looked as its appointed deliverer? From him, whose once honored name will now be regarded with execration?'[94]

Wallace then urges Bruce to '"Awake to thyself."' The king too must equate his own person with the cause of freedom, struggling alongside fellow Scots for the '"glorious prize [. . .] of national independence!"'[95] Eventually Bruce is won round. Wallace, speaking as the voice of his people, makes his ruler see sense.

Dramatising this encounter in popular prose, Porter revitalised it, taking it to international audiences. Tapping into fashionable popular literary culture as well as parts of the historical record, she received fan-mail from France, Germany, India and Scotland too. As in Hary's and Hamilton's *Wallace*, Porter's hero travels south as a minstrel. A man at a cottage tells him that '"Our renowned Wallace [. . .] is worth King Arthur and all the stranger knights of his round table, for he not only conquers for us in war, but establishes us in happy peace."'[96] Peace is not the most evident commodity in *The Scottish Chiefs,* but the book has its breathing spaces. Travelling incognito with his harp, and meeting King Edward I's French Queen, Margaret, and Piers Gaveston at Durham, Wallace sings to them. He even flirts with the queen who feels herself attracted. Bruce's father, the elderly Earl of Carrick, urges his son to '"Join the virtuous and triumphant Wallace."'[97] Henceforth Bruce and Wallace are united as 'the Scottish chiefs'.[98] Yet the Countess of Mar's intensifying jealousy of her step-daughter leads her to denounce '"the rebel Wallace"'. To him the Countess exclaims, '"When on the scaffold [. . .] remember that it was Joanna of Strathearn who laid thy matchless head upon the block; who consigned those limbs, of Heaven's own statuary, to decorate the spires of Scotland!"'[99] Eventually, plotted against by the Countess and Sir John Monteith, Wallace is betrayed to the English, then taken to the Tower of London. In a noble piece of cross-dressing, Lady Helen disguises herself as a page and manages to make her way to the imprisoned Wallace, awaiting his 'mortal sentence'. The pair pledge themselves to each other. Helen 'with a saint-like smile' resolves to follow him '"into the grave itself!"'[100]

Porter's narrative of Wallace's last hours is supremely melodramatic and irrepressibly pious. Yet these very elements helped ensure the book's nineteenth-century popularity, fitting it for audiences to whom it offered virtuous and boundless adventure. Wallace goes to his death 'with a martyr's confidence in the Power he served'; his beloved Helen embraces him on the scaffold. A footnote even assures readers that his 'last words' were 'from the 71st Psalm'.[101] Probably this piety was derived from popular traditions Jane Porter remembered from her Edinburgh childhood: 'a venerable old woman called Luckie Forbes' had told her tales of Wallace mixed up with bible narratives – stories of 'the Scottish heroes, whom almost deifying tradition had taught me to worship'.[102]

Still, Porter's Wallace is no mere martyr. He also spurs Bruce, who cries out, '"Oh! Let me die, covered with the blood of thy enemies, my murdered Wallace!"'[103] Histrionic male bonding unites the two 'Scottish chiefs', but the final lip-to-lip kiss that Bruce bestows on Wallace is more pledge than homoerotic token. Telling the Scottish nobles he will act '"in the spirit of my heart's sovereign and friend"', Bruce commits himself afresh: '"I offer you a way to recover our hereditary independence."'[104] After he has killed the 'traitor' Cummin [Comyn], with the words '"remember William Wallace!"' the novel moves to its climactic chapter: 'Bannockburn'.[105]

Here Porter telescopes and rewrites history to imaginative effect. Strengthening links between Wallace and Bruce, she places the carnage of Bannockburn so soon after Wallace's death that his 'sable hearse' is parked beside the battle-site. Above it flies the Scottish flag, set in the Bannockburn bore-stone. Conveniently, Porter's fictional Wallace has not been hanged, drawn or quartered; undisfigured, his corpse's presence inspires Scotland's Bannockburn troops: '"By that Heaven-sent palladium of our freedom," cried Bruce, pointing to the bier, "we must this day stand or fall. He who deserts it, murders William Wallace anew."'[106] As the battle progresses, Wallace's betrayer Monteith, dragged to the dead hero's hearse, is struck down by a hundred swords. After the fight – and Bruce's ensuing marriage to Wallace's daughter Isabella – Helen lies prostrate on Sir William's coffin: '"I waited only for this!"'[107] Then, having pronounced that '"Scotland is free, and Bruce a king indeed!"' the victor of Bannockburn notices that Lady Helen, her hands still clasped on Wallace's coffin, has expired. The novel's final two paragraphs unite Helen with Wallace, link Wallace to Bruce and Scottish freedom, then signal that Scotland may flourish with 'prosperity and happiness throughout the land'.[108] So, glancing towards Helen and Wallace, while adapting to het-erosexual ends Old Testament words about men who 'in their death [. . .] were not divided', Porter concludes her expansive, supercharged narrative.[109]

To suggest Porter was a deliberate Scottish nationalist would be absurd. Yet her tale's repeated conflicts climax enthusiasti-cally with Bannockburn. The ensuing peace holds little interest.

Clearly it was possible for nineteenth-century British readers to enjoy this novel without feeling it threatened their modern constitutional arrangements; however, its imaginative sympathy was so clearly on the side of Scottish independence that the overall effect made the ideals of Wallace once again excitingly resonant. Authored beyond Scotland, this English novel kept alive sympathy with Scottish political liberty, even if it may have been possible to respond in a way that made Bannockburn seem a mere youthful episode in the conflicted prehistory of the Hanoverian British state.

Across the Atlantic, such narratives were read differently. Some Americans were responding already to the links between Wallace, Bannockburn and George Washington that George Galloway, Burns and the Earl of Buchan had perceived. In Virginia, for instance, 'A Scotch Historical Note' is appended to the 1800 volume *Washingtoniana*:

> What Wallace began, Bruce completed – By the decisive battle of Bannockburn, in the year 1314, he freed his country from the yoke of England, and obtained the crown as the reward of his valour. ROBERT BRUCE, even at this day, is deservedly a favourite of his nation; unquestionably he was the ablest Monarch that ever swayed the Scottish scepter; and he may, with some propriety, be called the *Washington of Scotland*, because he was successful. – If *our* Washington had been unsuccessful, had fallen a victim to English vengeance, and had suffered a shameful death, then Lord Buchan's parallel had been complete with respect to Wallace – Washington himself, for a time, was in danger of the block or the gibbet – Washington defeated would have been a traitor; but, Washington victorious, became a hero.[110]

The author of this note, who signs himself simply 'R', laments that 'What the sword of Edward could not achieve in the 13th English gold has fully effected in the 17th Century [. . .] and ancient Caledonia is become an obscure province, subject to the pride and power of England!'[111] Those words 'English gold' and 'province' suggest a Scotland seen in terms of Burns's 'Such a Parcel of Rogues in a Nation'. In Burns-loving America a taste for Scottish patriotic verse developed. William Crawford brought out in New York an 1820 edition of Hamilton's 'revised and improved' version of *The History of the Life, Adventures, and Heroic Actions of the Celebrated Sir William Wallace, General, and Governor of Scotland [. . .] translated into metre, from the original Latin of Mr. John Blair, Chaplain to Wallace, by one called Blind Harry.*[112] This was the first publication of Hamilton's poem beyond Scotland, and an American fondness for the heroes of Scottish independence would continue: Bannockburn is invoked in Bayard Taylor's 'Gettysburg Ode' for the 'Dedication of the National Monument, July 1, 1869'. Perhaps, though, the most revealing American literary allegiance had been declared in the year that marked Bannockburn's 500th anniversary.

For July 1814, just days after that anniversary and while British imperial troops advanced to burn Washington DC in the still ongoing War of 1812, America's patriotic poet Philip Freneau (who had denounced in 1778 the 'haughty empire' of Britain) wrote 'The Volunteer's March', a 'little ode [which], with the addition of two new stanzas is somewhat altered from one of Robert Burns' compositions, and applied to an American occasion: the original being Bruce's supposed address to his army, a little before the battle of Bannockbourne'. With a brio that might have appealed to the Scot who hymned General Washington's fight for freedom, Freneau shows how the cause of Bannockburn could be taken over lock, stock and barrel for American ends:

> Ye, whom Washington has led,
> Ye, who in his footsteps tread,
> Ye, who death nor danger dread,
> Haste to glorious victory.
>
> Now's the day and now's the hour;
> See the British navy lour,
> See approach proud George's power,
> England! chains and slavery.[113]

Rechannelling 'Robert Bruce's March to Bannockburn', Freneau urges readers to heed 'Columbia's patriot call' and 'Lay the proud invaders low'. His echoic, committed rhetoric shows just how readily Bannockburn resonated alongside American struggles to defy British imperialism.

Throughout an America alert to such parallels, *The Scottish Chiefs* found eager generations of readers. In July 1810, just months after the book's London publication, it also appeared in New York. United States reprints continued across succeeding decades, their popularity spurring further American publications such as Peter Donaldson's 1851 *Life of Sir William Wallace, the Governor General of Scotland, and Hero of the Scottish Chiefs*, itself soon reprinted. As later historical studies would do, James Paterson's *Wallace, the Hero of Scotland* (reissued on both sides of the Atlantic from 1861 onwards) tries to establish its own authority: 'Miss Porter has already done enough in fiction', writes Paterson, making clear his work is 'not a *romance*'.[114] Porter's pervasive influence explains the presence of 'Helen, Wife of Wallace' in English public schoolboy C. E. Walker's 1820 *Wallace: A Tragedy* (available in print from 1823), which amalgamates aspects of Porter's novel with Burns's words. This dramatic Wallace (first played by the celebrated Victorian actor William Macready) surges into battle exclaiming,

> let the shout of liberty resound
> From hill to hill – till the loud echo shake
> The tyrant's inmost soul! – forward! –
> Death! – death or victory![115]

Later, as in Porter's novel, Helen and Wallace embrace on the scaffold: 'encircled in each other's arms / [. . .] we'll die together!' About to expire, Wallace learns that Bruce has gone to Scotland to lead a rebellion. 'My native land is free!' The curtain falls on the passionate Helen collapsing after 'a wild shreik'.[116]

In England, it seems to have been felt that slight cajoling might be necessary to get London theatre-goers to side with Wallace. In book form, at least, C. E. Walker's tragedy with its passionate Helen and her Scottish hero came with a prologue reminding Scottish and English former antagonists that

> Those times are fled – no longer jealous foes,
> Together bloom the Thistle and the Rose
> United still, oh, make one common cause,
> And give to freedom's son your joint applause![117]

No 'better together' pleading seems to have been required for William Barrymore's *Wallace, the Hero of Scotland*. First performed in 1820, it enjoyed a New York run, was published in Boston and toured as far as Cincinnati. This play's featuring 'Lady Helen Marr' again confirms it as drawing on Porter's fiction. 'A favorite stock drama', it was revived in 1840, 1845, 1846, 1848 and 1856. Early on, its Wallace announces his love for 'lovely Helen' who is assailed by other, wicked suitors; in a final *'Grand tableau* [. . .] WALLACE *and* HELEN *meet and rush into one another's arms'*.[118] Such a celebration of Scotland's independence struggle was true, in its fashion, to *The Scottish Chiefs*. When Graeme Morton (who mentions several similar 1820s dramas) points out that in 'Hodgeson's Juvenile Drama's version of *Wallace, the Hero of Scotland'*, there are 'two women competing to earn the love of Wallace', this too indicates a debt to Porter's fiction.[119]

More than any other nineteenth-century work, Porter's made Wallace and the ideal of Scottish independence welcomed beyond Scotland – whether by Americans or British imperialists. As the nineteenth century advanced, for some 'Southrons', Wallace and Bruce might even figure as heroic appendages to English valour. Writing for children, English versifier Menella Bruce Smedley published her *Lays and Ballads from English History* in 1845. Its table of contents contains such works as 'The Black Prince of England', and is faced by a medallion-style illustration of St George slaying the dragon 'for merrie England'. It seemed to Smedley quite appropriate to include in her volume also 'The Lay of Sir William Wallace' as well as poetry celebrating Bannockburn and Robert the Bruce.[120]

This might seem an improbable fate for such staunch upholders of Scottish independence. Yet the way Wallace was reinvented beyond Scotland by a succession of writers with Porter at their head also had an effect at home. In 1813 R. P. Gillies published in Edinburgh his mannered versification of scenes from *The Scottish Chiefs* in *Wallace: A Fragment*. Its preface calls Porter a 'powerful magician'. Perhaps spurred by Gillies's work, poet and dramatist Joanna Baillie (another admirer of *The Scottish Chiefs*) authored her 'Metrical Legend of William Wallace'. Written in 1814, this was not published until 1821 in

Baillie's *Metrical Legends of Exalted Characters*. Mentioning Bannockburn and imperial soldiering, her Wallace poem opens with a wordier version of Scott's 'Breathes there the man, with soul so dead'. One modern critic argues that for Baillie 'Wallace's heirs have a special mission – or burden – to prod the larger [British] state into recognizing the liberties of its marginal groups', and in Linda Colley's terms Baillie's 'Metrical Legend' can be seen as part of the British work of 'forging the nation'.[121] Yet while early nineteenth-century audiences enjoyed Baillie's British Empire rhetoric, to turn a freedom-fighter who spent his whole life battling against English invaders into a poster-boy for imperialism may be a forgery too far.

However odd such a transformation of Wallace can appear today, many in Scotland and beyond took it for granted. Still, writing of the Wallace legend's 'liberating potential', the twenty-first-century scholar Nancy Goslee is surely right to contend that in such works Wallace's 'power seems only to lend itself temporarily to Union, or to other structures of the status quo in Britain'.[122] Nevertheless, it became easy for English poet Felicia Hemans to sing Wallace's praises even to that 'generous and enlightened people', the English. When in 1819 'A Native of Edinburgh, and Member of the Highland Society of London' offered a prize for the best poem about Wallace inviting Bruce to the Scottish throne, fifty-seven poets entered, among them James Hogg and Hemans. Designed 'to give popularity to the prospect of rearing a suitable National Monument to the Memory of Wallace', the prize was won by Mrs Hemans, whose other works include 'The Heart of Bruce in Melrose Abbey'. The Wallace poems of Hemans, Hogg and Baillie (the last of whom did not enter the competition) have been discussed fully by Nancy Goslee as part of 'a debate over internal freedoms for Britain'.[123]

Hemans's 'Wallace's Invocation to Bruce', with its epigraph from Burns, mention of Ossian and evident knowledge of the Carron's significance for 'free and brave' Caledonians, is both readily and effortfully Scottish – all the more so, perhaps, because authored from beyond Scotland. In the wake of *The Scottish Chiefs*, Bruce is hailed by Wallace as 'yon Chief [. . .] England's [. . .] Royal Slave', and upbraided for his part in slaughtering his 'brethren', Scotland's 'martyr'd chiefs'. Hymning 'The glorious faith of Liberty', Hemans's Wallace calls Bruce a 'Vassal of England'. Eventually, Bruce asks forgiveness, returning to the cause of Caledonian freedom. The poem ends by pointing out to modern-day Scotland that if 'The stranger comes' he 'vainly seeks one votive stone / Raised to the hero all thine own!'[124] What seems needed is a national Wallace monument.

From beyond Scotland as well as from Scotland itself, demands grew for a signature Wallace memorial. Though there were local monuments, including the first Wallace statue, erected by the Earl of Buchan on his estate at Dryburgh in 1814, a grand statement was called for. Scottish historical researchers urged this, as did nationalists from elsewhere such as Hungary's Louis Kossuth and Italian patriots Giuseppe Garibaldi and Giuseppe Mazzini. By the time the national Wallace monument's foundation stone was laid, not far from Bannockburn, in 1861 the poet Janet Hamilton could marvel at how 'Baith Dukes and Lords' mingled with representatives of 'Kirk' and 'State' and 'tens o' thousands' of less exalted folk to mark the ceremony: 'Tae your immortal memories she [Scotland] will turn / For ever – Wallace, Bruce an' Bannockburn.'[125] Hamilton's phrase 'immortal memories' is redolent of Burns Suppers. Just as Burns was increasingly co-opted as an emblem of Scotland within Britain and the British Empire, so was Wallace. Yet for Hamilton the Wallace monument is a 'tower o' strength' raised in 'spite o' traitor Scot or Southern jeer'. Some Scots worried that this monument attracted an element of English mockery. Hamilton's tiny hint of resentment at internal divisions within Scotland, and at jeering from the 'Southern', serves as a reminder of a complex ideological climate. She signals, perhaps, that Wallace might still be an icon of internal strife and resistance within Britain, rather than simply a neo-British imperial pin-up. In London the *Times* newspaper, conscious of the monument project, had dismissed Wallace as 'the merest myth'.[126] The 'myth', strong in popular culture for centuries, was not about to disappear.

South of the Border, there was a consciousness of Scottish cultural difference. However, the only significant substantial Victorian poem from England to show considered interest in Scotland is Arthur Hugh Clough's 1848 'Long-Vacation

Pastoral', *The Bothie of Toper-na-Fuosich*. Part of a group of Oxford students on a reading-party in the Highlands, Clough's protagonist muses on 'Scotch and English', and thinks of 'the grand old times of bows, and bills, and claymores, / At the old Flodden-field – Bannockburn – Culloden'. He concludes that

> We are the better friends, I fancy, for that old fighting,
> Better friends, inasmuch as we know each other better,
> We can now shake hands without subterfuge or shuffling.[127]

Not many subsequent English writers thought as much about Scotland as Clough. When they did, these lines might well sum up their attitudes. North of the Border, 1852 brought the launch of the National Association for the Vindication of Scottish Rights which sought to improve Scotland's standing within the Union.[128] If the NAVSR's political orientation favoured 'a traditional, even a deliberately antiquarian, view of the nature of the Scottish polity', nonetheless, as Murray Pittock argues, their 'antiquarianism was active and vital, not passive and defeatist'.[129] Prominent in this National Association was the Jacobite-inclined poet and Professor of Rhetoric and Belles Lettres at Edinburgh University, W. E. Aytoun, whose works had such titles as 'The Heart of the Bruce'. Aytoun argued in *Blackwood's Edinburgh Magazine* for the British government to create a new post: a secretary of state for Scotland. The NAVSR's founder was Walter Scott's second cousin, James Grant, prolific author of historical novels like *The Scottish Cavalier* (1850). Though short-lived, the National Association (1852–6) sent a clear message: 'We are not a province.'[130] *Punch* mocked its list of Scottish grievances; an 1853 cartoonist pictured 'The sad Scottish lion' slumped in an armchair, swaddled under a tartan travelling rug.[131] The NAVSR indicated that literary imaginations and distinctively Scottish politics could come together, but it did so rather feebly.

Embarrassingly for supporters of Scottish independence, William Wallace became the subject of a 'Summary History' by another William, whom many now regard the world's worst poet. William McGonagall's contribution begins, 'Sir William Wallace of Ellerslie, / I'm told he went to the High School in Dundee.'[132] It gets no better. For most Victorians Wallace and

Bruce might be regarded as precursors of imperialist Britons. The English patriotic versifier H. D. Rawnsley, author of *Ballads of Brave Deeds* (1896), penned 'Brave Beresford, an Incident of the Zulu War' and glorified 'Skelton, the Birthplace of Robert Bruce's Ancestors' in 'A Dream of Robert the Bruce'. Readiness to merge Bruce with English and British imperial triumphs might be summed up in the novel *In Freedom's Cause: A Story of Wallace and Bruce* (1894) by G. A. Henty, author of popular fictions for boys that included *Under Drake's Flag* (1883) and *With Clive in India* (1884). Henty's attitudes were at one, surely, with the placing of imposing early twentieth-century statues of Wallace and Bruce on either side of the arched gateway to Edinburgh Castle, welcoming visitors to what was for many decades a British Army barracks.

Braveheart

Yet if those 'Scottish chiefs', so celebrated in the nineteenth century, were increasingly appropriated for imperial Britishness, then the disruptive power of their association with the struggle for Scottish independence would return later with a vengeance. Again, the resurgence was powered from beyond Scotland. The immediate prompt for this twentieth-century upsurge of interest was international tourism. Entering Edinburgh Castle and seeing there 'the statue' of Wallace alongside that of Bruce, visiting American novelist and scriptwriter Randall Wallace became intrigued by his medieval Scottish namesake.[133] The creative result of his subsequent investigations were a novel and the screenplay for Mel Gibson's 1995 box-office hit, *Braveheart*.

A global as well as an Oscar-winning popular success, Gibson's movie made historians splutter. Deploying uncertain Latin, Gaelic, English, Scots and French, the film is, though, largely true to the Wallace myth as it had been developed through literary imaginations. Randall Wallace's 'best source' was found at the University of California Los Angeles. Hunting there for Wallace narratives, the screenwriter could locate few major historical studies, but grew fascinated with a book which it took the librarians some time to locate: 'a 1722 Hamilton edition of BLIND HARRY which the library was preparing to discard as worthless'.[134]

Randall Wallace had already envisaged his namesake's story as a martyrdom patterned on the Gospel narrative of Jesus Christ. Portraying Wallace as a martyr had appealed to writers from Hary to Porter. Recognising that Hamilton, in revising Hary, had been 'embellishing the story, as poets will do', Randall Wallace read the 1722 *Wallace* with excitement. He took from it, for instance, the notion of Wallace's relationship with 'the Princess, though I changed her age, and made her the wife of Edward II, while Harry made her the wife of Longshanks'.[135] Whether or not he was familiar with *The Scottish Chiefs*, Randall Wallace, like Porter before him, sought to add more female interest. In *Braveheart* the imprisoned Scottish hero is visited by his French-born royal lover who has clearly shifted her allegiance from England to Wallace. Already pregnant with his child, she gives him a long farewell kiss before he is taken for execution. However historically absurd, this Hollywood realignment of the Wallace story develops elements from earlier literary imaginations, both in Scotland and beyond.

Very much a globalised Hollywood blockbuster, *Braveheart* was filmed partly on location in Ireland; its soundtrack is played by the London Symphony Orchestra; its star-cum-director is Australian. Randall Wallace's novel, whose hero crushes 'like pecans' the heads of English soldiers, has a discernibly American accent.[136] Purists may be discomfited that both book and movie come from beyond Scotland. But from the eighteenth century onwards part of the strength of the way the Wallace myth entered the literary imagination was its transportability. Taken up in England and America, it also travelled to Australia. For the Wallace Memorial erected in 1889 at Ballarat, New South Wales, Frances Lauderdale Adams wrote his lines,

This is Scotch William Wallace. It was he
Who in dark hours first raised his face to see:
    Who watched the English tyrant nobles spurn,
Steel-clad, with iron hoofs the Scottish free:

Who armed and drilled the simple footman Kern,
Yea, bade in blood and rout the proud Knight learn

His Feudalism was dead, and Scotland stand
Dauntless to wait the day of Bannockburn!

O Wallace, peerless lover of thy land,
We need thee still, thy moulding brain and hand!
For us, thy poor, again proud tyrants spurn,
The robber rich, a yet more hateful band![137]

This Australian Wallace has lost his title 'Sir'. Outdistancing feudalism, he has become even more a man of the people, one of 'the Scottish free'. Like Canadian poets Isabella Whiteford Rogerson, William Wye Smith, Mary McIver and Evan MacColl who also hymned Bruce and Wallace, Lauderdale in Australia sings a hero who, while still recognisable, has gone far beyond his native Scotland. In today's Australia Les Murray in 'The Physical Diaspora of William Wallace' writes of a Wallace whose reputation is global, his fate in India or Australia 'to be Scots for some lifetimes / and then Scots no more'.[138] The Australian-American-English-Irish-Scottish *Braveheart* brings back Wallace from a post-colonial beyond, but Randall Wallace's novel still carries the sense of a Scottish 'patriot: he wanted Scotland ruled by Scots'.[139]

Though avoiding several set pieces from earlier imaginings, such as the meeting between Bruce and Wallace on the banks of the River Carron, Randall Wallace's version includes the political argument crucial to that encounter. More than once it presents Wallace as a subject whose ideological strength lets him reproach Bruce for failure to lead Scots committed to independence. As often in earlier tellings, Wallace seems nobler than his king. Hamilton of Gilbertfield is not Randall Wallace's sole source; the scriptwriter glances, too, for instance, at English Renaissance dramatist Christopher Marlowe's *Edward II* with its homoerotic intrigue. Understandably, some have found notes of homophobia accompanying Anglophobia in *Braveheart*. Yet overt Anglophobia and pejorative homosexual hints have been part of the literary discourse of Wallace narratives from at least the *Scotichronicon* in which Wallace accuses Bruce of being a 'semivir' and suffering from 'effeminata ignavia' – effeminate cowardice.[140]

As Elspeth King has recognised, *Braveheart*'s scriptwriter

draws from Blind Hary's narrative elements including the slaughter at the Barns of Ayr, Wallace's entanglement with female English royalty, the siege of York and the hero's sending a severed head to King Edward. Elspeth King points out that 'Even one of the most criticized aspects of the film, the appearance of the Scots with blue face paint, has its origin in BLIND HARRY, where in a supernatural incident at the beginning of BOOK VII, Wallace has a saltire painted on his face by a woman with a sapphire.'[141]

No doubt encouraged by the scriptwriter's early decision to draw on New Testament accounts of the crucifixion, and by the preoccupations of controversial star/director Mel Gibson (whose later gory films include a Mayan epic and *The Passion of the Christ*), *Braveheart* the motion picture is replete with slaughter. Reductively, it makes its Englishmen consistently unattractive. The literary scholar Gary Kelly has suggested that *The Scottish Chiefs*, so enduringly popular in North America, may have been a source.[142] Perhaps he is right. Yet although, like Porter's novel whose Wallace is surrounded by 'a chain of brave hearts', the movie adds sexual excitement to the hero's story, unlike *The Scottish Chiefs* it makes no attempt to present English virtue.[143] In its eye-stabbing, beheading bloodthirstiness, as in its depiction of the English as tyrannically villainous, *Braveheart* is quite consistent with Hary and Hamilton who constantly present 'the Southron' as two-dimensionally murderous. Readers appalled by the Anglocidal violence of Gibson's movie would do well to remind themselves of the text that excited its scriptwriter. Hamilton's poem is replete with moments such as Wallace's slaughter of 'Southrons' at Dumbarton.

> Wallace thought then, it was not time to stand
> His noble sword, fast gripped in his hand;
> With such a stroke the captain did surprise,
> As cut off all that stood above the eyes.
> Another then he killed in great ire,
> A third he threw into the burning fire [. . .][144]

In their battle scenes the poems on which *Braveheart* draws are every bit as bloody as the film. When *Braveheart*'s Bruce says to his massed troops at Bannockburn, 'You have bled with Wallace. Now bleed with me,' his phraseology may call to mind Burns's Bannockburn poem; but, as Burns too recognised, imagery of blood and bleeding is fundamental to Hary's version of the Wallace tale, not least as mediated by Hamilton.

What everyone remembers about Mel Gibson's film is the hero, as he is being disembowelled, yelling out, '*Freedom!*' Arresting and improbable as this may be, no single word is truer to the Wallace of popular poetic imagination. The same word is also the very last one heard in the movie, whose voice-over tells how in 1314 at Bannockburn the 'patriots of Scotland [. . .] fought like warrior-poets. They fought like Scotsmen and won their freedom.'[145] Identical phrasing occurs in *Braveheart* the novel.[146] That term 'warrior-poets' is surely Hollywood's glance towards the ex-soldier Hamilton of Gilbertfield's version of Hary. 'I had to see through the eyes of a poet,' writes Randall Wallace in his prologue.[147]

This story of the 'charismatic' leader who can 'unite both noble and common Scot' carries forward crucial elements of earlier literary imaginings' narrative and tone. Yet *Braveheart* also demonstrates why these are now insufficient and even damaging when it comes to envisioning a modern ideology of Scottish independence.[148] Derided for its gender politics, the film has been turned into a witty homosexual fantasia ('O Mel! Mel of the hair extenders! Braveheart!') by Scottish poet David Kinloch whose Whitmanesque, exclamatory 'Braveheart!' makes Wallace, however ironically, an icon of gay liberation as well as of liberties more generally: that is what Kinloch's poem's last word – 'free' – invokes.[149] Nonetheless, in a rather different, more po-faced way, *Braveheart* has been subjected to scathing attack by critic Colin McArthur who writes of Gibson's movie as 'the modern "Ur-Fascist" text *par excellence*', complaining that it 'has convulsed Scottish society'.[150] Some might see these claims as exaggerated, but McArthur's analysis is not simplistic. He subjects this 'most gory of films' to a scene-by-scene micro-analysis dependent on the technique of Roland Barthes's *S/Z*. Perhaps the oddest thing about McArthur's scrutiny is that, while it notes the way 'At various points in the execution process the *mise-en-scène* presents Wallace as the crucified Christ', his lengthy analysis pays no attention to Wallace's final crying aloud of the word '*Freedom!*'[151]

Though this yelled word, the ideological climax of the film, maintains a fidelity to the core of the Wallace narrative in earlier fictions, McArthur's only interest in Blind Harry's *Wallace* is to attach it to his denunciations of the film's 'historical distortion'.[152] Elsewhere in his analysis, this critic – who sees *Braveheart* as 'primarily "about" Hollywood cinema', and links it to 'United States dominance in military, diplomatic and (less extremely) economic terms' – maintains that 'Part of the dubious appeal of *Braveheart* was its mobilizing of two of the most potent discourses of the modern world – nationalism and populism. The key (naturally undefined) terms of *Braveheart*'s rhetoric – "Scotland", "freedom" and "the people" – are empty vessels into which can be poured the most noxious of contents.'[153] McArthur shows convincingly how aspects of the movie have been appropriated by racist and neo-Fascist groups, and may readily lend themselves to such appropriation. Yet there seems a recurrent implication that the linked rhetorical 'empty vessels' he singles out as key to the movie – '"Scotland", "freedom" and "the people"' – invite *only* noxious contents. Seeing the Wallace myth in *Braveheart* as wholly negative, 'vulgar' and 'contemptible', he uses it (as Unionist politicians have done) to attack present-day Scottish aspirations for independence; he also deploys it to combat globalised cinematic imperatives operating largely beyond Scotland.[154]

McArthur's excoriating critique of *Braveheart* quotes Alex Salmond telling the 1995 Scottish National Party Conference in Perth that 'we can say with Wallace – head and heart – the one word which encapsulates all our hopes – *Freedom, Freedom, Freedom*'. McArthur shows how, for a time at least, some SNP politicians drew on words and images from the film.[155] Given that *Braveheart* was released, was much discussed, and won five Oscars during a decade when unignorable pressure was building in Scotland for a referendum on the issue of political devolution, it would have been surprising if no use had been made of the film by political campaigners. Yet it may also be to the credit of activists who favour Scottish independence that, conscious of charges like those of McArthur, their use of *Braveheart* has been limited. As far as literary imaginings go, for many of the contemporary poets in the 2005 anthology *The Wallace Muse*,

Mel Gibson's Wallace and earlier depictions of the hero have grown inextricably blended; Hollywood seems as much part of the story as Hary, Hamilton or Burns.

Today's Unionists like nothing better than to refer to Scottish Nationalists as 'Bravehearts', seeking at times to portray them as neo-Fascists; in particular, Scotland's First Minister Alex Salmond has been caricatured by some as a Great Dictator. Yet, in the run-up to Scotland's 2014 independence referendum the Scottish Government's minister responsible for constitutional affairs, Deputy First Minister Nicola Sturgeon, has shown little inclination to associate herself with Mel Gibson's Hollywood hero. Instead, she more cannily invoked the progressive small-nation politics of the internationally lauded Danish television series *Borgen* – a world away in terms of gender politics and democratic values from the blade-wielding 'Mel Wallace'. Photographed in Edinburgh in 2013 beside a tartan-suited Sidse Babett Knudsen, who plays the shrewd Danish Prime Minister Birgitte Nyborg in *Borgen*, and even 'interviewing her for Scottish Television', Sturgeon implied an imaginative counter-narrative to that of the 'Braveheart Nat'.[156] As she has said of Nyborg and her drama,

> I should say it's fiction! [. . .] She's not real! But I do like the way it portrays politics: decent folk getting it wrong sometimes but doing it for the right reasons. I like to see a confident, intelligent, articulate woman, portrayed in a position like that. Denmark – a small, independent country, doing politics quite nicely. It certainly appeals to me.[157]

Sturgeon made these remarks shortly after an opinion poll had shown her to be the politician most highly regarded among Scots. Though her admiration for *Borgen* has been mocked, it indicates a clear commitment to an intelligently scripted modern democratic pluralism in 'a small, independent country'. As the next chapter will indicate, the shrewdest ideology of modern official Scottish nationalism has arrived at a very deliberate pluralism, associated with literary imaginations very different from those behind *Braveheart*.

Chapter 4

Difficult Modern Scots

Stirrings

Twentieth-century Scottish political nationalism is about self-respect. It grew from a wish to reassert the dignity of the nation. Initially ambivalent about the British Empire, Scottish nationalists came to argue for a post-imperial Scotland governed from Edinburgh, not London. In less than a century their ideology moved from being regarded (sometimes rightly) as the preoccupation of a well-nigh lunatic fringe to becoming the policy of a Scottish government. Though their contribution is sometimes passed over, many of the independence movement's founders were creative writers whose poetry, prose, editing and polemic reshaped Scotland's intellectual landscape. Like most twentieth-century politicians, almost all these nationalists were male. Several relished a difficult Modernist literary spikiness, mixing avant-garde aesthetics with commitments to minority languages. But their difficulty was also temperamental, even strategic. A number were 'difficult' in the sense of being weirdly eccentric. They opposed the status quo and, sometimes, each other. Even if few, like the outspoken nationalist and minor poet Wendy Wood, blew up pillar boxes, most could be provocatively combustible.

Some writers, most notably Hugh MacDiarmid, made wildly incendiary, anti-English pronouncements, committing themselves to a visionary Communism; others, again including MacDiarmid, flirted with Fascism.[1] Yet, as the membership list of the extremist 'Right Club' reveals, in the 1920s and 1930s

Fascism attracted more Unionists than nationalists. Richard Griffiths has shown that whereas nationalists invoked the 1320 Declaration of Arbroath, the notoriously anti-Semitic, Scottish Tory Unionist MP Archibald Ramsay and his wife the Honourable Mrs Ismay Ramsay preferred to trumpet in Arbroath, Peebles and elsewhere their denunciations of Jews and Communists alongside their admiration for Hitler.[2] In his valuable study, *Fascist Scotland*, Gavin Bowd has detailed how Fascists in twentieth-century Scotland belted out 'Rule, Britannia' and the British national anthem, singing how they would 'for ever be true / To the Red, White and Blue / And British will always remain'.[3] Fascism attracted Unionists from the left as well as the right of the political spectrum: Scottish Labour MP Robert Forgan became a Fascist in 1931. The Scottish Nationalists too had Fascist sympathisers, sometimes including literati. While writers including Hugh MacDiarmid and Sorley MacLean are thought of as inclining towards Communism, on occasion MacDiarmid could invoke Fascist ideals, while the poet Douglas Young – 'future leader of the SNP', as Gavin Bowd points out – wrote to the Gaelic poet George Campbell Hay in January 1939 that 'If Hitler could neatly remove our imperial breeks somehow and thus dissipate the mirage of Imperial partnership with England etc he would do a great service to Scottish Nationalism.'[4] No one has yet provided a full comparative examination of Irish and Scottish literary and political attitudes towards Hitler's regime, but such a work – likely to be controversial on both sides of the Irish Sea – is needed. Bowd's survey suggests that though in Scotland there were appeasers and Fascists among both Unionists and nationalists, nonetheless they were a small minority. The Scottish nationalists' struggle was on the whole peaceful and democratic. Quickened by the Russian Revolution and 1930s European crises, their imaginings were part of a literary efflorescence that came to be called 'the Scottish Renaissance'; but no one was killed for Scottish nationalism. Long before it began to succeed at the ballot box, its struggles were waged, strikingly effectively, through acts of literary imagination.

Arguably, decades before the birth of the Scottish National Party, later nineteenth-century Scots such as Arthur Conan

Doyle, J. M. Barrie and even the Robert Louis Stevenson of *Strange Case of Dr Jekyll and Mr Hyde* had done more to define modern London in literature than to define modern Scotland. Yet Stevenson could maintain that 'Despite their proximity, there are no other two peoples in the world so different from each other as the Scots and the English'; while the 1890s Edinburgh cultural patriot John Stuart Blackie continued to write of 'Wallace and Bruce', denouncing those who had ' sold / Scotland's grace and Scotland's honour / For a bag of English gold'. Professor Blackie hymned medieval 'Aberdonia' and 'Dunedin', but his phrasing recalls Burns's eighteenth-century complaint, 'We're bought and sold for English gold.' Some co-opted Wallace and Bruce for Britain's empire; Blackie remembered their stubborn resistance:

> Fought and won is Freedom's battle;
>   Scotland's muse no more shall mourn;
> England no more toss her haughty
>   Crest o'er glorious Bannockburn.[5]

Seeking home rule, Blackie and others wanted to articulate Scotland's cultural distinctiveness, but few readers of his poetry detect a renaissance.

Associated with the 'Kailyard [cabbage-patch] School', J. M. Barrie in *Auld Licht Idylls* (1888) and Ian Maclaren in *The Days of Auld Lang Syne* (1895) simply accepted Scotland's provincial status. London-centred publishers found such tales of quaint Presbyterian small-town life commercially successful. In Edinburgh Blackie's literary admirer Patrick Geddes titled his 1890s magazine *The Evergreen*, invoking Allan Ramsay's patriotic eighteenth-century anthology of the same name. Geddes mixed with Ossianically-toned writers of the Celtic Twilight, but longed for a Scottish Renaissance; he also pioneered modern ideas of town-planning and authored *The Biology of Sex* (1890). As in Yeats's Ireland, so in Geddes's Edinburgh nostalgic or eccentric longing for the national past might accompany radical ideas. Spurred by Ireland's example, several Scottish writers nurtured a wish for a more modern political identity beyond that of the British state.

Some such authors were markedly exotic. Nicknamed 'Don

Roberto' – his mother was part Spanish – Robert Bontine
Cunninghame Graham boasted Scottish aristocratic descent,
ultimately from the noble Graham who died fighting alongside
William Wallace. Distant family ties with the Bruces led to
Cunninghame Graham's being termed the 'uncrowned King of
Scotland' – a claim apparently backed by the polymath Andrew
Lang.[6] Born in London and heir to estates in Scotland, Graham
was upper-class yet politically radical. Larger than life, as a
seventeen-year-old he worked on the Argentinan pampas; in
his twenties he accompanied a Chilean poetess to teach fencing
in Mexico City; afterwards in rural Texas he lost everything to
Native American raiders.

Globetrotting in Africa, the Americas and Europe, Graham
chronicled all those places. *Mogreb-el-Acksa* (1898) records
his attempt to reach the Moroccan forbidden city of Tarudant.
His other writings range from *A Vanished Arcadia, Being Some
Account of the Jesuits in Paraguay* (1901) to literary sketches
of the Scottish district of Menteith. Politically radicalised in
South America, in Scotland Graham became a Liberal MP in
the 1880s. Eccentrically for the time, he grew increasingly anti-
imperialist, supporting universal suffrage, land nationalisation,
Irish and Scottish Home Rule, and the abolition of the House of
Lords. Some thought him a traitor, or at best a Don Quixote. In
1888, having allied himself to Keir Hardie, he became founding
president of the new Scottish Labour Party. During an era when
the Westminster government had recently set up the Scottish
Office (an Edinburgh branch of the British Civil Service, helping
to administer Scotland) Graham was among several authors
who were born outside Scotland, yet came to feel themselves
deeply Scottish, pressing for not just cultural but also political
recognition of the northern nation's distinctiveness.

Some of these campaigners from beyond Scotland were dash-
ingly eccentric neo-Jacobites. The Australian Scot Theodore
Napier, editor of a political and literary magazine, *The Fiery
Cross*, wrote about Stuart monarchs as well as *Scotland's
Demand for Home Rule or Local National Self-Government*
(1892) and *Bannockburn and Liberty, An Appeal to Scotsmen*
(1893). Napier wanted the date of Bannockburn celebrated as
Independence Day. Photographed in full Highland dress with

rakish feathers in his bonnet, in 1896 he published *Scotland's Relationship to England, Past and Present: A Plea for the National Rights of Scotland*. He denounced Scots for being 'more interested in a football or a golf match than in the political welfare and freedom of their country'. Invoking Wallace and Bruce for having won 'freedom from English thralldom', he argued that 'a country that does not govern itself cannot be regarded as free'. Graeme Morton has shown how verse was part of Napier's campaigning: 'Shades o' the immortal Wallace, / Bruce an' Burns tae duty call us.'[7] Deploying the 'chains and slavery' rhetoric of Burns's 'Scots, Wha Hae', Napier urged late Victorian Scots to 'Hark to the voice of Liberty!'

> Land of the Bruce, awake, reply,
> Assert your rights, avenge or die!
> Break now your chain, be free, ye brave,
> Nor live degraded – England's Slave![8]

In 1901, when *The Fiery Cross* called for a National Party in Scotland, Napier addressed the Scottish Patriotic Association's first gathering at Bannockburn, 'kissing his dirk', as Murray Pittock points out, and denying his allegiance to the king.[9]

At Bannockburn the spiritedly difficult Napier championed 'national rights'. So, as Home Rule was more widely debated, did Cunninghame Graham at Wallace's Elderslie. Demonstrations of Scottish political restlessness had been held there since 1905. Early assertions of the possibility of devolved government or even independence, these convocations celebrated Bruce and Wallace, but also looked ahead. A extreme nationalist website still cites Graham's rousing speeches at 'Wallace Day' rallies: in 1925 he maintained Wallace had 'laid down his life for the cause of Scottish Home Rule'; seven years later, Graham determined to 'repeal the Union'.[10]

If the London-born, Harrow-schooled Cunninghame Graham was a literary man and a credible politician, albeit one regarded as eccentrically difficult, he was joined as an advocate of Scottish independence by West Hartlepool-born Edward Montague Compton Mackenzie. Educated at another English public school, then at Oxford, Mackenzie made his name as a novelist with *Sinister Street* (1913). This semi-autobiographical exploration of youthful sexuality scandalously dealt with gay *mores*, and was admired by Henry James. Widely travelled in America and Europe, the sophisticated, prolific Mackenzie was a late, committed convert to Scottish nationalism. Like Graham, he had felt attracted to Scotland since childhood. In 1926 he visited the Highlands, inspired by Gaelic enthusiast Ruaraidh Erskine of Marr whose Scots National League, founded five years earlier, advocated confiscating estates from absentee landlords and contesting English ascendancy. Mackenzie wrote articles for Erskine's *Pictish Review*, then edited by Hugh MacDiarmid. Soon, in his early forties, Mackenzie relocated to the Hebridean island of Barra. Authoring novels, travel books and memoirs on Scottish and non-Scottish subjects, this adoptive Scot went on to write *The Monarch of the Glen* (1941) and *Whisky Galore* (1947). In their own right and when adapted to form the bases of film and television productions, these witty, gentle fictions achieved widespread popular success.

A friend of MacDiarmid and Graham, Mackenzie had moved to a Scotland where an increasing number of organisations sought political change. In 1926 the poet Lewis Spence had founded the Scottish National Movement. Author of *The Story of William Wallace* (1919) and an advocate of Scots-language verse, Spence shared Graham's interest in Mexico and South America; while his movement aimed to promote a distinctively Scottish cultural outlook, Spence's horizons, like those of Mackenzie and Graham, were wide. His 'patriotism [. . .] a religion, deep, passionate, intense', Spence's William Wallace had 'not only a British but a European reputation', appealing intensely to 'Mazzini, the Italian patriot'.[11] Spence's poetry, though, can sound nostalgic. At its best, it links the Scots tongue to a similar international outlook, and contains unexpected imaginative glints. 'The Prows o' Reekie', wishes that the 'high-heapit toun' of Edinburgh might 'Sail aff like an enchanted ship', crossing the world's seas to 'kiss wi' Venice lip to lip'.[12] Fascinated by the occult (though he called Hitler 'Satanic', he had his own anti-Semitic streak), Spence could be eccentrically difficult, again like Graham and Mackenzie.[13] Each of these writers is, in his way, fascinating. Yet rather than surveying the full, often bristling extent of Modernist-era Scottish writing and its engagement with nationalist ideals (something done expertly elsewhere by Margery Palmer McCulloch), the rest of this chapter will focus firstly on the most imaginative Scottish Modernist literary nationalist, Hugh MacDiarmid; then on MacDiarmid's important American literary ally, James H. Whyte. It will conclude by considering how aspects of Whyte's legacy conditioned the education of the First Minister who leads first Scotland's pro-independence majority government – Alex Salmond.[14]

Hugh MacDiarmid's Scottish cause

When the National Party of Scotland was established in 1928, Lewis Spence was one of its founders, and wrote about it in the *Edinburgh Review*. Though he lists among the 'prominent Scottish Nationalists' who are acting on the 'provisional council' of the new party 'Mr R. B. Cunninghame Graham, the well-known litterateur and authority on Latin-America, Mr. Compton Mackenzie, the novelist', and 'Mr. C. M. Grieve, J.P., the leader of the "Scottish Literary Renaissance"'(who wrote under the pen-name 'Hugh MacDiarmid'), Spence does not discuss literary or artistic aspects of Scottish nationalism. Instead, he concentrates on economic and governmental matters. These range from anxiety about emigration to 'the tyranny of sport' in the Highlands, and the headquartering in London of formerly Scottish commercial institutions.[15] If anything, the early National Party, like the modern SNP, seems to have played down its literary strengths. Yet, despite trying not to sound like a poet, Spence indicates the new party was dominated by authors. Its first president was Cunninghame Graham, dissatisfied with the Scottish Labour Party's luke-warm commitment to Home Rule. In Glasgow in 1928, when organisations dedicated to independence met to discuss forming a new political grouping, Graham, Mackenzie and MacDiarmid all featured in a photograph of the nascent National Party's principal leaders.[16] Six years later the National Party of Scotland merged with the more culturally nationalist Scottish Party to form the modern Scottish National Party. The SNP's origins were bound up with literary imagination, and by 1928 the independence cause had been given an inspiring literary aesthetic through the arresting, difficult verse of Hugh MacDiarmid.

One of MacDiarmid's earliest surviving poems, written before Borders-born Christopher Murray Grieve first styled himself 'Hugh MacDiarmid' in 1922, is 'Allegiance'. Apparently composed late in World War I, when MacDiarmid served with the Royal Army Medical Corps in Salonika and Marseilles, this poem celebrates Mediterranean 'treasures of the antique great'. Yet it asserts that the deepest 'allegiance' of the 'Scots Borderman' remains with local streams and 'shy, light eyes' in Scotland. These have 'sealed me the servant of a cause forlorn'.[17] This dynamic of maintaining allegiance not to the great but to the more vulnerably local undergirds some of MacDiarmid's finest poems. At times his politics might seem 'a cause forlorn'. However, confident that Scotland was culturally, intellectually and politically as good as anywhere else, he encouraged it to take its place in the wider universe.

MacDiarmid shared this aspiration with Graham, and recalled his first meeting with that older writer as a turning point: 'I was introduced to R. B. Cunninghame Graham by William Archer in London in the early 1920s. My decision to make the Scottish Cause, cultural and political, my life-work dates from that moment.'[18] What appealed to MacDiarmid about Graham was how he combined support for Scottish independence with a clearly internationalist vision. MacDiarmid's imagination was excited by Scotland, Scottish words, images and places, but also by the sheer scale of the universe, and by world literature. Convinced any 'Scottish literary revival' would require 'get[ting] rid of our provinciality of outlook', in astonishing lyric poems written throughout his thirties, as well as in longer works, he articulated a relationship between intense local and national commitment and his sense of the dizzying vastness of the cosmos.[19] Boosted by Nietzschean daring, this relationship is signalled in one of his earliest printed poems, 'Edinburgh'. The Scottish capital is 'a mad god's dream'; from Edinburgh Castle's 'soaring battlements [. . .] Earth eyes Eternity'.[20]

Relating Scottish places to the great scheme of things is crucial to MacDiarmid's poetry. 'Parnassus and Schiehallion are one' he asserts in a 1921 sonnet, relishing the name of a Highland mountain; also 'Schiehallion and Calvary are one'.[21] Soon MacDiarmid was exulting in the Scots language, not as a vehicle for the provincially pawky, but as potentially attuned to the Modernist aesthetics of Joyce, Eliot and Dostoevsky. A politics was implicit in this approach. Calling Graham's *Mogreb-el-Acksa* 'one of the best books of travel ever written', MacDiarmid admired Graham's mix of internationalism and nationalism: 'For almost ten years he regularly addressed the two chief nationalist demonstrations at Stirling and Elderslie.'[22] Yet, though the nationalist-internationalist MacDiarmid respected and participated in such gestures of homage to Bruce and Wallace, those Scottish heroes of independence seldom feature in his verse. He argued that 'The field of Bannockburn', while capable of attracting tourists, 'has been a singular failure as a national rallying ground'.[23] He distanced himself deliberately from nostalgic Scottish versifying, which was all too prone to invoke old heroes in a lazily sub-Burnsian manner.

An inveterate editor of short-lived literary periodicals, MacDiarmid unleashed torrents of nationalist propaganda. He linked these to his advocacy of a renaissance in Scottish litera-ture. Looking back on 1920s and early 1930s nationalism in Scotland, he complained in 1952 that 'as had happened in the Labour and Socialist Movement, a gang of dullards with no cul-tural interests' had taken over from an initial political leadership distinguished by its literary imagination:

> At that time the Scottish National Movement was largely led by writers – Lewis Spence, Neil M. Gunn, the Hon Ruaraidh Erskine of Marr, William Gillies, Eric Linklater, and others, above all, a little later, Compton Mackenzie. Cunninghame Graham could get along well enough with men like these [. . .][24]

Yet when it came to Scottish independence and the literary imagination, MacDiarmid's genius lay not so much in often scandalously splenetic prose as in making great poetry out of the most vulnerable aspect of the emergent movements for Scottish independence: eccentricity. Scottish nationalism in the early twentieth century may have attracted support from writers who came to Scotland from Australia, England and elsewhere, but it was generally regarded as completely eccentric. Scottish Nationalists were 'difficult', unrealistic. As Mackenzie's biographer writes,

> To the great majority of Scots, the British Empire, with the emphasis on British, offered an umbrella nationality which they were happy to adopt as their own. The corollary was that Scotland could not be more than a region of the Home Country [. . .][25]

In such circumstances, to see Scotland as potentially independent seemed perverse. Yet MacDiarmid's finest Scots poetry repeatedly exploits perspectives of eccentricity to masterly effect, encouraging readers to relish the rewards of siding with the utterly marginal. This is true of his explicitly political poems, and of those without explicit political content. The strength of his eccentric approach generates a politics, an oblique angle on the cosmos and human society, subtly reinforcing imaginative commitment to Scottish independence. Such a politics is all the more fertile for being implicit.

Dedicated to his young wife, Peggy, who had recently given birth to their first child, 'The Bonnie Broukit Bairn' dates from 1925. In it the poet imagines the earth as a dirty-faced baby–neglected in a universe where grandly coutured planets process across the sky.

Mars is braw in crammasy,	*handsome in crimson*
Venus in a green silk goun,	
The auld mune shak's her gowden feathers,	*shakes; golden*
Their starry talk's a wheen o' blethers,	*[lot of nonsense]*
Nane for thee a thochtie sparin',	*thought*
Earth, thou bonnie broukit bairn!	*smudge-covered child*
But greet, an' in your tears ye'll droun	*weep*
The haill clanjamfrie![26]	*[whole rabble of them]*

This poem's language is markedly Scottish in sound as well as vocabulary. Its first line invites a vigorously rolled 'r'; its italicised concluding lines deftly offset the polysyllabic last word with a long preceding run of monosyllables, and contain some shrewdly finessed acoustics as the 'r', then 'ee', then 't' of '*greet*' are reversed in the 't', then 'ee', then 'r' of '*tears*'. Yet, however musical, MacDiarmid's lyric is also somewhat difficult; removed from standard English, it deploys a Scots perspective on reality that is ec-centric. Winningly, 'The Bonnie Broukit Bairn' presents such a shift of perspective as almost irresistible: its changed viewpoint is allied with the hard-wired human instinct to attend to a crying child. The value system of a universe dominated by the grand is overthrown as soon as the infant weeps. Until then, clad in green silk, crimson and gold, the other planets command attention; the dirty 'bairn', introduced in offhand fashion, seems marginal, even embarrassing – a provincial nobody in the vast scheme of things. The child's crying upsets all that. What was marginal becomes compellingly significant, counting for more than all the rest –'*The haill clanjamfrie*'. Overturning initial assumptions about what matters most, this powerful lyric subtly implies a politics as well as a parental concern. Using a difficult modern Scots and a perspective of cosmic eccentricity, it works.

None of the poems in MacDiarmid's first Scots collection, *Sangschaw* (1925), mentions Scotland. Occasionally he uses a Scottish place name, but language, metaphysics and striking (often religious) imagery preoccupy him – not the discussion of nationalism: no William Wallace here. However, these poems are thoroughly and determinedly Scottish in their use of language MacDiarmid took from Scots dictionaries. Especially he used the lexicon produced by John Jamieson, an early nineteenth-century minor poet who had written of William Wallace and who had edited the work of Blind Hary.[27] MacDiarmid had a taste for recondite words. His work in English and 'Synthetic Scots' is linguistically bristling, but hardly antiquarian. A synthesising Modernist imagination produces this sparky, challengingly difficult modern Scots whose use foregrounds the politics of language.

Formally, MacDiarmid's use of the traditional Scots ballad stanza reinforces a sense of rootedness in Scottish tradition. Yet *Sangschaw* contains, too, poems drawing on work by Germany's Stefan George and the Russian Dmitry Merezhkovsky; there is even a poem in French. The effect is both manifestly Scottish and committedly international. 'Au Clair de la lune' presents an earth littered with what is left of 'Empires', and asserts that 'Muckle [great] nations are dust'. Change appears inevitable, politics a sparky, dynamic process, not a perpetual status quo.[28] Ideology and the politics of language combust.

MacDiarmid's deployment of the figure of Christ is comparably radical. Sometimes the divine being represents committed energy: the 'bairnie [infant] Christ' has 'nae thocht o' sleep' in the lullaby-like 'O Jesu Parvule'; repeated images of death and resurrection indicate insistent renaissance.[29] In one sense Christ's resurrection parallels MacDiarmid's galvanic revival of the Scots tongue; it also signals that what has been written off can come back, against the odds, with startling energy. More than one poem imagines resurrection at the last trump. In 'Crowdieknowe', another powerful lyric from this strikingly alliterative poet, men from an old Scottish graveyard are resurrected to 'glower at God an' a' his gang'.[30] Poems full of resurgent energies threaten to topple received opinion. They imply restlessly metamorphic possibility. MacDiarmid's Scotland just might be reborn.

Often eccentric, insistently challenging, at once full of Nietzschean insurrection and of an acoustic familiar to Scottish readers from the ballads, Burns and medieval verse, these poems seem at once a continuation and a new beginning. Despite allusion to a story about Robert the Bruce's murder of John Comyn in the conclusion of 'I Heard Christ Sing', the only Robert Bruce mentioned in *Sangschaw* is a twentieth-century one: MacDiarmid dedicates 'Ballad of the Five Senses' *'To Sir Robert Bruce, President of the Burns Federation, in appreciation of his efforts to foster a Scottish Literary Revival.'*[31] That poem ends by envisaging a 'flourishing tree' and 'gowden [golden] sun'.[32] In planning his Scottish Renaissance and in his early Scots lyrics MacDiarmid was shaped by engagement with Burns clubs and the 'Burns movement'.[33] His aesthetic of exalting the little over the grand owes something to the poet of 'To a Louse'. MacDiarmid sought nothing less than to be a twentieth-century Burns, writing for a country on its way to independence.

Keen on manifestos, he published his clarion-call 'Gairmscoile' (Singing School) in his second Scots collection, *Penny Wheep* (1926), whose Burnsian title denotes small ale. In 'Gairmscoile' this poet who valorises what others dismiss as smallness celebrates the sound of that minority language, the Scots tongue, linking it to imagined ancient creatures – 'beasts in wha's wild cries a' Scotland's destiny thrills'. There is a determination to press ahead with a difficult cause despite those who question the apparently eccentric stance,

> For we ha'e faith in Scotland's hidden poo'ers,
> The present's theirs, but a' the past and future's oors.[34]

In such work MacDiarmid links his literary and political campaigning both to an older, independent Scotland and to an envisaged future. This is the dream state that he and his literary allies – from Cunninghame Graham to poems' dedicatees such as nationalist novelist and political campaigner Neil Gunn – aim for. Allying himself with past and future, MacDiarmid seeks to circumvent present difficulties. Sometimes his visionary imagination parts company with immediate political reality. Matthew Hart, in *Nations of Nothing But Poetry* (2010), regards MacDiarmid's project as impossibilist.[35] Yet the poet's bookish utopianism could be exaggerated: while writing some of his most imaginative early Scots verse MacDiarmid was an effective local councillor; his most successful overtly political long poem, *A Drunk Man Looks at the Thistle* (1926), acknowledges mundane difficulties as well as visionary possibilities.

A Drunk Man is dazzlingly exciting but ultimately perhaps less satisfying than MacDiarmid's shorter Scots lyrics. Formally, as in those lyrics, the poet often deploys ballad metres. This gives his work a popular intonation even as it includes sometimes recondite materials. It serves, too, to conjure up the feuding milieu of traditional Border ballads where Scottish and English reivers clash. The protean rhetorical excess of *A Drunk Man* includes objectionable moments. Early on, its boozy speaker mentions 'some wizened scrunt o' a knock-knee / Chinee'.[36] Twenty-first-century audiences may find the work's ready association of Scottishness with drunkenness and often belligerent masculinity problematic. *A Drunk Man* can seem an incarnation of entrenched, rebarbative aspects of Scottish culture, but is surely aware of that fact and repeatedly interrogates it. Haunted by other texts, including *The Waste Land*, the 'Drunk Man' speaker can be abusive. Yet he is also resolutely intellectual, conscious of a Scotland filled with possibilities of rebirth, while in danger, too, of becoming a waste land where people lead a 'livin' death!'[37] Such is MacDiarmid's commitment to decentred or ec-centric energies that he seeks to make his speaker's 'Montrose or Nazareth' – his supposedly provincial location – a place of potentially metamorphic energy. He wants Scotland to have its own confident vision, an ability truly to perceive.

Much of his poem involves the struggle to achieve this. So mired in social and psychological problems that it is imaged as 'THE barren fig', Scotland requires a difficult, even miraculous, new start:

> *Pu' Scotland up,*   Pull
> *And wha can say*
> *It winna bud*
> *And blossom tae.*
>
> *A miracle's*
> *Oor only chance.*
> *Up, carles, up*   men
> *And let us dance!*[38]

Sounding sometimes like a prophet, and sometimes like a man dancing a jig, the speaker is overcome at many points by his own and Scotland's problems. Though his wife, 'Jean', is granted some authority over him towards the poem's conclusion, the lines 'And nae Scot wi' a wumman lies, / But I am he', seem to assume that to be Scottish means to be heterosexually male.[39] The poem can be read as an examination of Scottish masculinity and male sexuality, but may be compromised at times by blokeish bluster. Still, a certain slapstick humour is one of its rewards, as is a very different sense of profound struggle to reconceive national identity. Plumbing the 'deeps' of the conscious and unconscious mind – both his own intelligence and 'Whaur [where] the soul o' Scotland sleeps' – the speaker aims to breathe new life into a 'deid' (dead) nation, letting it see itself and be seen as a fully realised part of the world and the universe.[40] He seeks for it both dignity and imaginative fire.

> I wad ha'e Scotland to my eye
> Until I saw a timeless flame
> Tak' Auchtermuchty for a name,
> And kent that Ecclefechan stood   *knew*
> As pairt o' an eternal mood.[41]

Attempting to bring to birth a new vision of Scotland, the speaker faces up to the damage, pain and repression that are also part of its (and his) inheritance. All are imaged as the thistle, at once distinctive national emblem and 'infernal', tumour-like growth.[42] Just as MacDiarmid's early Scots lyrics are saturated with sometimes heretical Christian imagery, so too is *A Drunk Man*. Determined to acknowledge Scotland's miseries, including those of the 1926 General Strike, the poem hopes to transcend the whinge of '"*Puir Auld Scotland*"'. The Scottish poet must offer himself up, Christlike, to set his country free.

> *A Scottish poet maun assume*   must
> *The burden o' his people's doom,*
> *And dee to brak' their livin' tomb.*[43]   die to break

Part of an idealistic, ambitious attempt to galvanise a nation through an act of literary imagination, these plain words can sound self-aggrandising. The poem's voice – or one of its most compelling voices – tries to get Scottish people to '*learn*' and '*move*', rather than remain in '*their auld groove*'.[44]

Eventually, this formally eclectic poem's thistle with rose-like flowers, sharp, branching thorns and formidable roots emblematises not just Scotland but the human situation. It partakes alike of dream and inescapable hurt. Yet the nation it represents is as valid as any other. The 'King and System' that represent England or Anglocentric Britain are something the speaker may 'admire', but they exercise 'nae claim upon my hert'.[45] Heart and head are committed to a vision of Scotland that takes on cosmological intensity as the poem nears its conclusion. The nation is glimpsed, albeit 'like a flea', taking its place on the 'birlin' [spinning] edge' of the great wheel of the universe: eccentric, yet a fully distinct national part of the whole.[46]

This wheeling universe in MacDiarmid's poem can seem medieval or Dantescan; yet also, with its mention of Einstein as well as Euclid, modern. *A Drunk Man* seeks to acknowledge the difficulty of the Scottish past and present, while perceiving nation and cosmos in all their glory.

> He canna Scotland see wha yet
> Canna see the Infinite,
> And Scotland in true scale to it.[47]

From this perspective 'Bannockburn and Flodden' appear mere 'Little wars', minutiae in the great scheme of things.[48] Yet in this grand, galactic pattern, to be small is not to be worthless.

The poem's metaphysics and politics combine as it concludes. After its huge, cosmic wheeling, the speaker glimpses figures from Scottish history including 'Rabbie Burns and Weelum Wallace'. Then, beyond a vision of the stars as themselves resembling 'thistle's roses' in flower across the universe, the exhausted Drunk Man gains a fleeting perception of a great celestial 'Silence', a Scots counterpart to that 'Shantih' which is the last word of Eliot's 1922 *The Waste Land*. Then he imagines being brought down to earth firmly by his wife:

> O I ha'e Silence left,
>
> – 'And weel ye micht,'
> Sae Jean'll say, 'efter sic a nicht!'[49]

Written when MacDiarmid was at the height of his powers in the mid-1920s, *A Drunk Man Looks at the Thistle* may be invoked more frequently than it is read in full. Less demanding than *The Waste Land*, its difficulty, too, pays dividends. Marking a decisive turn away from retelling old tales of Bannockburn, this spiky 1926 production offers a vision of Scotland attuned to modern circumstances, political possibilities and literary culture.

Often with scandal and aplomb, MacDiarmid continued to set forth a difficult articulation of modernity. Right from its title, which refers to the problem of confining a curly snake, *To Circumjack Cencrastus* (1930) challenges readers. As much anthology as poem, it worries whether '*a Scot*' can be '*weel-eneuch read*' to '*scrawl a phrase frae Scotland yet / On the palimpsest o' th' Infinite*'.[50] Artistically challenged, Scotland is seen as hobbled by unthinkingly accepting the value of the Union, which too many people assume 'brocht / Puir Scotland into being / As a country worth a thocht'. Scotland must make its own voice heard, not succumb to 'the Balliol accent' associated with an English or Anglo-Scots leadership.[51] In a country whose academic assumptions about literature were still substantially bound by the rhetoric and belles lettres tradition, MacDiarmid detects cultural betrayal. A professoriate refuses to acknowledge Scotland's distinctiveness.

> *Oor four Universities*
> *Are Scots but in name;*
> *They wadna be here*
> *If ither folk did the same*
> *– Paid heed to a' lear*   learning
> *Exceptin' their ain,*   own
> *For they'd cancel oot syne*   then
> *And leave us wi' nane.*[52]

As often, this poem's rhetoric may be exaggerated, but when it was written no academic in all Scotland had the title 'Professor of Scottish Literature'. In his long poem, MacDiarmid pays tribute to authors including Burns and the eighteenth-century Gaelic poet Alexander MacDonald. Doing so, he celebrates Scottish cultural traditions: part of his work to bolster Scotland's inheritance of literary imagination, one that connects with the word-hoards of other countries too.

All this boosts his case for matching literary imaginings to political independence that can see beyond '*the British Empire*'.[53] Not isolated, his Scotland has different cultural co-ordinates from England. Resolutely suspicious of narrow ideas about '"Oor Scots tradition"', he wants a Scottish writing alive to both Burns and Proust, to Gaelic poetry and the fiction of James Joyce. In pursuit of his Modernist ideal, he takes an iconoclastic view of even the greatest traditional exemplars. *To Circumjack Cencrastus* argues that 'Bruce, a hero in certain airts [parts], / Was Norman first and Scotsman second / And aye o' self, no' Scotland, reckoned.'[54] Like much of MacDiarmid's work, *Cencrastus* is nowhere more gleeful than when provoking readers into reconsidering presuppositions. Still, this questioning of the consistency of the victor of Bannockburn goes no further than the accusations against Bruce voiced in earlier literature by a fictionalised William Wallace.

Ever the gadfly, when MacDiarmid gives to a lyric section the title '*Separatism*', he chooses a term usually deployed pejoratively by Unionist opponents of Scottish independence. In these lines (later produced as a poster), the word carries a subtly different inflection:

If there's a sword-like sang
That can cut Scotland clear
O' a' the warld beside
Rax me the hilt o't here.   *Reach*

For there's nae jewel till
Frae the rest o' earth it's free,
Wi' the starry separateness
I'd fain to Scotland gie [. . .][55]   *give*

With its sword-song image, this might seem MacDiarmid at his
most *Braveheart*-ish, and even isolationist. Yet the word 'starry'
in the second verse suggests that the aspiration is for a Scotland
that may be stellar alongside all sorts of other jewel-like stars,
independent from them – separate – yet also one among many.
This 'separatism' is subtler than first appears, while still deliberately provocative.

The insurrectionary, 'difficult' side of MacDiarmid produced
poems with titles like 'Ode to All Rebels'. Such instincts intensified his verse, leading to enliveningly stinging prose tirades:

> Scottish literature, like all other literatures, has been *written*
> almost exclusively by blasphemers, immoralists, dipsomaniacs, and
> madmen, but, unlike most other literatures, has been *written about*
> almost exclusively by ministers [. . .][56]

Besotted with the Scots tongue, he could maintain in *To
Circumjack Cencrastus* that '*Speakin' o' Scotland in English
words*' was like listening to '*Beethoven chirpt by birds*'; he
might even think it possible to find through research and
imaginative engagement 'the Omnific Word' in Jamieson's Scots
dictionary.[57] Published at the start of a decade when many
writers perceived something was politically amiss in Scotland,
To Circumjack Cencrastus has more in common with Edwin
Muir's later *Scott and Scotland* (1936) than most critics have
cared to admit. MacDiarmid regarded that book as a betrayal,
but Muir's polemic, too, was designed to provoke. It urged
readers to re-evaluate Scottish culture and politics, not least
from an international perspective. Where Scotland's capital city
should be, Muir saw 'a blank, an Edinburgh'; Muir's claim that
'The prerequisite of an autonomous literature is a homogeneous

language' highlighted wider questions about Scotland's lack of autonomy.[58] Influenced not least by the Anglophile T. S. Eliot who saw Scottish culture as irredeemably fragmented, Muir turned against the political nationalism that fascinated him when he was MacDiarmid's 1920s neighbour. Articulating an anxious national self-loathing not unfamiliar among Scots, he later called Burns and Scott 'sham bards of a sham nation'.[59] Condemning Scotland's greatest poet as a mere 'sham' was too far even for MacDiarmid, however much he liked to shock his contemporaries.

Among these was the novelist Lewis Grassic Gibbon, who thought MacDiarmid 'seems to have done, seen, and read everything': ' He launched the ship of Scottish Nationalism. Probably [. . .] he invented the Celts, staged the rising of William Wallace, led a schiltroun at Falkirk, and wrote Dunbar's poetry for him.'[60] The tone here mixes amusement with admiration. MacDiarmid and Gibbon collaborated on the wonderfully provocative *Scottish Scene*. The poet, then resident in the Shetland Islands, presents Edinburgh as 'a highly educated community in which any genuine intellectual life is out of the question.'[61] Though the two authors sometimes clashed politically, Gibbon and MacDiarmid spurred each other on. *Scottish Scene* (1934) contains Gibbon's finest short story, 'Smeddum' – outstandingly alert to the politics of gender as well as to the politics of language. Yet Gibbon affords MacDiarmid the last word: in their book's final essay, 'The Future', the poet conjures up the spirit of Bannockburn through linking what he wants for Scotland with the most wistfully idealistic lines in John Barbour's medieval *Bruce*. This is surprising, since elsewhere MacDiarmid destabilises Bruce as a Scottish icon: in *To Circumjack Cencrastus* he aligns that monarch with his modern namesake, the editor of the *Glasgow Herald*, arguing that the king fought for Scotland at a time when 'it was *less* imperilled'.[62] Nonetheless, 'The Future' opens with a resonant medieval epigraph and a characteristically definitive statement. Quoting the twelve lines of *The Bruce* which begin 'A! fredome is a noble thing!', MacDiarmid asserts that

This is the quintessential note of the Scottish genius struck wherever throughout the centuries a Scotsman for however brief an interval has risen above the dodges of every dialectical system and struck a major note.[63]

Next, MacDiarmid connects this note with Burns, citing the revolutionary words,

> A fig for those by law protected!
>   Liberty's a glorious feast!
> Courts for cowards were erected,
>   Churches built to please the priest.[64]

Arguing that 'everything else in Scotland must be measured up against that glorious stanza', he invokes 'the Arbroath Declaration of Independence', then argues the modern case for Scottish political autonomy.[65] In this prose piece MacDiarmid's literary imagination is bound up with now discredited political details such as Douglasite economics. As often, he mixes insight with vitriol. References to Scotland's having 'a national character singularly unaffected by a cosmopolitanism only equalled by that of the Jews' sound philosemitic, but, for all that the phrasing probably refers to Scottish Presbyterians, other mentions of 'Scottish Jews' with 'stany herts' at the very end of *Scottish Scene* disconcert post-Holocaust readers.[66]

Matching MacDiarmid in intelligence, Grassic Gibbon outshone him as a writer of imaginative prose. Like Lewis Spence, Gibbon was fascinated by ancient civilisations, not least those of Central and South America. His fiction ranges from classical Rome in the 1933 *Spartacus* (its politics conditioned by Red Clydeside and modern German 'Spartacist' Communist revolutionaries) to science fiction. By far Gibbon's finest novel, however, is *Sunset Song* (1932), the first part of his trilogy *A Scots Quair*, which surveys modern Scottish society. Like 'Smeddum', this trilogy engages insightfully with revolution and nationalism. In remarkable prose that fuses an older Scots acoustic with English, *Sunset Song*'s opening ranges across centuries of Scottish history, taking in matter passed down through literature since before the days of Blind Hary.

> But Wallace came through the Howe right swiftly and he heard of Dunnottar and laid siege to it and it was a right strong place and

he had but small patience with strong places. So, in the dead of one night, when the thunder of the sea drowned the noise of his feint, he climbed the Dunnottar rocks and was over the wall, he and the vagabond Scots, and they took Dunnottar and put to the slaughter the noble folk gathered there, and all the English, and spoiled them of their meat and gear, and marched away.[67]

Yet with its sexually abused female protagonist Chris Guthrie, this sometimes Lawrentian novel focuses not on the medieval past but on early twentieth-century north-east Scotland whose menfolk go off to World War I and in many cases do not return. Instead of celebrating British military victory, the book chronicles the passing of a way of life. The 'sunset song' is 'The Flowers of the Forest'. Quoted in Gibbon's text, it laments Scotland's dead at the 1513 Battle of Flodden – in Scottish culture the very opposite of Bannockburn.

As Gibbon's trilogy develops, rural Scots try to come to terms with predominantly urban modernity. His characters encounter what most perceive as nationalist eccentricity: 'the nationalist candidate was Hugo MacDownall, the chap who wrote in Synthetic Scots. Ewan asked *Why synthetic? Can't he write the real stuff?* And Archie said *I'm damned if I know. Sounds more epileptic to me* [. . .]'[68] Gibbon's Ewan Tavendale is attracted by political radicalism. He feels modern 'Masters' simply tell lies 'even as they'd lied in the days of Spartacus', but Gibbon portrays a Scotland unable to find a clear political direction.[69] A socialist but not, ultimately, a nationalist, he has his heroine Chris return to her natal landscape in a conclusion partly satisfying, yet partly, in a sense, regressive.

> Time she went home herself.
> But she still sat on as one by one the lights went out and the rain came beating the stones about her, and falling all that night while she still sat there, presently feeling no longer the touch of the rain or hearing the sound of the lapwings going by.[70]

As well as highlighting, sometimes subtly, the politics of gender – a topic more usually examined in this period by Scottish writers such as Nan Shepherd or Catherine Carswell, who seem to have had much less time for Scottish nationalism – *A Scots Quair* looks at political extremes, but eventually backs away from them. In 1935 Gibbon, whose *Sunset Song* may sound more nationalist than its author, died at the age of thirty-four. Whether or not they shared his suspicion of nationalism, generations of younger writers came to admire his wholehearted imaginative engagement with language, gender and class, as well as his ambition (paralleling that of Ireland's James Joyce) to produce a national epic. Some of the most interesting of those younger writers, however, sought to produce a 'song' that looked to a new dawn rather than a 'sunset'.

Among these younger figures whose ideas and expression still resonate with twenty-first-century debates was Hamish Henderson. Born in Perthshire then brought up in London, at the end of his teens, in the summer of 1939, the Cambridge-educated Henderson stood within spitting distance of Adolf Hitler; in his twenties he fought in the British Army at El Alamein and made his name as a poet of desert warfare; in his thirties he impressed alike photographer Paul Strand and film-maker Pier Paolo Pasolini, and he dandled the infant Annie Lennox on his knee. Genial, bisexual, at once forthright and elusive, this polymathic champion of a Scottish republic became a great and generous folksong writer and collector. Having returned from World War II to a Scotland he saw as full of 'Vichy Scots' Unionists content with their government in London, Henderson initially allied himself with republican nationalist poets, not least Sorley MacLean and MacDiarmid. Wanting a synthesis of poetry and politics that would harness popular energies in his reinvigorated nation, he wrote in 1947 of the National Assembly, which was campaigning for a Scottish Parliament, that its struggle was 'Scotland's Alamein'.[71]

Not everyone heeded his rallying-cry. Despite his enthusiasm for *Sunset Song*, MacDiarmid had little time for modern folk-singers; and Norman MacCaig, for all his nationalist sympathies, complained about 'the Scottish working class, with its interest in football, and beer, and nothing beyond'.[72] Henderson, who found his greatest folk material among tinkers and the poor, acknowledged a working-class 'philistinism', but thought it far from the whole picture. Returning to Italy, he worked on translating the *Letters from Prison* of his hero Antonio Gramsci; he also spent time in Northern Ireland where he developed his theories of 'the poet or bard [. . .] integrally part of the community'.[73] In many ways Gaelic models, and the vernacular example of Burns formed Henderson more than did MacDiarmid with whom he was sometimes uneasily linked. In Glasgow in 1948 he organised celebrations marking the thirtieth anniversary of the trial of Glasgow radical John Maclean whose 'Red Clydeside' ideals Lewis Grassic Gibbon had known at first hand. MacDiarmid, Sorley MacLean and others contributed to these celebrations. Henderson's biographer Timothy Neat argues 'this was the day when Hamish's Scottish Folk Revival joined MacDiarmid's Scottish Renaissance as an equal partner, in the process by which the twentieth-century culture of Scotland was to be transformed'.[74] In his new 'John Maclean March' Henderson sang of Lenin and how 'The red will be worn, my lads, an' Scotland will march again.'[75] His folksongs also achieved wide circulation in World War II and after. Sometimes disappointing in print, their own verbal tunes require the boost of music and, ideally, of communal singing, to achieve true vibrancy. Henderson's most famous song, the 'Freedom Come All Ye' of 1959/60, energised events from Edinburgh to New Zealand, and, invoking John Maclean, its paean to freedom for 'aa the bairns o Adam' is still sung as well as disseminated across the internet.

Encouraged by Sorley MacLean's brother Calum, Henderson developed his gifts as a folksong collector and guider of others, sometimes through his pioneering work for the School of Scottish Studies at Edinburgh University from 1952 onwards. Eager for a Scottish parliament and enthused by the 'terrorism without terror' which resulted in the swiping of the Stone of Destiny in 1950, he knew no nation has ever lived without treasuring its poetry and song. Fittingly, a phrase from his 'Freedom Come All Ye' is now part of an inscription at Bannockburn.

Very different from both the Henderson whose Scottish republicanism he shared and from the Grassic Gibbon whose Unionism he saw as backward-looking, since at least 1926 MacDiarmid had been attracted to being 'Whaur extremes meet'. Around this Modernist-inflected impulse he had developed his aesthetic of the 'Caledonian Antisyzygy'.[76] However fruitful for poetry, his willed extremism could be intensely problematic. Notoriously, this poet of 1930s hymns to Lenin was expelled from the Scottish National Party for communism; then, later, from the Communist Party of Great Britain for national-ist deviation. At the other extreme, while Stalin and Hitler were still allied, the MacDiarmid who had flirted with Fascism asked, scandalously, in his second-rate poem 'On the Imminent Destruction of London, June 1940',

> Is a Mussolini or a Hitler
> Worse than a Bevan or a Morrison?
> At least the former proclaim their foul purposes
> The latter practise what their words disown.[77]

Here MacDiarmid looked forward to London's destruction. Recent commentators have continued to debate the consistency or otherwise of his politics. Scott Lyall defends the integrity of his political thought against W. N. Herbert, who, while admir-ing MacDiarmid's poetry, describes him as 'an appalling politi-cal thinker'.[78]

The positive use of eccentricity that quickened MacDiarmid's best poetry and energised – for good and for ill – his vision of politics could also take him in very different directions. So his greatest 1930s poem, 'On a Raised Beach', considers the rela-tionship of human beings to geology. From the perspective of geological time, humanity is completely eccentric.

> What happens to us
> Is irrelevant to the world's geology
> But what happens to the world's geology
> Is not irrelevant to us.
> We must reconcile ourselves to the stones,
> Not the stones to us.[79]

This remarkable long poem is again a work of cosmological imagination. Whereas in *To Circumjack Cencrastus* the poet had thought to locate 'the Omnific Word' in Jamieson's Scots dictionary, now he finds it in the world of stone.[80] Compared with the powerful longevity of even a pebble, 'All human culture' is 'a Goliath to fall'.[81] At times MacDiarmid's speaker is more attracted to the alien world of stone than to humanity. 'On a Raised Beach' marks an extreme limit to this poet's explora-tion of difficult imaginative standpoints that are both eccentric and productive for poetry. Yet to take his geological poem as articulating the politics of Scottish nationalism would be absolutely distorting. MacDiarmid's oeuvre is about far more than simply Scottish independence and the political imagination. He was, though, determined to advance the independence cause as it emerged onto the stage of serious politics. Taking him far beyond notions of bread-and-butter political issues, his imagination confirmed him as a poet. It did not, however, make him the subtlest political theorist. That role in Scottish nationalism fell to another man of letters, J. H. Whyte, dedicatee of 'On a Raised Beach'.

James H. Whyte's pluralist Scottish nationalism

James H. Whyte's most important contribution to Scottish literature came not through poetry but through brilliant editing. In his avant-garde magazine 'On a Raised Beach' and other MacDiarmid poems first appeared alongside a nuanced theory of modern Scotland as an independent nation. Though the twenty-first-century art historian Tom Normand has presented part of Whyte's story, the rest has gone untold.[82] Today in a Scotland that has regained its parliament and which looks like recovering even greater autonomy, it is time to set out in full this young American's background and achievement. Like so many other people, Whyte found MacDiarmid infuriatingly difficult at times, while respecting his best work. In response, MacDiarmid saluted Whyte by dedicating to him not one but two of his most outstanding poems.

Whyte's background conditioned his work in Scotland. Dreicer, not Whyte, was his original surname. James Huntington Dreicer was born in 1909 into a spectacularly wealthy Manhattan family. His mother, Maisie Saville Shainwald, was the daughter of Ralph Louis Shainwald of Madison Avenue, an industrialist from a German Jewish background. James's father, Michael Dreicer from Minsk, had become a highly successful New York jeweller with substantial property investments on Fifth Avenue. Paintings the family collected are now among the holdings of the National Gallery in Washington and New York's Metropolitan

Museum. When James was four his father sold a Fifth Avenue property for a million dollars. The family fortune increased and the boy spent summers on Long Island, at Deepdale, Michael and Maisie's summer residence, previously owned by one of the Vanderbilts. With his younger brother Donald, James Huntington Dreicer enjoyed a plutocratic childhood.[83]

In 1921 Michael Dreicer died, aged fifty-three. His properties around Fifth Avenue were worth over $3.5m. Remaining jewellery stock was sold to Cartier for $2.5m. Much of the art collection was given away.[84] Soon his widow moved to Britain where she married a Scottish consulting engineer and naval architect. Jardine Bell Whyte had worked previously as technical director for the British Ministry of Shipping, New York and Canada.[85] So it was that James Huntington Dreicer became James H. Whyte. In Britain his boyhood remained privileged; his brother Donald, who became a photographer, took some of his earliest pictures in childhood, which show members of the British royal family at Balmoral.[86] The Whyte family mixed in high society.

James Whyte attended England's Stow public school, then Trinity College, Cambridge, for session 1928–9. He passed the Qualifying Examinations for the Law Tripos in 1929.[87] At Trinity's Magpie and Stump debating society, a contemporary wrote, 'Mr. J. H. Whyte's seriousness is not very serious.'[88] In October 1928, when Whyte was elected a member, the society debated the motion, 'That films should be seen and not heard'.[89] Whyte's brother went to Oxford where, with a friend, he started Christ Church's first film club, later the Oxford University Film Society, then went on to work for London's Lefevre Gallery.[90] James Whyte's career took a different, but related turn. He moved to Scotland soon after abandoning his Cambridge degree; in April 1931 the *Scotsman* mentions him as president of the Edinburgh Film Guild. That month Whyte put up a prize of £10 for the best 'rough shooting script' for a documentary film about contemporary Edinburgh and its people. Though John Grierson had pioneered film documentary, the *Scotsman* considered that 'This would seem to be the first attempt adequately to represent Edinburgh on a film.'[91]

Conceivably it was love brought Whyte northwards. He was involved in a relationship with Scottish art critic John Tonge, a recent graduate of St Andrews University. Residing in North Street, St Andrews, Whyte had established his magazine *The Modern Scot*, published from Dundee and printed in Montrose by James Foreman of the *Montrose Review*, the newspaper for which MacDiarmid had worked as a journalist. Its second (summer 1930) issue carried MacDiarmid's highly polemical 'Clan Albainn' essay. Building on the poet's recent 'demand for a far more strongly worded new Covenant for signature at Bannockburn', this urged 'militant action' as the only way for Scotland to secure independence. It appeared to advocate armed struggle: 'I simply assert that Scotland will never secure a measure of independence worth having without having been forced to adopt means similar to those taken by the Irish.'[92] Gavin Bowd has drawn attention to a May 1931 Glasgow *Evening Times* cartoon showing kilted Nazis of the 'Scottish Nationalist Original Socialist Conservatives' parading 'under Hamish MacHitler' and carrying swastika banners, one of which also shows 'Bruce & the Spider', and Bowd points out that in the same year in the summer issue of *The Modern Scot* an anonymous review (attributed by Duncan Glen to Hugh MacDiarmid) deals with 'Wyndham Lewis's book on Hitler', arguing that

> Hitler's 'Nazis' wear their socialism with precisely the difference which post-socialist Scottish nationalists must adopt. Class-consciousness is anathema to them, and in contradistinction to it they set up the principle of race-consciousness.

MacDiarmid (I assume he is the author) then urges the Scots as 'a Gaelic people' to side with Ireland and Wales in rivalling English dominance in the British Isles. He calls for 'the acceptance of Blutsgefuhl [blood feeling] in Scotland'.[93] Yet if in one mood he could argue this in *The Modern Scot* – and have Whyte print it – then, nevertheless, MacDiarmid eschewed the Fascist manoeuvres of Scots such as Captain Ramsay, whom he later feared Hitler might choose to rule a conquered Scotland.[94] Even the sometimes wildly extremist poet had no time for those who denounced, as he put it, 'Irish, Poles, English, and other aliens' in Scotland; rather in 'Clan Albainn' he thought that 'these aliens are citizens of Scotland and their interests are bound up with its condition'.[95]

While MacDiarmid welcomed immigrants, on paper at least at this time he advocated on occasion a potentially violent nationalism that Whyte (though he did not censor MacDiarmid's views) made clear he had no time for. However, admiring the poet's imaginative gifts at their best, Whyte wrote enthusiastically to encourage his 'good work' in 1933; he greeted MacDiarmid on visits to St Andrews, and thought nothing of sending telegrams to Whalsay – the Shetland island where MacDiarmid lived for part of the 1930s – commissioning material for *The Modern Scot*.[96] From the start Whyte demonstrated that he had his own political ideas and that it was he who called the editorial shots – not least because his financial standing enabled him to pay for work with a generosity rare in Scottish literary publishing.

Travelling as far north as Barra, and familiar with London society, Whyte met Grassic Gibbon, Catherine and Donald Carswell, Edwin and Willa Muir, and a host of other Scottish writers; he also enjoyed excellent contacts abroad. His magazine has been described as nothing less than 'the principal forum for Scottish intellectual debate in the 1930s'.[97] Tom Normand's work on Whyte is salutary, but unfortunately Whyte's own essays on nationalism and the arts in *The Modern Scot* were omitted by Margery Palmer McCulloch from her otherwise admirable anthology of Scottish background documents, *Modernism and Nationalism* (2004). In *Scottish Modernism and its Contexts* (2009) McCulloch pays tribute to *The Modern Scot* as 'a splendidly interactive and cosmopolitan modern journal', but again passes over Whyte's own writing.[98] Whyte has tended to be remembered, if at all, as an editor, rather than as an important theorist of modern Scottish nationalism.

Looking again at his magazine, its striking cosmopolitanism surely owes more than a little to Whyte's background. While this is certainly a Scottish, predominantly nationalist periodical, publishing from its early numbers onward Compton Mackenzie, Hugh MacDiarmid, Neil Gunn, Naomi Mitchison and others, their work soon appears alongside that of W. H. Auden, Hermann Broch, Hermann Hesse, Herbert Read, Franz Kafka, Lydia Seyfoollina, Luigi Pirandello and further writers from beyond Scotland. Book reviews cover publications by André

Gide, T. S. Eliot, William Empson and Thomas Mann, as well as the productions of Gibbon, MacDiarmid, Muir and others. Whyte's editorial standards were high. A man of letters, he knew that for the sake of art as well as for the cause of Scottish independence they had to remain so. As he put it in 1932, replying to the question 'Whither Scotland?' in a symposium organised by *The Free Man*,

> In literature, as in the other arts, our obvious need is still to make up the leeway between Scottish literature and the literature of Ireland, Poland, Czecho-Slovakia, and those other 'new' countries that have developed a national literature following the gaining of national independence and now move on a European plane. To aid in this, it is essential to eschew the log-rolling indulged in by those mediocrities who see in the Scottish Renaissance merely a new publicity medium for their mouldy wares; to judge our literature as good or bad, rather than as Scottish [. . .][99]

In 1934 Edwin Muir, by then no Scottish nationalist, wrote in the *Spectator* that *The Modern Scot* was 'the best literary review that has appeared in Scotland for many decades, and has now maintained for several years a critical level which is unique there'.[100] Though even a cursory glance reveals that the magazine's focus is principally literary, *The Modern Scot* also reflects Whyte's interest in the visual arts and music. He writes, for example, praising the painter S. J. Peploe, and publishes song settings by Francis George Scott to whom MacDiarmid had dedicated *A Drunk Man Looks at the Thistle*. Staying with her family in Whyte's St Andrews, Lillias Scott Forbes (daughter of F. G. Scott, and now the last surviving member of the 1930s St Andrews artistic circle) recalls seeing for the first time examples of the art of Paul Klee, some of whose work was featured in the 1935 *Modern Scot*.[101] Whyte's partner John Tonge sometimes wrote under the pseudonym A. T. Cunninghame, and had a keen eye for painting. He was interested, too, in Joyce, T. E. Hulme, Oswald Spengler, Gide and D. H. Lawrence. In 1938 he published *The Arts in Scotland*.

As well as editing *The Modern Scot*, Whyte in St Andrews ran the Abbey Bookshop. Its customers included bohemian visitors as well as more reserved locals such as the Scottish history student and (from 1936) St Andrews University lecturer Ronald Cant. In Whyte's shop, MacDiarmid contended, 'all the important books and periodicals of Europe can be seen as they appear'.[102] Whyte was at the centre of a cosmopolitan community. During 1931, however, his correspondence with Edwin Muir indicates that he thought there was 'little immediate hope of an economically self-supporting Scottish literature'; he bankrolled *The Modern Scot* with his own money.[103] T. S. Eliot, then editing the *Criterion*, told MacDiarmid he would like to meet Whyte, and in November 1931 when Whyte was in London for a week, MacDiarmid wrote to Eliot to set up an encounter.[104] As Tom Normand points out, Whyte was consciously trying to create in 1930s St Andrews what would now be called a cultural hub. In 1932 he wrote to the painter William McCance, inviting him and his artist wife Agnes Miller Parker to visit.

> If the Muirs ever come to live here we might someday make it a centre of contemporary Scottish art and literature. You and Flora Grierson might remove your hand-presses hither. I should open up a little restaurant where we could all meet, as well as a picture gallery for exhibitions. But I'm afraid that is very much a dream at the moment.[105]

Some aspects of Whyte's aspirations did not remain 'a dream' for long. From St Andrews he oversaw production not just of his magazine, but also of related limited editions among which was a translation of Gaelic poet Alexander MacDonald's 'The Birlinn of Clanranald', rendered into English by MacDiarmid using notes supplied by the young Sorley MacLean. MacLean was surprised when MacDiarmid went ahead with publishing the poem in English verse without allowing him to proofread it; but, MacLean told me decades later, 'I would have forgiven him anything.'[106] Nationalists including MacDiarmid regarded the integration of Gaelic culture into the identity of modern Scotland as an important cultural as well as political project. MacDiarmid's poetic translation appeared both in Whyte's magazine and in an elegant, signed, limited-edition pamphlet. At Whyte's invitation, Willa Muir (a St Andrews Classics graduate) and her husband Edwin moved to the Fife town. She recalls, a little waspishly, going with Edwin to dine with James in his house, an old one in South Street thoroughly modernized inside. It was padded everywhere with cushions; the sitting-room ceiling had been painted blue to match them and silvered with stars. James was obviously a young man who liked to be in the fashion and could afford it [. . .][107]

Once owned by John Tonge, Dundee artist David Foggie's expert 1933 drawing of Whyte is now in the Scottish National Portrait Gallery. It shows the twenty-four-year-old American neat in jacket and tie, looking intellectual and introspective. By that time Whyte had not only established himself as editor of *The Modern Scot*; helped, perhaps, by John Tonge, he had also embarked on the most sophisticated articulation of a theory of Scottish nationalism.

At Cambridge Whyte had taken a course on the 'History of International Relations, 1815–1914' – arguably the great age of European nationalism. Constitutional History was also part of his Qualifying Examination in Law.[108] We know from his correspondence in the National Library of Scotland that he was an SNP member by 1934; but as early as Mayday 1930, when it noticed the first issue of *The Modern Scot*, the *Scotsman* quoted Whyte's contention that 'whatever lasting benefits Scotland may receive will come through the re-establishment of an independent Government and of an individual Scottish culture'. The Edinburgh newspaper maintained that 'Whether political propaganda and the highest literary expression can be successfully combined in this way remains to be seen', but it commended the magazine.[109]

In the first issue of *The Modern Scot* Compton Mackenzie explains how

> I still hold as one of the most precious moments in my reading life the memory of turning the pages of *A Drunk Man Looks at the Thistle* [. . .] That first reading of *A Drunk Man Looks at the Thistle* was followed by the formation of the National Party of Scotland, so that for me they will always be linked with the appearance of cause and effect, though I know perfectly well, of course, that Grieve's genius is only one manifestation of the surging impulse of national life which evoked the Party.

Yet no sooner has he written this than Mackenzie argues defensively that 'to say that the National Party of Scotland is run by cranks and poets is equivalent to saying that the English are not a nation of shopkeepers because Shelley was an Englishman'. Mackenzie is clearly aware that having a poet as a controversial figure in a political party need not be an asset. Perhaps awkwardly, he argues that 'the very absence of a constructive policy which our critics so scornfully deride is the best possible testimony that the National Party of Scotland is not in the hands of wild poets and papists'.[110] Catholics and politically dangerous poets were, he knew, easy targets.

Around this time Whyte began to develop not quite so much a 'constructive policy' as a more modulated and subtle theorising of Scottish nationalism. In part, this young English-educated American may have done so in reaction against the politics of his step-father, a Unionist Tory MP from 1931 to 1935. There may have been tensions within the Whyte family: James's mother left Jardine Bell Whyte during the mid-1930s; in Monaco in 1935 she married Belgian baron René de Kerchove. However, to see Whyte's nationalism as a crude reaction to family turmoil would be naïve. He and Tonge had been debating Scottish independence in an international context since at least early 1931.

Though he realised that 'A nationalism founded upon the personality of a single individual would be a perilous one', Whyte was fascinated not by Hitler but by the recently imprisoned Gandhi.[111] It is clear from Tonge's writings in *The Modern Scot* that he and Whyte discussed Scottish nationalism in the context of anti-imperialist struggles elsewhere in the British Empire; Scotland enjoyed imperial power, but, as the Empire weakened, desire for Scottish independence might increase. Tonge quotes with approval Whyte's controversial lecture to the International Club of Glasgow University:

> 'How much better it would have been if we had had for Scotland and England the concern we have had for the Empire: if our eyes had been centred nearer home than the Colonies. Does not Spengler regard Imperialism as one of the last stages in a civilization's decay?'

For Tonge

> Imperialism and Nationalism as I understand them are incompatible: Gandhi and Winston Churchill can never be on speaking terms;

the belief that every nation, however small, has its own peculiar part to play in the world cuts right across the idea of a world-wide Empire looking to London as the source of its light and strength.[112]

Such thoughts were at one with the verse of MacDiarmid, whose 'The Little White Rose of Scotland', published 'With acknowledgments to Compton Mackenzie', appeared unsigned immediately after Tonge's piece on 'Scottish Nationalism and Imperialism' in the second volume of *The Modern Scot*:

> The Rose of all the World is not for me.
>   I want, for my part,
> Only the little white rose of Scotland
> That smells sharp and sweet – and breaks the heart![113]

Like the MacDiarmid who had incorporated versions of French and Russian-language poetry into *A Drunk Man Looks at the Thistle*, Whyte sought to balance considerations of Scotland with international concerns. Though no poet, he writes with clarity and honesty: 'At a time when the words *nation* and *nationality* and *nationalism* are so often on the lips of Scotsmen one might expect some clear idea of the precise meaning of these words to prevail. But no.' For Whyte 'a nation' is simply 'a social group sharing a corporate sentiment engendered by a historical process'. Citing the Swiss thinker, Bernard Joseph, who argues that nationality 'cannot be said to be based on an *a priori* philosophy', Whyte acknowledges nationality's contingency and changing nature. He has little time for essentialist petrification or nostalgia. Instead, in line with his enthusiasms for the new medium of film and for modernity, he states that 'National identity is not a concrete thing given to a people in its beginnings, but a corporate sentiment that is moulded by history: hence the unreality of the arguments of those Scottish Nationalists whose chief desire is to recapture pre-Union traits we have lost.' Happy to admit that 'Chance to a large extent decreed what elements went to produce modern nationalities', Whyte is alert to recent thinkers on nationality, not least C. G. Seligman who argued that 'Nationality stands apart from race and is in the main a matter of *history* and *politics*.'[114] Such thinking countered MacDiarmid's dangerous attraction towards race and 'Blutsgefuhl'. Moreover, with his Jewish ancestry, Whyte is conscious in 1932 of how 'a Jew [. . .] in France will find the hand of the *Action Française* turned against him, and in Germany the anti-Jewish campaigns of Herr Hitler may seriously inconvenience him.' Whyte does see art as linked to national identity:

> Nationalism is the political manifestation of that national consciousness of which the great artist and the great representative genius of any kind is the fullest expression. Chaucer and Dante, for instance, were the fathers of great *national* literatures.

Yet at the same time he is wary of assertive essentialising, arguing that 'few Nationalists could be found today to applaud, for example, Treitsche's and Fichte's impassioned invocations of the racial superiority and achievements of the Germans'. Whyte has no patience with any 'worship of the race, or similar relic of nineteenth-century romanticism. Nationalism must not seek to subordinate philosophy, art, science or religion'.[115]

Here in *The Modern Scot* is a philosophy of nationalism developed to counter 'racial mysticism'.[116] Whyte acknowledges that 'the two chief Nationalist movements in Europe – Hitlerism and Fascism – are a menace to the peace of the world' and 'express not the nobler, but the baser and most aggressive and barbarous side of a nation'. This perceptive man of letters realises very early as a 'political pluralist' that Nationalists across Europe – and certainly in Scotland – need to face up to such issues and think them through, however 'difficult' they may be.[117]

Though MacDiarmid some years earlier had flirted with 'The Need for a Scottish Fascism', and Whyte (who purchased a painting by Edward Baird of the Scottish nationalist novelist Fionn MacColla wearing what looks suspiciously like a Fascist uniform) admits that 'In the Scotland of the future a Scottish Fascist party may evolve', he makes it quite clear that he is as opposed to Fascism as to bolshevism. He desires a Scotland with 'a large measure of political pluralism' and has little time for art as mere nationalist political propaganda: 'The artists who seek to "put over" Nationalism in the way H. G. Wells does Socialism or "sex reform" are transparent failures.'[118] What Whyte wants is 'to see Scotland a free country like Norway; and yet [we] should not like to see our fellow-countrymen imitating the frantic insularity of the Fascists or the Hitlerites'. Holding up the example of distinguished Irish writers such as Yeats and George Moore who wrote in English rather than in Irish Gaelic, and in Yeats's case belonged to a religious minority, Whyte argues against essentialist searching for 'Scottishness' in politics or art.[119]

Whyte's Scots are 'racially [. . .] diverse'. He admires Walter Scott (not always a Scottish nationalist icon) for his ability to 'conceive of Scotland as a whole' and for being 'devoid of sectarianism'. An independent Scotland would be free to enter into 'certain agreements with England' since both nations would share some common interests.[120] Well aware of 'the tragic farce of Herr Hitler's *Judenfrage*', repeatedly Whyte makes the point that the National Party of Scotland does not advocate 'such a Nationalist *Kulturkampf* as the Nazis are fostering in Germany and the newly formed Scottish Fascist Party would like to see inaugurated in this country'. The aims of this last he sees as 'destructive of goodness', not least in their opportunistic 'anti-Catholic, anti-Irish bias'. He advocates

> such an ideal as Thomas Mann and others of like mind framed for Germany. They visualized a Germany tolerant of individualisms, in which the good German was the good European and in which the traitor was the Prussian Chauvinist [. . .] In taking our stand by such a form of nationalism as Herr Mann's we are not unmindful of the more favoured position of Scotland. Scotland's centuries of free education and democratic institutionalism of all sorts have not had entirely bad results.[121]

Whyte wants no nationalistic brainwashing, but does argue that

> education in Scotland today is by no means propaganda-free: whilst the teacher may profess no personal opinions on the matter, the 'system' does its best to make the children little Union Jack-waving Imperialists. To urge Scottish children to think of themselves as Scots would be propaganda: to help them to forget their native speech, to neglect their traditional culture, misread their nation's history – that is not propaganda in the eyes of the Scottish Education Department.

Whyte longs for a 'school text-book' that would 'take all Scottish literature for its sphere', including work in Gaelic and

Scots as well as English. Without that, he fears a continuing 'provincialization of the Scottish outlook'.[122] Putting forward such arguments from St Andrews in 1934, Whyte was both prescient and courageous. In the university, students attending the Union Debating Society had voted the previous year in support of the motion, 'This House approves of the Nazi Party, and congratulates it on its splendid work in the reformation of Germany', though a few months afterwards they had also supported the motion, 'This House deplores the rise of Fascism'.[123] In a volatile ideological climate, Whyte was distrusted by many local people – inside and outside the university. Driving around Fife in his large expensive car, he and his bohemian companions unsettled their neighbours; this Anglo-American was considered exasperatingly difficult, even a potential spy. His magazine was nicknamed by at least one member of the St Andrews University principal's family '*The Modern Blot*'.[124] When local artist Horne Shepherd painted on Whyte's bookshop's interior wall a fresco featuring a leering John Knox 'astride a beer cask, raising a reaming tankard', the lasses of nearby St Leonard's School were forbidden by their teachers to enter Whyte's establishment.[125]

Like Edwin Muir for whom the Reformation had 'bundled all the harvesters away', Whyte, living within sight of the devastated St Andrews Cathedral, regarded Reformation iconoclasts as a blight:

> They killed the architectural movement of the Renaissance that had so many gracious achievements to its credit, and strangled the drama that was so promising. In routing Catholicism, they destroyed more of the indigenous culture of the country than, say, the Bolshevists have in Russia.

Countering complaints about Irish immigration into Scotland, Whyte maintained that 'If ever there is again an independent Scotland, Ireland will be found to be one of its firmest friends.'[126] His behaviour and attitudes may have alienated him from the straitlaced Scottish Presbyterians among whom he lived. Yet, more than anything else, this difficult immigrant, drawing on thinkers as different as John Macmurray, Thomas Mann and Leonard Woolf, as well as on friends and sparring partners such as Tonge, MacDiarmid and the Muirs, articulated a sophisticated twentieth-century theory of Scottish nationalism. *The Modern Scot*, as he put it in the final issue of 1936, 'came into being in order to provide Scottish writers with such a platform as Irish writers enjoy in *The Dublin Magazine*, and to focuss [sic] attention on the cultural activities and aims of the Scottish Nationalist movement generally'.[127]

Whyte's sense of political issues, however, was not infallible. While he was editing his magazine, just around the corner Willa Muir was writing *Mrs Grundy in Scotland*, a classic Scottish consideration of assumptions about gender. When Muir ends that work by claiming that 'It is Mrs MacGrundy who is to be dreaded, because she may persuade people that she is the national spirit of Scotland', she points towards questions about the relationship between gender and national identity that Whyte, ironically perhaps, simply fails to tackle.[128] Muir's book appeared in 1936, the last year of *The Modern Scot* to which she, Catherine Carswell and several other women were at least occasional contributors.

As the clouds gathered over continental Europe in the mid-1930s, Whyte's activities faltered. An editorial piece in the final volume of *The Modern Scot* is headed 'This Affligit [Afflicted] Realm', and appears disaffected – even exhausted. It sounds notes reminiscent of Burns's 'Such a Parcel of Rogues in a Nation', that song which bids farewell to 'Scottish fame' in a country reduced to 'England's province'. Though Whyte does not quite quote Burns's poem, he alludes to it: 'What was once a nation is now a province [. . .] One cannot be very optimistic.'[129]

Not so long after typing these words, Whyte ceased publishing *The Modern Scot*. In 1936 as a representative of PEN he stood among the mourners on the island of Inchmahome on the Lake of Menteith in Perthshire when the body of one of the founders of the National Party of Scotland, Joseph Conrad's friend Robert Bontine Cunninghame Graham, who had died 6,000 miles away in Buenos Aires some weeks earlier, was finally laid to rest.[130] That summer was acrimonious. After the publication of Muir's *Scott and Scotland* MacDiarmid completely unfairly accused Whyte in an open letter of taking a 'Fascistic line', and maintained that 'all the decent work done in connection with the Scottish Movement has been, and can only continue to be, done along the Communist proletarian separatist-Republican line'. Given MacDiarmid's own earlier invocation of Fascism, this was rich. *The Modern Scot* had dared to publish a less than wholly enthusiastic review of his *Second Hymn to Lenin and Other Poems* in its final, January 1936, issue. Whyte wrote to MacDiarmid seeking 'to put an end to a very unfortunate mis-understanding which seems to have arisen between us'. He com-plained of 'indiscriminate abuse of Muir'.[131] Attacking Whyte, MacDiarmid denied being 'basely ungrateful and [. . .] biting the hand that has fed me', but it is hard not to feel the poet was indeed biting Whyte's generous hand.[132] Writing from Compton Mackenzie's Barra, Whyte accused MacDiarmid of behaving like 'a spoilt schoolgirl'.[133] Later that year MacDiarmid stated he had 'of course broken completely with [. . .] Whyte and Muir'. He accused them of being 'responsible for preventing the publication of *Red Scotland*', a work in which the now vehemently Communist poet aimed to present views much more extreme than those of Whyte.[134]

Unsuccessfully, Whyte tried to make peace: 'This is my last offer – and perhaps the last time you may hear from me again.'[135] He then returned to the United States, where with his brother he set up a Washington art gallery.[136] Tom Normand reports that there is evidence in 1951 Whyte married a woman called Polly Robinson, with whom he had a son.[137] Towards the end of his life the founding editor of *The Modern Scot* wrote a book about Washington in the 1860s and 1870s, *The Uncivil War* (1958). It mentions Scotland only once, making the point that it is a different country from England.

James Huntington Whyte died in 1962 at the same age as his father. While the SNP, like several pro-Union parties, has not lacked in members and adherents with Fascist sympathies, to the thinking of James Whyte modern Scottish nationalism owes much of its tolerance, non-violence and pluralism; also the best of its open-ness towards Europe and the world. His wisdom helped steer it away from Fascism and, contra MacDiarmid, from Communism too. Many years after dedicating to him 'On a Raised Beach', belatedly and movingly, MacDiarmid made Whyte a dedicatee of his late long poem *In Memoriam James Joyce*. Well known this rich, Manhattan-born, English-educated bisexual intellectual is not. Yet, thanks to Whyte's astute theorising and editing, literary imagination in that earlier twentieth-century Scotland whose greatest and most difficult exemplar was MacDiarmid came to be linked not just with the sustained poetic achievement of a poet who sometimes trumpeted his Anglophobia, but also with a credible and subtle theory of Scottish nationalism. Eschewing both Anglophobia and wistful harking back to Bannockburn, Whyte's theory articulated a pluralism appropriate to a modern nation, one ready to join in the fight against Fascism, without abandoning ideals of independence.

Legacies to Alex Salmond

There is a clear link between James Whyte's pre-World War II St Andrews and the famous painting of seven Scottish poets by Sandy Moffat which now hangs in the Scottish National Portrait Gallery: walking downstairs in the painting's background is Whyte's partner John Tonge. Moffat has quoted Alan Bold's statement 'that "St Andrews in 1935 could claim to be the cultural centre of the Scottish Renaissance"', and acknowledges that Tonge continued to have an impact on Edinburgh-based artists and poets of the 1950s and 1960s.[138] His presence in Moffat's 1979 artwork indicates that Tonge's impact lasted even longer. Most of the poets in this picture, including Sorley MacLean, Sydney Goodsir Smith, Norman MacCaig and Edwin Morgan, had strong political convictions: MacLean fused left-wing commitment with a longing to have 'Alba saor' ('Scotland free'), as one of the poems from his 1943 *Dàin do Eimhir* (published with the encouragement of MacLean's nationalist friend from Fife, Douglas Young) puts it.[139] Others too among that generation of later twentieth-century poets may have voted for the SNP, as Norman MacCaig told me he did; yet their poetry does not always carry any strong political inflection. In 'A Man in Assynt' MacCaig refers to 'a remote and ignorant government', but that note hardly dominates his verse.[140] Nevertheless, throughout the twentieth century, politics, and particularly pro-independence campaigning, continued to be entangled with

Scottish writing – from Alasdair Gray's *Why Scots Should Rule Scotland* to Douglas Dunn's *Poll Tax: The Fiscal Fake*. In the early twenty-first century the SNP, once associated with a bohemian fringe, came into government. It would be easy to suggest their political transition to power has taken them far from Whyte and his radical circle in St Andrews; but, as Moffat's painting reminds us, a legacy connects that St Andrews and its once scorned nationalism with modern Scottish literature and politics.

Sorley MacLean's close wartime friend, Tayport-born classicist and nationalist activist Douglas Young, attended St Andrews University from 1931 to 1935. He studied Greek with H. J. Rose (who thought him 'brilliant') and Latin with W. M. Lindsay.[141] Young's undergraduate years coincided with Whyte's period of residence. Along with MacDiarmid, Whyte and other intellectuals, Young campaigned for the SNP candidate Eric Linklater in the north-east Fife by-election of 1933, which the novelist Linklater (who lost) fictionalised gleefully in *Magnus Merriman* (1934). Linklater's election oratory quoted the Declaration of Arbroath and invoked the victor of Bannockburn.[142] Young's Scottish nationalist views intensified during postgraduate work at Oxford; perhaps aware of Ireland's stance as well as of Scottish history, with elaborate legal-historical reasoning and highly questionable ethics he argued that Scots should not be conscripted into the British Army to fight Hitler: 'The values on which Nazism is based are not entirely my values,' he wrote in 1939, 'but neither are the cash values of our social and economic and political system.'[143] This was an era when, as Gavin Bowd points out, the British Home Office 'reported on a leaflet beginning "1314 Bannockburn 1943", which stated that it was "high time for another Bannockburn" and for the clearing out of Scotland of her worst enemy, "the London imperialist Boss Class and the English would-be *Herrenvolk*."'[144] As well as corresponding with his friend the Communist-inclined Sorley MacLean, Young visited MacDiarmid in the Shetlands; had his home raided by the British Secret Service; and was imprisoned for his political convictions in Edinburgh during World War II. In prison he translated the twenty-third psalm into Scots, publishing it along with original verse and translations into Scots from MacLean and 'Psappho', Homer, Catullus and others in his 1943 collection *Autran Blads*. Young's autobiography, *Chasing an Ancient Greek*, recalls his wartime imprisonment and shows no Fascist sympathies; released, he was pleased that 'Dr Robert McIntyre, secretary of the National Party, organized a procession complete with bagpipes to serenade me at the prison-gates, the poet Hugh MacDiarmid being among the most demonstrative of the demonstrators.'[145]

There is patrician self-regard in Young's autobiography, and his views around the outbreak of World War II are dangerously quixotic, but he was not without political insight. In 1944 he contested the parliamentary seat of Kirkcaldy, coming second with 40 per cent of the vote; as SNP chairman he took the view that his party would do best as part of a Scottish anti-Tory, anti-Unionist coalition; and he foresaw the creation of a devolved Scottish parliament. Still, translating Burns's 'Ae Fond Kiss' into ancient Greek, the clever, sometimes deluded Young maintained much of the eccentricity familiar among early twentieth-century literary nationalists. MacDiarmid made remarkable poetic capital out of such eccentricity, but Young struggled. His poetry is too willed. At his best, from the early 1940s onward he recast Greek into Scots vernacular, bonding the accents of the Scots-speaking working class to 'Pan, the skeely piper wi the dansan horny feet'.[146] Such Scots classicism may not appeal to everyone, but T. S. Eliot called Young's 1958 version of Aristophanes, *The Puddocks*, 'a most delightful piece of work', remarking that 'Aristophanes seems to fit extraordinarily well into the Scots language', while Edwin Morgan thought the translation 'more comic than the original'.[147] Young's Aristophanes was part of a Scots-language classicism that included Robert Garioch's translations of plays by George Buchanan. It can smell at times of the lamp, but, taking that risk, these writers articulated in surprising ways the ideal of internationalism alongside support for Scottish independence. Aspects of Young's stance were reprehensible, especially when set beside the nationalist theorising of Whyte. The challenge for later campaigners would be to carry forward the best thinking from this era and to jettison the worst.

Young's war record and pro-independence views seem to have made it hard for him to find academic work in a Scotland whose universities were conservative and very largely Unionist. At St Andrews he was helped by the intervention of the writer and scholar William Laughton Lorimer, who had become assistant to the great classicist John Burnet in 1910 and who then worked as a Reader in Classics employed by the Fife university to teach in nearby Dundee. Eventually Lorimer became Professor of Greek at St Andrews. Living there, he was familiar with Whyte and his circle, while he admired Young's academic work and 'had much sympathy also with his nationalist views'; Lorimer overcame institutional opposition and hired Young as his assistant.[148]

Young lectured in Latin at University College, Dundee (then part of the University of St Andrews), from 1947 to 1953, before transferring to the St Andrews Greek Department (1953–68). Working on his Aristophanes translations, he left the SNP for the Labour Party, though he continued to campaign for Scottish autonomy. In 1968, while still adhering to Labour, he co-founded the 1320 Club, a secretive pro-independence pressure group encouraged by MacDiarmid and whose members included the extremist Ronald MacDonald Douglas who had been chief of the so-called Scottish Defence Force. All this explains why when he published *St Andrews: Town and Gown, Royal and Ancient* in 1969 Young described the place as a 'Headquarters of Militant Nationalism'.[149] At St Andrews the charismatic and sometimes suspect Labourite Young was neither the only experimenter with Scots, nor the sole literary nationalist. However, by the later 1970s the idea of St Andrews as a stronghold of Scottish nationalism came to seem strange, since, as novelist James Robertson puts it, the Thatcherite Poll Tax was dreamed up in that era by 'a group of radical right-wing intellectuals, who had first coalesced around the University of St Andrews'.[150] Round about the time when Michael Forsyth (later Margaret Thatcher's Secretary of State for Scotland, and now Lord Forsyth, a virulent opponent of Scottish independence) was a St Andrews student, these intellectuals included Norman Gash, Professor of Modern History, and his acolytes Madsen Pirie and Eamonn Butler, who founded the Adam Smith Institute, a right-wing, monetarist think-tank in 1977. However, it was the legacy of the older, Whyte-connected nationalist St Andrews which would come to resonate most strongly in terms of Scottish independence and which produced several notable works of Scottish literature.

With assistance from Young's friend Scots lexicographer David Murison, Kenneth Dover wrote an obituary of W. L. Lorimer for the *Proceedings of the British Academy*. He notes that in 1894 as a nine-year-old Lorimer began 'to collect material (now lost) on the dialect of Strathmartine', but states it is 'not clear' when or how Lorimer returned to the study of Scots.[151] Nonetheless, Lorimer's son recalled, 'my father and I both learnt plenty of Scots' from Ayrshire miner's daughter Helen Strachan (Mrs MacGregor) who was the suddenly widowed Lorimer's housekeeper at 19 Murray Park, St Andrews, from around 1922. Lorimer's interest in vernacular Scots continued alongside his Greek scholarship; and it would be surprising if his 1947 appointment of Douglas Young was not bound up with Lorimer's statement in late 1945 that he 'had tentatively decided to undertake the task of making his own Scots translation' from Greek.[152] Lorimer advanced this project after his retirement.

Its initial posthumous publication in 1983, made possible by donors ranging from poets Sorley MacLean and Edwin Morgan to classicists Kenneth Dover and Nan Dunbar, Lorimer's *New Testament in Scots* became a surprise bestseller. Soon republished by Penguin, then, later, as part of the Canongate Classics series, it was lauded by reviewers including Anthony Burgess. Lorimer's is both the finest work written in Scots prose, and the most important translation from Greek produced by a Scottish classicist. What it does for the English-speaking world is to draw on its translator's classical learning to produce a vernacular voice which often impresses listeners as insistently demotic. In his own synthetic Scots, Lorimer fuses willy-nilly classical learning and working-class eloquence in a scripture that ranks as a masterpiece of Scottish literary Modernism. The translator has managed to draw not just on his St Andrews study but also on the common speech heard first in childhood from 'Mrs Mollison, Mrs Haggart, and Mrs Hodge, three aged and impoverished pensioners who inhabited the cottar-houses behind his father's manse', as well as from his housekeepers.[153] Such Scots was treasured, too, by his colleague Young, but in Lorimer's work Classics and class come together with unique, lasting results that produce a Scottish acoustic akin to MacDiarmid's Modernist Scots in its synthetic assembly; yet also, again like MacDiarmid's poetry, convincingly vernacular in rhythm:

> Luve is patientfu; luve is couthie, an kind; luve is nane jailous; nane sprosie; nane bowdent wi pride; nane mislaired; nane hame-drauchtit; nane toustie. Luve keeps nae nickstick o the wrangs it drees; finds nae pleisur i the ill wark o ithers; is ey liftit up whan truith dings lies; kens ey tae keep a caum souch; is ey sweired tae misdout; ey howps the best; ey bides the warst.[154]

Published the year before the appearance of James Kelman's first novel, Lorimer's *New Testament in Scots* is no more a straightforwardly nationalist work than is Kelman's *The Busconductor Hines*. Yet both these landmark productions mark the assertion of a Scots voice that challenges linguistic hierarchies and gives dignity to an idiom markedly at odds with the King's or Queen's English. A cultural nationalist sympathetic towards aspects of independence, Lorimer became chairman of the *Scottish National Dictionary*. Famously, the only time he considered using English in his translation was for short speeches made by the Devil.[155]

Though Whyte, Young and Lorimer had vanished from the scene by the time the young Alex Salmond arrived as a student at St Andrews in 1973, they were well remembered locally. Members of their circle still lived in the town. Prominent among these was that former customer of Whyte's bookshop, the academic Ronald G. Cant who taught in the university's Department of Scottish History and who had been unusual in the 1930s, having circulated between conservative university circles and the much more radical group of writers, artists and intellectuals gathered around Whyte. Originally a St Andrews graduate, Cant (1908–1999) in his eighties spoke with me about Whyte, the Muirs and their many visitors; by then he was best known as an expert on the history of St Andrews University, and as an enthusiast for links between Scotland and Norway. After lecturing in medieval history, he worked as his university's first lecturer in Scottish history in 1948. A sponsor (along with MacDiarmid, MacLean, Goodsir Smith and other nationalist literary figures) of a 1970s selection of Young's writings, Cant was admired not least by Geoffrey Barrow, who became the first holder of a chair in Scottish history at St Andrews on Cant's retirement as reader in that subject in 1974. Barrow followed Cant not least in his sympathetic interest in the politics of Scottish independence.[156]

Later, like Wendy Wood, Neil MacCormick and other nationalists including Alex Salmond, Barrow would deliver the annual Fletcher of Saltoun lecture in tribute to that early eighteenth-century writer who had resisted the 1707 Act of Union. Though not overtly active in party politics, Barrow seems to have been attracted to St Andrews in part by the nationalist-inflected circle there. A scholar of distinction, he was author of *Robert Bruce and the Community of the Realm of Scotland* (1965), much of which had been read in typescript by D. E. R. Watt (Professor of Scottish Church History at St Andrews and editor of the *Scotichronicon*), by Douglas Young who had supplied 'extremely helpful criticism', and by the man Barrow acknowledged as 'my old friend Ronald Cant'. In 1970s St Andrews Barrow mixed with people who remembered the days of *The Modern Scot*; local memories of that time remained strong for many decades. Barrow has been described as 'Nationalist-inclined' and his biography of Bruce (now regarded as a classic of Scottish historiography) is alert to literary traditions; the title of its first chapter alludes to a medieval Scots poem, while that chapter's opening sentence includes a phrase from the Scots ballad 'Sir Patrick Spens', from which a stanza is soon quoted.[157]

Though Barrow is neither poet nor novelist, his biography of Bruce is an unusually writerly book, crafted to reveal the full importance of Bruce, Bannockburn and the Declaration of Arbroath to the Scottish nation. The work had wide appeal; a second edition was published as a popular-format paperback in 1976 by Edinburgh University Press which adorned it with photographs of the Bannockburn battlesite and of the Declaration of Arbroath, advertising it as containing 'one of the great stories of history, finely told by the Professor of Scottish History, St Andrews University'.[158] Often writing with flair, Barrow was revising his biography for its second edition around the time he started at St Andrews. 'To make a nation conscious of its identity,' he argues, 'you must first give it a history.' He chronicles 'the first emergence of "Scotland" in a modern sense', seeing Scotland 'Above all' as 'a North Sea country'.[159] Giving prominence to 'that "masterpiece of political rhetoric", the Declaration of Arbroath of 1320', Barrow presents a revisionary history, arguing that 'Contrary to a common belief, the concept of Scottish nationality and the fact that it was distinct from English nationality were clearly understood in the late thirteenth century.'[160] Cleverly, he quotes such popular English historians as G. M. Trevelyan to bolster notions of 'Wallace's amazing appeal to the Scottish democracy to save the Scottish nation'.[161] Disputing with modern historians who 'hold that Scottish nationalism was the product rather than the cause of the war of independence', Barrow stresses the Scottish ideal of a 'community of the realm' which brought the nation together to support – in the words of a 1301 document cited by Barrow – 'independence at all times'.[162]

For Barrow, Bruce's narrative possesses the highest imaginative excitement; it is fact that carries the allure of fiction: 'the story of one of the great heroic enterprises of history. If it were cast in the form of a romance it would possess at least one of romance's essential requirements, incredibility'.[163] Barrow quotes from Barbour's 'well-imagined' *Bruce*, even as he draws together more prosaic historical sources.[164] Noting that St Andrews was 'appropriately enough' the site of Bruce's 'first parliament', the modern historian goes on to set out in compelling detail how King Robert and his 'band of famous captains' won, against the odds, their great victory at Bannockburn.[165] He cites original sources including the *Scotichronicon* where Bruce addresses his men: 'Those barons you can see before you, clad in mail, are bent upon destroying me and obliterating my kingdom, nay, our whole nation. They do not believe that we can survive.' Heightening his narrative with medieval prose and poetry from the *Scotichronicon*, Barbour's *Bruce* and other sources, Barrow presents what remains the most impressively detailed and vivid account of the great victory for Scottish independence at 'Bannokburn'.[166]

Though Bannockburn is Barrow's centrepiece, he goes on to give a full account of the later years of Bruce's reign and of that 1320 Declaration of Arbroath whose 'crucial passages [...]

form a declaration of the independence of Scotland'.[167] Such phrasing has encouraged subsequent writers to link the Arbroath Declaration to the American Declaration of Independence, though Barrow avoids this. He does, however, emphasise that the Arbroath Declaration is not simply a kingly document, but a statement of 'the constitutional relationship between the king and the community'. Alert to the importance of that 'community of the realm of Scotland' regarded as vital to the Scottish constitution, Barrow presents the Declaration as 'a masterpiece among political manifestos'.[168]

Connections between Barrow's historiography and earlier Scottish literature are manifest. Moreover, he can be seen as belonging to that St Andrews nationalist lineage that goes back through such figures as Douglas Young to the era of *The Modern Scot*. Barrow's presence raised the profile of medieval Scottish history in St Andrews and spurred his colleague D. E. R. Watt in editing the *Scotichronicon*. However, links to twenty-first-century politics of Scottish independence are even more striking. For when Barrow's second edition appeared, the person whom Barrow later recalled as his 'star student' at St Andrews was Alex Salmond. A member of Barrow's intimate 'special subject' Honours-level class on the Scottish Wars of Independence, Salmond regards *Robert Bruce and the Community of the Realm of Scotland* as 'the best book about Scottish history ever written'. He was, his biographer records, 'particularly attracted by its emphasis on the phrase "Community of the Realm" as "one of the first expressions of national feeling in medieval Europe"'.[169] Responding eagerly to the strong narrative drive in Barrow's work, Salmond has praised his former teacher as one of a relatively small number of historians 'who can write, who can tell a story'.[170] Remembering the 'active part' that Salmond took in his class, Barrow recalls how the undergraduate politician 'was fond of teasing some of the English students when they jumped to the defence of King Edward I, and thought that Wallace and Bruce were rather a bad thing'. It was apparent even then to Barrow that Salmond 'was going places'.[171] Extremely active in student politics, Salmond was studying economics as well as medieval history, and would pursue a career as an economist. Yet Barrow's seems to have been the class that really quickened his imagination, and that did most to strengthen political convictions first nurtured in Salmond's boyhood. As a St Andrews student he relished having a tutor who chronicled so impressively the victor of Bannockburn and described the Declaration of Arbroath as 'a masterpiece among political manifestos'; at work on student manifestos of his own, Salmond even decorated his undergraduate room with a substantial reproduction of that declaration of independence.[172]

As had Whyte, the Muirs, MacDiarmid and others in 1930s St Andrews, so, four decades later, the young Salmond who had grown up in a Linlithgow council house felt something of an outsider. Though he was inspired by Barrow and met other nationalist-inclined intellectuals there, he was conscious that theirs was hardly the prevailing ideological milieu. He is on record as stating that 'St Andrews is a very Anglicised University, a very socially select university and so I went as a kind of Scottish punter because I wanted to demonstrate something.' As an SNP student politician, he allied himself not just with other Scots. Standing for the presidency of the Students' Representative Council, he 'enlisted virtually all the foreign students at St Andrews', but narrowly lost.[173] Salmond has quipped that this is the only election he ever did lose, but his tactic of enlisting minority and non-Scottish students as well as Scots can be aligned with the older, multi-national, cosmopolitan and pluralist St Andrews nationalism which had been encouraged by J. H. Whyte – and with the political ideology of today's SNP with its emphasis on including minorities and recent arrivals, rather than regarding independence as a cause to be supported solely by native-born Scots.

The Salmond who studied Robert the Bruce alongside modern economics participated in a 1977 debate in St Andrews University's Parliament Hall where the independent, pre-1707 Scottish Parliament had once met. This debate took place just along the road from where Bruce had held his own first parliament and where Whyte had run his Abbey Bookshop. The motion was 'This Government believes that Independence is in the best interests of the people of Scotland'. The independence debate was part of a St Andrews conference that Salmond, enthused by Barrow's teaching and by his own burgeoning role in student politics, helped organise on 'Scotland at the Crossroads'.[174] As part of a speech reported in detail in the *St Andrews Citizen* of 24 September 1977 Salmond argued for the huge potential of Scotland's natural resources in terms of 'wave, solar and wind power', while stressing that the country's greatest 'wealth' was 'the people of Scotland'. In the St Andrews where Barrow emphasised the importance of 'the community of the realm of Scotland' as well as its great 'manifesto' and its leader, the victor of Bannockburn, Salmond came of age as a politician. St Andrews was, as Douglas Young (quoting the university principal) pointed out shortly before Salmond arrived, determined to establish itself as '*par excellence*, "Scotland's International University"'.[175] Salmond learned from that, as well as from the place's nationalist inheritance. The student who displayed the Declaration of Arbroath in his room remains eager for an independent twenty-first-century Scotland to have its own written constitution.

Among fellow undergraduate supporters of independence, Salmond's closest friend was an Englishman, Peter Brunskill; Salmond delighted more in the music of African American singer Paul Robeson than in the sound of bagpipes; he sought political allies among English and overseas students as well as reaching out to a more predictable SNP demographic. The complex history that informs modern St Andrews; the teaching of Barrow; the strong subcurrent of pro-independence thought there that was at variance with the assumptions of the university authorities; as well as the intensely cosmopolitan mix: all these formed Salmond irrevocably. 'I just absolutely loved it,' he said in 2009 of his St Andrews student years, 'and if it hadn't been for the money and the lack of it, I'd still be there.'[176]

Not predominantly a literary man, Salmond possesses nonetheless a deep love of Burns's poetry. Moreover, his early commitment to nationalism was bound up with his teenage reading of the ascetic Welsh nationalist poet R. S. Thomas, with whom he corresponded at the age of sixteen. Thomas's essay, 'Contemporary Scottish Writing' (quoted by Salmond), may have introduced the teenager to the poetry of MacDiarmid, likened by Thomas to an 'unacknowledged legislator'. As Salmond's astute biographer, David Torrance, points out, in this piece Thomas also quotes William Power, a supporter of Scottish independence, who presents MacDiarmid as wanting to see

> Scotland 'respected like the lave [rest]', not for her ships and engines, banks and investment companies, prize bulls and sporting estates, Empire builders and 'heids o' depairtments'; not even for her kirks and her Sabbath; but for her intellect and art, her developed national culture, her social justice and equity.[177]

Salmond delights in quoting Burns, but seldom cites MacDiarmid in political speeches. Perhaps this is because if he mentions that Modernist poet, political opponents hit back by highlighting MacDiarmid's most outrageously extremist statements. Nonetheless, it is noticeable that after winning the 2011 election which allowed him to form the Scottish Parliament's first ever majority pro-independence government, Salmond did quote those lines from 'Gairmscoile',

> For we ha'e faith in Scotland's hidden poo'ers,
> The present's theirs, but a' the past and future's oors.[178]

Salmond linked this confident pronouncement to his own assertion that 'The Scottish people have shown a hunger for more powers in order to secure a fairer as well as a more prosperous future and I believe optimism has been chosen over pessimism.'[179] When re-elected as First Minister of the Scottish Parliament, Salmond, urging MSPs to 'act as one and demand Scotland's right', warned, too, against 'patronising' Scotland as 'small'. He cited MacDiarmid's poem 'Scotland Small?' which asks 'Our multiform, our infinite Scotland *small*?' and concludes with the line, '"Nothing but heather!" How marvellously descriptive! And incomplete!'[180] At the same time, Salmond stressed the increased pluralism in a parliament whose MSPs now included those whose native tongues were Urdu, Arabic and Italian, adding that 'We are proud as a parliament of having those languages spoken here, alongside English, Gaelic, Scots and Doric.' Emphasising that Scotland 'belongs to all who choose to call it home', he made clear that 'We offer a hand that's open to all, whether they hail from England, Ireland, Pakistan or Poland.'[181]

In quotation this speech drew on the imaginative literary legacy of MacDiarmid, but more importantly in its ideology it drew on that tradition of nationalist pluralism so effectively established by James H. Whyte.

Making it clear that 'My dearest wish is to see the countries of Scotland and England stand together as equals,' Salmond does not define modern Scotland in terms of Bannockburn; but, more than most people, the former student of Geoffrey Barrow has a sense of that historic conflict's meaning.[182] Though he avoided suggesting that the Scottish independence referendum should be held exactly on the 700th anniversary of the battle, that anniversary clearly matters to him. It is hard not to suspect that his preference for 2014 as the referendum date owes something to his undergraduate studies. Salmond realises that present-day arguments around Scottish independence are likely to be dominated by economics, rather than by medieval history or legacies from Scottish literature; but independence is more than a matter of money and there is a vestigial, discernible thread connecting the ideals of *The Modern Scot* and the difficult Scots inheritance of MacDiarmid with Salmond's study of Bruce, Bannockburn and the Declaration of Arbroath. In St Andrews, almost four decades after Whyte had left, Salmond began to develop into the most important and consciously pluralist leader in the modern history of Scottish nationalism, as well as (from the perspective of the Unionist government at Westminster) the most difficult of modern Scots.

Chapter 5

Voting for a Scottish Democracy

Across the half century preceding 2014, Scottish politics have been redefined. From the 1960s when Scottish voters elected for the first time a woman MP who supported independence – lawyer Winifred Ewing – to the early twenty-first century when they chose the first ever pro-independence Scottish government, campaigners for autonomy have passed many significant milestones. Though in *Dominion* (2012), aware of 'Douglas Young' and his stance around the start of World War II, crime writer C. J. Sansom (long resident in England, but born in Edinburgh in 1952) has accused present-day SNP supporters of wanting 'a people drugged on historical legend, replete with holy national sites (such as Bannockburn) and myths', the ballot box, not the battlefield, has been central to Scottish politics.[1] However, for supporters of devolution and independence it has not always been an emblem of victory.

The 1979 devolution referendum delivered a majority in favour of a 'Scottish Assembly' as it was then called, but no such parliament resulted. This was because, as novelist James Robertson points out, 'On Burns Night 1978 [. . .] a Scot called George Cunningham, the Honourable Member for Islington, proposed an amendment to the legislation, requiring 40 per cent of the registered electorate to vote in favour of an assembly before it could be established [. . .] In no General Election since the war had the victorious party won the votes of 40 per cent of the registered electorate.'[2] Cunningham's successful attempt to frustrate the establishment of the Assembly ignited literary resistance north of the Border, not least through poems in

Douglas Dunn's *St Kilda's Parliament* (1981), Edwin Morgan's *Sonnets from Scotland* (1984) and the present writer's *A Scottish Assembly* (1990); in fiction, landmark works included Alasdair Gray's *Lanark* (1981) and *1982 Janine* (1984) as well as the novels of James Kelman, then, later, Irvine Welsh and others, asserting the unignorable strength of predominantly male and mainly urban working-class Scottish voices.

Such books were votes for a Scottish democracy. Often their speakers were angrily conflicted. This is epitomised in *Trainspotting* when Welsh's protagonist reflects,

> It's nae good blamin it oan the English fir colonizing us. Ah don't hate the English. They're just wankers. We are colonized by wankers. We can't even pick a decent, vibrant, healthy culture to be colonized by [. . .] Ah don't hate the English. They just git oan wi the shite thuv goat. Ah hate the Scots.[3]

Shot through with various shades of bigotry, Mark Renton's musings carry a Scottish self-loathing detectable at times in earlier writers, but now scandalously energised and disturbingly funny. *Trainspotting* mocks notions of Scottish heroic masculinity: Begbie, a 'total fuckin crazy psycho', is 'held up as an archetypal model of manhood Ecosse'. The novel contains shrewd political asides ('Power devolved is power retained'), but in general *Trainspotting*'s politics of gender and nationalism intersect more as energy than analysis. Seeing a London pub sign, 'The Britannia', Renton muses,

> Rule Britannia. Ah've never felt British, because ah'm not. It's ugly and artificial. Ah've never really felt Scottish either, though. Scotland the brave, ma arse; Scotland the shitein cunt. We'd throttle the life oot ay each other fir the privilege ay rimmin some English aristocrat's piles. Ah've never felt a fuckin thing aboot countries, other than total disgust. They should abolish the fuckin lot ay them.[4]

Splenetic and disillusioned, here is a back-handed globalisation; Renton's next sentence about 'fuckin parasite' politicians' 'platitudes in a suit and a smarmy smile' anticipates a cynicism that has intensified among many twenty-first-century voters. Any supposed 'Bannockburn spirit' seems hard to invoke. Nonetheless, in 2004, Welsh joined Edwin Morgan, Alasdair

Gray, Iain Banks and other Scottish writers in supporting the Declaration of Calton Hill, which called for an independent Scottish republic.[5] In 2012, looking to the Scottish independence referendum, Welsh announced once more his clear support for Scottish independence.[6]

Late twentieth-century works as different in form and complexion as Morgan's sonnets and *Trainspotting* shared a stance of assertive resistance. Sometimes subtly, sometimes noisily, they played their part in a movement that outlasted the politics of Margaret Thatcher. Written about by Neal Ascherson and others, this political and cultural tendency sought an enhancement of Scotland's democratic control over its own affairs.[7] In time it led to political devolution after a 1997 referendum offered by newly elected British Prime Minister Tony Blair. A 'New Labour' Scot educated at Edinburgh's private Fettes College, Blair represented a northern English constituency and suppressed indications of his Scottish background. At Westminster, then in Edinburgh, Edwin Morgan's constituency MP, Donald Dewar, soon the inaugural Scottish First Minister, piloted the Scotland Bill, which in 1999 established a Scottish parliament. The Labour Unionist Dewar was well read in Scottish literature from George Buchanan's Renaissance constitutional theory to the contemporary poetry of Morgan. After Dewar's premature death, part of his library was housed in the splendid Holyrood Parliament building which he had helped commission. Though Dewar's family had harboured nationalist sympathies, he did not see Scotland's literature as tied to political independence. Instead, he regarded the independence struggle as substantially scotched by devolution; primly, perhaps, he flatly refused to read *Trainspotting*. Much Scottish literature in his era was pointing in political directions that he refused to follow. This concluding chapter presents a necessarily selective account of some works that both condition and are shaped by recent debates about Scottish independence. Though not deliberately attuned to one another, they share aspects of a common trajectory. In 2014, with Scotland nearing its independence referendum, literary imaginations continue to shape that approach.

Edwin Morgan

Edwin Morgan's most direct political action was posthumous. After his death in 2010, it was revealed that this most impressive Scottish poet of the second half of the twentieth century had left a bequest of nearly a million pounds to the Scottish National Party. If 'follow the money' is a shrewd motto when examining campaign funding, it may be revealing that while Morgan's bequest and a similarly big donation to the SNP from a lottery-winning Ayrshire couple, Chris and Colin Weir, came from Scottish voters to further the cause of independence, then when the Unionist 'Better Together' campaign revealed for the first time the identity of donors to their own '£2m war chest' in 2013 by far the largest sums were given by people ineligible to vote in the Scottish independence referendum and who were domiciled in England.[8] Controversial London businessman Ian Taylor, chief executive of a multinational oil and gas trading company and one of David Cameron's major funders, gave £500,000 – the biggest single donation at this stage of the 'Better Together' campaign; while the next largest gift (£161,000) came from Sussex-based C. J. Sansom who portrayed the Scottish nationalists as Nazi collaborators in the fictional Britain of his sometimes flat but impressively researched counter-factual thriller, *Dominion*. Sansom's book (set in a Britain that has capitulated to Hitler) is not principally about Scotland, but contains an appendix that attacks 'Alex Salmond' for fomenting a 'prospective breakup of Britain'.[9] While Sansom presents supporters of Scottish nationalism as Nazis in his fiction, the vehemently outspoken 'Better Together' donor has made it clear elsewhere that in the real world he regards Salmond as 'deeply dangerous' and that the SNP's choosing to hold an independence referendum 'around the anniversary of Bannockburn should make any Scot wonder what sort of party they will be putting in power in their newly independent state, perhaps forever'.[10] If you see Alex Salmond and Nicola Sturgeon as aspiring to set up in Scotland their thousand-year Reich, then, for all that it is set mainly in 1952, this is the intelligent, Nazi-era thriller for you.

Edwin Morgan, who served with the Royal Army Medical Corps during World War II in North Africa, was no Nazi.

However, poetry and the issue of independence were crucial to him, although he was not a member of a political party and only a few of his poems explicitly engage with Scottish politics. Journalists, when they mention Morgan's million, often refer to 'the poet Edwin Morgan', using an intonation which implies both that they think not everyone will know who Morgan was, and that some find it strange that a poet should have left so much money to a political party.

A Glasgow University professor of English, Morgan lived alone for much of his life. Some of his money was saved, some inherited from his middle-class parents. His poetry ranged 'from Glasgow to Saturn', as the title of his finest collection put it in 1973. Covering a wide spectrum, his work is so friskily astonishing that one might miss its political energies. To do so would be naïve. *Sonnets from Scotland* was written not least to strengthen and complicate Scotland's sense of itself after the 1979 referendum fiasco. In that volume Morgan's panoptic imagination runs from prehistory into the distant future, demonstrating throughout a commitment to what the poet had called elsewhere 'the resources of Scotland'.[11] For Morgan these resources are imaginative and historical, but also political and future-oriented. In his sonnet 'The Coin' future visitors – perhaps from outer space – discover a coin bearing on one side a deer's head and on the other the words '*One Pound*'; then, producing a 'shock' in the reader, the inscription '*Respublica Scotorum*'.[12]

Emanating from a Scottish republic viewed as historical from a far distant future, this coin is the most insistent token of Morgan's politics in his verse. Though he accepted the Queen's Gold Medal for Poetry, he maintained a commitment to a republican Scotland. His stance marked out his politics as more radical than those of, say, Alex Salmond, who supports retaining the monarch as an independent Scotland's head of state. However, 'The Coin' also signals Morgan's imaginative commitment to a distinct Scottish political entity. His coin may have been one Scots pound; in time, through his bequest to the SNP, it became a million pounds sterling.

That sounds neat, but the connections between poetry, politics and money are seldom tidy. Nor should they be. More nuanced and complex than political rhetoric, poetry often runs counter to valuations based on cash. Morgan's gift to the cause of Scottish independence is subtler, more lasting and more energising than a mere million pound coins. What his poetry did for Scottish life was to provide a vibrant articulation of change – not financial small change but extensive metamorphosis. Morgan's million may or may not represent the political game-changer he and the SNP hoped for; but games and game-changing were vital to this poet's imagination. Ludic and protean, his verse suggests that anything and anyone can alter.

Articulating such a sense of possibility in Scottish and non-Scottish contexts was a political act. With an internationalist's pluralism true to the spirit of James H. Whyte, Morgan took further an impulse important in MacDiarmid's best work. Yet where MacDiarmid and Whyte had been solemn, Morgan was frequently mischievous. The play of his poetry repeatedly brings delight, ambitious determination and political possibility. Politicians have come to understand this. After the Labour First Minister Jack McConnell gave Morgan the title of 'Makar' or official National Poet in 2004, Morgan subtly yet determinedly set forth his own politics: his first official publication was a translation of Robert Baston's decidedly serious fourteenth-century poem about Bannockburn. To translate an obscure Latin poem in which an Englishman pays tribute to an unexpected victory for Scottish independence may have seemed quixotically professorial. But in a Scotland which had regained its parliament in 1999, that act had clear political resonances. Nimbly, the independence-minded poet-professor outflanked the Unionist Labour politician.

Soon, at the age of eighty-four, Morgan produced his rhetorically Whitmanesque poem, 'For the Opening of the Scottish Parliament, 9 October 2004', marking the parliamentarians' move into their new Holyrood building. Morgan's trumpet-blast is a strikingly successful piece of twenty-first-century political public poetry. Linking accessible address to linguistic adroitness and oratorical gusto, it resonates into the parliament's and the nation's institutional future.

Rejecting 'classic columns', the poet celebrates the new Scottish Parliament's 'syncopations and surprises'; listeners should 'Leave symmetry to the cemetery'.[13] Too ill to declaim his poem at the parliament building's opening ceremony, Morgan had it read for him by friend and fellow poet, Liz Lochhead. She shares Morgan's pro-independence political stance, and, after his death in 2010, succeeded him as 'National Poet'. Beginning with the exclamation, 'Open the Doors!', the Morgan work that Lochhead read aloud avoids party-political statement; yet its whole impetus is to reject the status quo. Welcoming 'something more' than a cosy establishment that belongs to the past, and addressing the whole parliament as well as the nation beyond, Morgan's poem eschews the word 'independence'. It does, however, alert the 'reconvening' parliament to a 'sense of what was once in the honour of your grasp'. Morgan summons up the older, independent pre-1707 Scottish Parliament even as he urges a need to move on. In this sure-footed piece of ceremonial verse, he implies, too, that the new parliament is part of an unfinished process. His 'something more' remains undefined: 'What is it? We, the people, cannot tell you yet, but you will know about it when we do tell you.' Morgan's pointed use of the phrase 'We, the people' echoes the American Declaration of Independence, and so subtly calls to mind the ideal of political independence in the context of the Holyrood Parliament.[14]

Culminating with the word 'begin', Morgan's fanfare for the opening of this parliament regained after 300 years signals not just history being shuffled off, but also a fresh start. Published in his 2007 collection, *A Book of Lives*, this poem preceded another, less subtly pitched piece, 'Acknowledge the Unacknowledged Legislators!', in which Morgan, invoking among others Robert Burns, makes clear his Shelleyan belief in the poet as an unacknowledged legislator who makes things happen politically. When Morgan sees 'poet and legislator / plugged into the future of the race', that last word could have unfortunate overtones, but this pluralist writer seems to mean simply the human race.[15]

Morgan's dedication to a specifically Scottish democracy was strong. He showed how commitment to Scottish independence and cosmopolitanism could not just co-exist but nurture one another. His articulation of ideals appropriate to the Scottish public sphere is one reason why at the 2010 celebration of his life – in effect his funeral service – the principal eulogist was

George Reid, the former SNP politician who became Speaker of the Scottish Parliament, while in the audience sat First Minister Salmond. Impressive for his dignified tribute of silence, the First Minister (not a man renowned for buttoning his lip) spoke no public word at this event. He simply listened as readers read aloud poetry by Morgan, Yury Pankratov and Robert Burns. On the back of the order of service was Morgan's sonnet 'The Coin'.

In their commitment to change, including political change, Morgan's poems carry a restless, continuing energy, built up over many decades and in no sense confined to Scottish themes or models. His early unpublished and published verse reveals that in adolescence this 1930s reader of Eliot and Pound savoured most the diction of Romanticism in its nineteenth-century, Hopkinsian and Dylan Thomas incarnations. Morgan's first poems (written before he schooled himself to produce a modern voice) are also shot through with Old English accents. For all his commitment to the future, he understood the medieval. Yet Morgan's Middle Ages were not principally the era of Bruce and Wallace. He learned most from Old English verse and from the poetry of the 'makar' William Dunbar. Morgan entitles a 1940 poem, one of a series of erotic pieces, 'Drihten Dryhtna, Gemiltsa Me' (Old English for 'Lord of Lords, Pity Me'); his scrapbooks from the 1930s contain alongside cuttings about robots, primitive peoples, monsters and men in kilts a quotation from the lament over change and transience in the Anglo-Saxon poem 'The Wanderer'.[16] As he matured, however, Morgan would exult in metamorphosis, and his lifelong commitment to Scotland would reflect that.

The bulk of Morgan's 1952 *Beowulf* introduction, with its epigraph from Russian Revolutionary poet Vladimir Mayakovsky, pinpoints lasting concerns: 'What literary activity is more powerful than translation?' After mentioning Ezra Pound, Morgan stresses the need for a genuinely modern tone. Translation for him was bound up not just with moving from one language to another, but also with change; it was, by definition, metamorphic. Like many of his admired Modernist poets, he ranged among different times as well as different tongues: to flit from *Beowulf* to Mayakovsky and the urgency of 'original poetry' was a characteristic glissade.[17]

However, a conception of the modern poet as translator and medievalist was scarcely new. Recasting 'The Seafarer' in 1954, Morgan followed cheekily in Pound's footsteps. He shared this enthusiasm with his first poet friend, W. S. Graham. Graham, too, would write constantly of language's peculiarities and of voyages, spurred by having 'read Pound's translation of the Seafarer'.[18] Auden, another poet admired by Morgan and Graham, had echoed Anglo-Saxon sound-effects in his early verse; when living on Clydeside he had drawn on medieval visionary verse in works including 'A Happy New Year' (1932) – a poem alert to possibilities opened up by nationalism in Scottish politics. This was the Auden who was in touch with James H. Whyte at *The Modern Scot*; in Whyte's Scottish nationalist oriented magazine Auden had published part of his spirited experimental 'English Study', *The Orators*.

Translating not only 'The Ruin' and those heroic-elegiac poems 'The Seafarer' and 'The Wanderer' but also Anglo-Saxon riddles as well as the whole of *Beowulf*, the Anglophile Morgan outdid Pound and Auden. Medieval legacies keep resurfacing in his later work, whether in 'Grendel' or in 'Newspoems' such as 'Caedmon's Second Hymn' or in 'Harrowing Heaven, 1924', first published in 1954. Familiar alike with Old English and Glasgow's 'Red Clydeside', Morgan in 'Harrowing Heaven, 1924' invokes 'Vladimir!', linking Mayakovsky with an ironic upending of the medieval harrowing of Hell: 'Tell the archangels in their cells of divinity / They must levitate like larks, for LENIN is coming.'[19] The political excitement, energy and occasional images in this poem anticipate some of Morgan's later work. Sometimes even his heroic elegy could have a political slant, as in his celebration of the revolutionary Glasgow socialist John Maclean, the hero of Red Clydeside who has been praised by Hamish Henderson and who stayed true to the belief 'that Scotland was not Britain'.[20]

Morgan's revealing 1952 essay, 'Dunbar and the Language of Poetry', involves a medieval subject, and a Scottish one at that, but is written by a thirty-two-year-old poet eager to take his imaginative bearings from world literature as a whole. For all his belief in 'Registering the Reality of Scotland' (to cite the title of his 1971 essay), Morgan's lifelong internationalism was as important as his sense of national inheritance: each quickened the other, but when he left Scotland for North Africa during World War II, he became more conscious of what it meant to him to be Scottish, experiencing 'a kind of revelation' while reading M. M. Gray's anthology *Scottish Poetry from Barbour to James VI*, in which William Dunbar's work figured prominently. When Morgan began to write about Scottish medieval poetry it was Dunbar, rather than the Barbour of *The Bruce*, that he chose to focus on; yet his wartime encounter with Barbour's verse may have conditioned his much later decision to reanimate Robert Baston's Bannockburn.[21]

If Morgan's early 'Vision of Cathkin Braes' culminates in an absurd dance, then in so doing it connects with his study of Dunbar, from whose 'Dance in the Quenis Chalmer' Morgan singles out the lines 'Than cam in Dunbar the mackar, / On all the flure [dancefloor] thair was nane frackar [more nimble]', commenting that they 'might well describe his [Dunbar's] equally nimble and lively entry into poetry'.[22] Nimbleness is surely among the most striking features of Morgan's own work, at one with his eagerness for liberating change, not least when it comes to the politics of gender or nationhood. Agility in Morgan holds implicit political possibility, generating, too, an infectious sense of fun. He argues that 'one of Dunbar's greatest pleasures' is 'the approach towards' a scene 'where either dancing or some other vivid movement is described'. Morgan adds that this is 'A recurrent pleasure in Scots verse, as witness *Colkelbie Sow*, *Tam o' Shanter*, and *The Witch's Ballad*'.[23] Consciously or not, Morgan is supplying a Scottish poetic background against which his own work can be read.

Just as striking, in view of Morgan's later career, is the problem the young poet sees posed by Dunbar's oeuvre: that of apparently outrageous diversity. Morgan points out that Dunbar lacked Burns's talent for intimate erotic lyrics, but his 'startling indifference to theme in poetry' lets him glide 'from fantasy to ethics, from ethics to satire, and from satire to stately elegy and eulogy'.[24] Describing Dunbar, Morgan outlines the sort of poet he would himself become. His Dunbar, one of the greatest poets of the independent Scottish kingdom, possesses 'restless and nervous force' and a 'darting quick-silver personality'.[25]

Morgan's own verse, also, delights in presenting such figures. His is an oeuvre, like that of Miroslav Holub, produced by a poet committed to remaining in his own country even when he regarded its politics and attitudes as frustrating. In an era when contemporaries such as W. S. Graham and Muriel Spark elected to leave a Scotland they found constricting, Morgan's fusion of internationalism with determined empowering emplacement was an example to younger writers including Liz Lochhead, Alasdair Gray, Tom Leonard and James Kelman.

Morgan's long dialogue-poem 'The Whittrick', begun in the 1950s, celebrates an elusive, mercurial essence imaged in Scots as a 'whittrick' or weasel – the spirit of creativity. Such an uncatchable essence is celebrated, too, in the endlessly 'displaced person' of the juggler Cinquevalli in his poem of that title.[26] 'Cinquevalli' presents a Polish political refugee in London, and its celebration of freedom is at one with Morgan's more general wish for independence. Whittrick-energy is seen as vital both to individuals and to society; it lets poet and reader travel far and fast – 'what I love about poetry is its ion engine'.[27] When asked if he was particularly attracted to mercurial figures, Morgan replied with an eager yes, adding that for him such a quality of energy had always been represented by MacDiarmid, Burns and Dunbar.[28] He saw openness to change as vital to Scottish tradition, and strove to rearticulate it in Scotland's present, letting it go on sounding throughout the future. Whatever else, Morgan's project (as his final financial bequest confirmed) fused the political with the poetic, balancing clear intellectual commitment with a dancing openness to popular engagement.

As in politics, so in poetry, tradition was a jumping-off point for change. For Dunbar and Morgan energy is manifested as controlled alteration through the poet's ability to deploy form after form, genre after genre. Morgan's faith in change was probably connected to the politics of gender. A gay man in mid-twentieth-century Scotland, he found his sexuality criminalised. Coming out could have put his job in danger; homosexual sex acts were punishable with imprisonment. For Morgan (who kept his sexuality secret, or at least veiled, until he retired from his university post) change was important in terms of personal independence, not just in terms of the autonomy of Scotland.

An early poem, 'Those Clouds are Drunken with Unearthly Light', suggests that verse is built out of storm and strife, beauty resulting from often painful metamorphosis. Poetry for Morgan is like a release of pent-up force for change: whether water located by dowsing in the desert or the power of suns whose energy, in the words of the 1940 erotic sequence, could waken 'flowerless acres into light'. Significantly, his scrapbooks, crammed with homoerotic images, articles about art, poetry, natural history, monsters, robots, astronauts – a whole private hoard and energy-bank – end in the mid-1960s, when he was able publicly to acknowledge at least some of his hitherto private concerns in his own increasingly successful poetry of change.

His breakthrough collection was *The Second Life* (1968), published by Edinburgh University Press. A large flower on its yellow cover, it was a book synchronised with, though not confined by, its political moment. Morgan found the 1960s liberating; public discussion of wide-ranging changes in sexual, economic, religious and technological living patterns came to be taken for granted. His outspoken poem 'The Flowers of Scotland', published in 1969, maintains 'it is too cold in Scotland for flower people', but is in tune with its era in denouncing the Scottish 'Kirk' for trying to stamp out 'change'. Morgan also complains about 'a Scottish National Party that refuses to discuss Vietnam and is even applauded for doing so, do they think no lesson is to be learned from what is going on there?'[29]

Liberated by the sixties, whose beatnik-influenced art the ageing MacDiarmid scorned, Morgan wrote while Noam Chomsky's ideas about generating verbal patterns out of deep structures shared by all humanity were becoming intellectual currency. Translinguistic speculations like Chomsky's surely relate not only to international movements with which Morgan was associated, such as concrete poetry and sound poetry, but also to computational linguistics and to further areas of Morgan's more idiosyncratic interest in linguistic alteration. 'Message Clear' and other poems apparently computer-generated, but actually plotted by Morgan on his sturdy typewriter, carry with them a gleeful machinery of change.

Old English poetry's most celebrated refrain – 'that passed away, so may this' – sees change as inevitable, but also as a potential relief from melancholy or oppression.[30] So does Morgan's 'The Change' which, addressing tyrannies and over-rigid systems, celebrates the way the sun sets on orthodoxy as 'other fruits ripen for other lips'.[31] Those sentiments are in line with the urge in an unpublished 1939 poem 'Sculptures' 'to change / The unchangeable'.[32] In poetry as in politics, Morgan refuses to accept that the status quo is unalterable. I have heard Douglas Dunn censure Morgan's 'Stalinist optimism', but a mischievous sense of humour keeps Morgan's love of metamorphosis vital; where MacDiarmid's often humourless poetry more readily risks Stalinism in its weaker moments, Morgan was less of a party-political man: his independent-mindedness led him to back Scottish independence, but not to become a party stalwart. Like the very different SNP-supporting poet Norman MacCaig, Morgan maintained his own autonomy.[33]

His poetry is less wedded to party than to partying, though the commitment to change and translation is also profound. 'The First Men on Mercury' opens with English-speakers confronting aliens:

> – We come in peace from the third planet.
> Would you take us to your leader?
>
> – Bawr stretter! Bawr. Bawr. Stretterhawl?[34]

This is a wonderful poem for two speakers to read aloud in a room full of different nationalities. It engenders laughter and admiration, as well as signalling attunement to a postcolonial sensibility. As it develops, languages converge and are exchanged, each translated into the other; eventually the Earthmen speak Mercurian, the people of Mercury bid farewell in English. What happens parallels a movement in Morgan's 'Memories of Earth', where alien experience changes the speaker: 'She's changed. / I'm changing.'[35] 'The First Men on Mercury' wittily models cultural crossover, the transition from one language community and its assumptions into another different one – a theme pertinent to

any multicultural, multilinguistic society, not least Scotland. As
the flick of the tail reminds us, 'nothing is ever the same, / now
is it?'[36] This politically dynamic poem upsets an assumed power
balance. It can be read in terms of cultural and political
imperialism – as well as the 'Mercurian' resistance they engender.
A sense of optimistic change connects Morgan's poems of
outer space with those of Glasgow. That city, too, is a site
of 'endless [...] interchange'; Morgan is for translating it,
rather than embalming a status quo.[37] 'Glasgow Sonnets'
vividly encapsulates problems of his city, but shows that while
'Environmentalists, ecologists / and conservationists are fine
no doubt', he sides controversially with the bulldozer, with
metamorphic energy that might 'displease the watchers from
the grave' yet still delight Charles Rennie Mackintosh.[38] Despite
his sense of history, for Morgan hope and energy always lie in
reinvention. What he dislikes most are forces that impede this –
like the speakers repeating proverbial platitudes in 'The Clone
Poem' or like people responsible for the death of a foetus in
the 'Stobhill' sequence, which terminates in verbal ossification.
Sharply contrasting is the energetic buzz of 'Bees' Nest', whose
shape emphasises we are dealing with a wild, if contained,
energy. Resisting linguistic (and, by implication, other forms of)
petrification, these works resemble Morgan's computer poems
where line is constantly translated into line, unscrambling what
may or may not be a 'correct answer':

```
m e r r y C h r i s
a m m e r r y a s a
C h r i s m e r r y
A s M E R R Y C H R
Y S A N T H E M U M39
```

Morgan's early poems such as 'The Cape of Good Hope'
had begun to connect physical translation with metamorphic
energy, but had sometimes done so longwindedly. As his work
develops, it manifests more clearly and wittily his celebration of
energetic changes, praising not just computers but also Hugh
MacDiarmid for placing man 'with all the world he changes as
it changes him'.[40]
    Poet and artist Ian Hamilton Finlay and painter Joan Eardley,

like MacDiarmid, are seen by Morgan as sharing his creative impatience. Theirs is the eagerness of a St Columba whose 'Altus Prosator' – Englished as 'The Maker on High' – is Morgan's greatest translation. In 'Columba's Song' Morgan presents a saint appreciative of the beauty of nature, but hastening on to effect change: 'It wasn't for a fox or an eagle I set sail!'[41] Such figures translate us into the new. Morgan sings them as he sings bridges, spacemen, remakers of Glasgow, persevering computers, because they can allow everyone to 'Make, and take, your crossing', translating readers through a rite of passage into a 'second life'.

Prefacing his 1974 *Essays*, Morgan declared punningly, 'CHANGE RULES is the supreme graffito. Gathering up the shards – "performances, assortments, resumes" – can hope perhaps to scatter values through a reticulation that surprises thought rather than traps it.'[42] 'CHANGE RULES' is a credo appropriate to this poet, connecting apparently outré parts of his work with documentary ones. Morgan lets us hear 'The Loch Ness Monster's Song', leaving the reader to translate it from the original. Opening with a sort of whale's-blowhole blast, that sound-poem presents the creature's emergence into our world, its interrogation of its new surroundings, and its final submergence: the last line a farewell bubble of 'blp'.[43] The alien and scary are not to be fended off, but decoded. 'Deplore what is to be deplored, / and then find out the rest' ends 'King Billy', yet another poem focused on a strange energy, a disrupting force.[44]

Small verbal 'translations' can alter our perception completely. Metamorphosis becomes ethically potent. The poem 'Rules for Dwarf-Throwing' concludes with a hint of how a slight translation or rearticulation can transform reactions:

> 10. It is strictly forbidden, in dwarf-throwing literature and publicity, to refer to dwarfs as 'persons of restricted growth' or 'small people'.[45]

Whether Morgan provides a poem structured like a rulebook or a computer printout or a map in a linguistic atlas, he is concerned, too, with what destroys or evades such systems, and with how they might be rerouted. Sometimes implicit, sometimes explicit,

in his work is an ideology. Clearly Morgan likes the closely
structured form of the sonnet, yet he also recalled thinking of
shuffling his more overtly political *Sonnets from Scotland* on
index cards in order to arrive at an unsystematic final arrange-
ment: a new system of government that unsettles the old one.

A reviewer once remarked that Morgan had the ability to
write whole themes on a variation; Morgan liked this so much
that he made it the title of his 1988 collection.[46] All this is true,
yet the themes and the variations are related because throughout
Morgan's oeuvre from the Persian-inflected 'New Divan' to
his Glasgow poems, and from the level of individual words to
larger-scale patterns, change – variation – is the guiding theme.
His literary imagination is the reverse of conservative. Yet, from
its start, it is inflected by history and precedent.

Late in life, and after the controversial movie *Braveheart*,
Morgan wrote 'Lines for Wallace', a poem grouped with his
2004 piece for the opening of the new Scottish Parliament.
Despite his work's insistence on the future, Morgan states that
when it comes to Wallace, 'It is better not to forget.' He praises
Burns for realising that Scots would follow Wallace not only
on a battlefield but also 'with brains and books / Where the
idea of liberty / Is impregnated and impregnates'. Mentioning
Soviet dissident writer Yevgeny Zamyatin, the poem is hardly
the product of a small-minded, 'Little Scotland' mentality; it
acknowledges that 'Cinema sophisticates / Fizzed with disgust
at the crudities / *Braveheart* held out to them', while upholding
the validity of the response which involved crying 'a tear' at the
movie.[47] In the end, Morgan's Wallace is confined neither by
Braveheart's detractors nor by its admirers; he becomes simply
an emblem of the persistent, potentially scary, yet compellingly
exciting possibility of Scottish independence. It is Morgan
more than any other late twentieth-century Scottish poet who
has articulated Scotland's desire for change, including political
change. His legacy is aesthetic and enjoyable as well as political;
the financial legacy of a million pounds to further the political
aim of Scottish independence is simply a consequence of his
poetry's metamorphic impulse.

Alasdair Gray

If liberation through metamorphic change typifies Morgan's verse, then a contrasting fear of entrapment and domination runs throughout much of the prose of his Glaswegian near-contemporary the artist and writer Alasdair Gray. Gray's obsessive theme of resistance to being boxed in extends from the personal to the realm of national politics and back. As in Morgan's work, so Gray's notions of freedom extend into areas far beyond party politics; yet there is also Scottish political commitment, signalled most obviously in the title of Gray's book *Why Scots Should Rule Scotland*. From its earliest edition, this work involved arguments for independence that were based on a sustained engagement with Scotland's political and literary past, as well as a sometimes controversial assertion of Scottish distinctiveness: 'The Bannockburn victory made Scotland the first European nation state – the first to have territorial unity under one king.'[48]

Again, like that of Morgan, Gray's explicit support for Scottish independence is part and parcel of a longstanding interest in kinds of liberation and freedom from external dominance that sometimes finds playful imaginative expression. Gray can be mischievous as well as didactic; he may link modern Scottish MPs – all too ready to enjoy 'Westminster Palace (sometimes called "the best club in London")' – to Scots who, before Bannockburn, 'accepted subordinate places in the court of Edward, Hammerer of the Scots'. Yet, winkingly, Gray also introduces into *Why Scots Should Rule Scotland* a fictional Editor figure who accuses the author of 'bellowing' and 'resorting to rhetoric'.[49] Gray's political conviction is clear: 'I believe an independent country run by a government not much richer than the People has more hope than one governed by a big rich neighbour'; but this writer's political commitment is far from po-faced.[50] He delights in unsettling orthodoxies and, sometimes to shrewd effect, flouting taboos. In a country where Anglophobia remains detectable and where an organisation called Settler Watch not so long ago highlighted English immigration as a threat, Gray in a 2012 essay praised 'settlers' who have become 'more effectively Scottish than most born natives'.[51] Yet alongside this he also complained about Scottish,

English and American 'colonists' who have trapped Scotland and other countries in an imperial paradigm. Gray's attempts to valorise the term 'settlers' and his provocative argument about 'colonists' attracted wide press coverage in Scotland in 2012 and 2013. He made the mistake of naming several living 'settlers' and 'colonists' and, though he denied Anglophobia, his rhetoric was not always sure-footed. Most of the nuance of his arguments was lost in the ensuing mêlée, with the staunchly Unionist *Sunday Times* presenting the topic of Scottish independence under the one-word headline 'Free-dumb'.[52]

One of Gray's English teachers at Glasgow's Whitehill Senior Secondary School, Arthur E. Meikle, recalled Gray as determinedly provocative, independent-minded and humorous from the start.[53] A very early Gray story is recalled in the Mr Meikle episode in *Lanark*, a novel whose remote origins go back to this period in Gray's schoolboy writing. In *Lanark* (1981) Mr Meikle, 'Head English teacher', encourages the Scottish protagonist Duncan Thaw to write a piece for the school magazine, only to reject it as 'a blend of realism and fantasy which even an adult would have found difficult'.[54] In fact, Arthur Meikle, then an assistant English teacher in charge of the school magazine, did not reject Gray's story but advised self-censorship in the form of bowdlerisation. It is emblematic of Gray's imagination that in *Lanark* these facts are reworked to emphasise the controlling nature of authority at the same time as paying tribute to Mr Meikle's nurturing of the young writer. Gray's story appeared as 'The Wise Mouse' in the *Whitehill School Magazine* for Summer 1949. It describes how an engulfing monster, after defeating human might, is beaten by a mouse who goes to Honolulu, tricks his way into the creature's mouth, then proceeds down its trachea into a lung, and thence to the heart. There the mouse lets off a hand-grenade before exiting through the monster's nostril. In the original, unpublished version, Arthur Meikle recalled that

> We were given a much fuller account of the mouse's adventures inside the monster, and his final exit was made through an inferior orifice. I had a man-to-man talk with this Second Year Smout and we agreed that the details were reasonable but unsuitable for a school magazine.[55]

This small but significant incident was probably one of Gray's earliest direct experiences of a form of censorship. Much later, entrapment in systematised censorship would be the theme of his finest short story, the more overtly political 'Five Letters from an Eastern Empire', which Gray refers to in the context of cultural imperialism in his 2012 'Settlers and Colonists' polemic, and which is the author's personal favourite among his short fictions. But his much earlier story 'The Wise Mouse' is also notable for its fascination with being literally trapped inside an engulfing monster from which one must try to escape. Later, Lanark, the eponymous protagonist of Gray's novel, will be physically swallowed by a giant mouth and so eventually enter the entrapping, labyrinthine Institute from which he will at last exit through an 'inferior orifice'. Continually in combat with monstrous, quasi-imperial systems that try to engulf him, Lanark has to confront the view that the universe is 'a stinking trap'.[56] A frightening, eczema-like Dragonhide threatens to encase his body, imprisoning him in his own self, while on a larger scale the Institute, Glasgow, and Unthank too are traps from which he seeks to escape through physical flight or erotic love, art or fantasy. In *Lanark*, and more directly in the later *1982, Janine*, these themes of personal and psychological entrapment are associated explicitly with the arena of Scottish politics, and with a need for social and national as well as personal liberation.

That Gray's developing imagination was obsessed with monstrous traps is confirmed by the subject of one of his earliest mature works, the remarkably accomplished depiction of 'Theseus and the Minotaur' published in the *Whitehill School Magazine* for summer 1952. The Minotaur's huge, entrapping arm and claw and its bestial legs on either side of Theseus surround the hero, as if the monster itself is part of the labyrinth behind it. Ariadne, and even Theseus's ship, seen in the distance at the top of the picture, are confined by concentric rings of water, as if even the means of escape is caught at the centre of a maze. Much later, Bohu, writer-hero of 'Five Letters from an Eastern Empire', also arrives by boat at his labyrinth, the crammed chessboard city whose layout is illustrated on page 97 of the original edition of *Unlikely Stories, Mostly*. Like Gray at school and like Duncan Thaw in *Lanark*, the young Bohu is educated to write within the acceptable structures of authority. But his nurturing is much more extreme and sophisticated, taking place within the rigid, Kafkaesque design of the Empire's physical and intellectual architecture.

Here is a structure so labyrinthine that it can turn release into an entrapment serving the ruling élite's political agenda: '*The emperor grants Bohu permission to do anything he likes, write anything he likes, and die however, wherever, and whenever he chooses.*' Bohu goes on to achieve what Gray has called elsewhere 'orgiastic release' before attempting a means of escape by 'separating himself from this ruling clique through death'; as a literary artist he strives to 'separate himself through language, through the poem'.[57] Yet this release is turned easily by the headmasterly imperialist Gigadib into utter bondage to the very authority Bohu has sought to defy. Gigadib, '*Headmaster of modern and classical literature*', subtly alters the writer's text to purify it of dissident meaning.[58] In treating of imperialism, gender, sexuality and freedom, Gray has continued to nudge at the boundaries of censorship, while acutely and astutely acknowledging the bondage of propriety. A lifelong socialist, he has maintained a determined and spirited sense of personal independence as well as a staunch commitment to the independence of his country.

For Gray's political imagination the theme of a contest against physical and ideological entrapment has remained compelling. In *1982, Janine* (published in 1984) Jock McLeish is at the same time a Scottish supervisor of security installations and a man constantly compelled to flee from reality through fantasies which not only involve bondage but also become a form of further entrapment. Again, with horrible ease, escape seems to result in renewed imprisonment. Paralleling Jock's sexual fantasies are his musings on Scottish politics: Scotland too seems in thrall, but no liberation is envisaged which would not be another form of trap.

Who spread the story that the Scots are an INDEPENDENT people?
Robert Burns.

> Is there, for honest poverty
>   That hangs his head, and a' that?
> The coward-slave, we pass him by –
>   We dare be poor for a' that!
> For a' that, and a' that,
>   Our toils obscure and a' that,
> The rank is but the guinea's stamp –
>   The man's the gowd for a' that.

The truth is that we are a nation of arselickers, though we disguise it with surfaces: a surface of generous, openhanded manliness, a surface of dour practical integrity, a surface of futile maudlin defiance like when we break goalposts and windows after football matches on foreign soil and commit suicide on Hogmanay by leaping from fountains in Trafalgar Square. Which is why, when England allowed us a referendum on the subject, I voted for Scottish self-government. Not for one moment did I think it would make us more prosperous, we are a poor little country, always have been, always will be, but it would be a luxury to blame ourselves for the mess we are in instead of the bloody old Westminster parliament. 'We see the problems of Scotland in a totally different perspective when we get to Westminster,' a Scottish M.P. once told me. Of course they do, the arselickers.[59]

So reflects Gray's Scottish Tory, Jock, as he ponders the failure of the 1979 devolution referendum. In this Thatcher-era novel Jock goes on to conclude as 'a comfortable selfish shit' that Cold War 'militarisation and depression of Scotland has been good for the security business'. Jock's Scottish self-loathing to some extent prefigures that of Renton in Irvine Welsh's 1993 *Trainspotting*. Gray's Jock, with his fantasies of bondage and security, mixes the political and sexual as shockingly as does Welsh, and Gray is alert to the way national politics intersects uneasily with the politics of sex and gender. *1982, Janine*'s treatment of pornography develops a theme in Gray's earlier work. *Lanark*'s Duncan Thaw writes in his diary about '*June Haig, no, not real June Haig, an imaginary June Haig in a world without sympathy or conscience*', while Lanark argues about *No Orchids for Miss Blandish* as 'a male sex fantasy' and denies 'that life is more of a trap for women than men'.[60]

Among Gray's most memorable comic scenes is the meeting between Lanark and his author when 'A Damned Conjuror Starts Lecturing' in the epilogue to Gray's largest novel.[61]

Significantly, with the labyrinthine book scattered round him, the author himself seems 'confused', caught within the expanding web of his own fiction, which he cannot entirely control or map.[62] As the text itself splits in two, shooting off in innumerable directions through both an 'Index of Plagiarisms' and a long catalogue of epic books, *Lanark* is revealed as clearly caught in a centreless network of intertextuality with which its author aims to fuel critics, to entertain readers and to demonstrate the condition of authorship. It becomes unclear whether writer or protagonist can find a way out of the novel – a predicament no doubt mirroring Gray's own years of struggle to bring the book to conclusion. Eventually, it seems that the protagonist both is and is not a successful searcher for freedom. The final escape of author and character (for it is not obvious whose are the novel's very last lines) records both a deathly incarceration and a movement of release:

THE LAND LIES OVER ME NOW.
I CANNOT MOVE. IT IS TIME TO GO.

GOODBYE[63]

Here Gray exits from, yet also inters himself within, his labyrinthine, quasi-autobiographical novel. Such an escape, which is also from another perspective an act of enclosure, is typical of his imagination as a whole.

Though, understandably, it has been discussed in terms of the postmodern imagination, whether of Jorge Luis Borges's *Labyrinths* or of Fredric Jameson's *The Prison-House of Language*, Gray's writing is also widely indebted to Scottish tradition. His characters' very names – Monboddo, Lanark, Kelvin – help anchor his work in a Scottish cultural and political milieu, while his manifest commitment to Scottish independence has sometimes a bleak dimension, but also an enlivening clear-headedness evident in his 1992 dialogue between 'Publisher' and 'Author':

Publisher: Will a separate Scottish parliament improve things?

Author: I think Scottish poverty will get worse whether we have a Scottish government or not. I think it almost certain that the London government will regard an independent Scottish one as an excuse to strip assets from this country even more blatantly. I also think a new Scottish parliament will be squabblesome and disunited and full of people justifying themselves by denouncing others – the London parliament on a tiny scale. But it will offer hope for the future. The London parliament has stopped even pretending to do that.[64]

Written in 1992, these words may have been unduly pessimistic, but, like much of Gray's work, they derive from a period in relatively recent Scottish history when the struggle for a Scottish parliament still seemed forlorn and when Scottish independence was not on offer. More recently, Gray's explicit support for independence has seemed, perhaps, too overt for Rodge Glass who writes in *Alasdair Gray: A Secretary's Biography* (2008) of how in 2007 Gray 'has written a piece called "Scottish Politics Now", which he hopes his most recent agent Zoe Waldie will be able to get printed somewhere – a response to the arrival of the new Scottish Nationalist government – although the piece itself sounds more like he's telling Alex Salmond how to do his job'.[65]

As elsewhere, so in Scotland the relationship between literature and politics remains hard to negotiate. Gray, whose artwork 'Bella Caledonia' has featured on First Minister Salmond's Christmas card, may seem to have grown closer to a governing politician than is customary for authors or artists; yet the writer remains his own man and his rhetoric of 'Settlers and Colonists' was hardly welcomed by the Scottish Government.[66] Influential on younger generations of writers from Janice Galloway to Ewan Morrison, he has become a national treasure but also a restless national gadfly. It seems right that the words by Canadian author Dennis Lee, which Gray quoted on several of his book covers, 'WORK AS IF YOU LIVED IN THE EARLY DAYS OF A BETTER NATION', are now incorporated into the Canongate Wall of the Scottish Parliament building at Holyrood; but the fact that they are there attributed to Gray and that Gray's first name is misspelled on the inscription emblematises the way that the fit between literature and politics in Scotland, as elsewhere, remains awkward. Nevertheless, through explicitly political polemic; through an unflinching interrogation of Scotland's predicament; and through sheer imaginative daring, Gray, Morgan and younger writers from

Liz Lochhead to James Robertson have produced over the last few decades volatile imaginative works in which concerns about Scottish independence came face to face with other urgent pre-occupations, not least issues pertinent to apparent entrapment in oppressive identities and to the insistent politics of gender.

Liz Lochhead's *Mary Queen of Scots*

Through restlessly energetic language and stagecraft Liz Lochhead's most impressive play gives gender its full part in the jostling political life of the nation. The first words audiences hear at a performance of *Mary Queen of Scots Got Her Head Chopped Off* (1987) are 'Country: Scotland.' Whatever else matters here, the play's politics of nation and gender are specifically, though not exclusively, Scottish. Lochhead has acknowledged that she found the writings of Morgan and Gray inspirational. However, where those authors (each of whom also wrote drama) made their greatest impact outside the theatre, Lochhead, who came to prominence as a poet, has created her most important work for the stage. Previous plays by Scottish dramatists, whether J. M. Barrie's early twentieth-century *Peter Pan* or Ena Lamont Stewart's *Men Should Weep*, had explored issues of gender identity in very different ways. But *Mary Queen of Scots Got Her Head Chopped Off*, aware alike of Brechtian theatre and of issues surrounding modern feminism, does so with fresh gusto. Moreover, this Scottish dramatic milestone builds on a 1980s context where, as never before, the British state was being ruled by powerful women: the monarch Elizabeth II and Prime Minister Margaret Thatcher.

In Thatcher, particularly, Britain elected a strong woman whose politics many regarded as horrifying. After the 1979 referendum, Scotland came to seem increasingly at odds with Tory governments in London. So a play whose opening speech deals with 'wan green island [. . .] split inty twa kingdoms. But no equal kingdoms, naebody in their richt mind would insist on that' had clear political resonances in 1987. Interviewed that year, Lochhead said of her character, Queen Elizabeth, 'she's somebody you love to hate, and so it was easy to compare her with the Thatcher monster'.[67] Having grown up in Lanarkshire, Lochhead came from a place where one of the most important industries was coal-mining; the 1984 miners' strike led to that sector epitomising clashes with Thatcher's government. When *Mary Queen of Scots Got Her Head Chopped Off* was premiered on the Edinburgh Festival Fringe and later toured in England, reviewers readily picked up how it might connect with contemporary politics. A critic in the *Manchester Evening News* of 1991, for instance, wrote about Lochhead's Queen Elizabeth that 'there is no handbag but author and actress clearly have Thatcher in mind'.[68]

Lochhead's Elizabeth I is not Margaret Thatcher. However, the play was interpreted at the time of its first appearance not only as a drama commissioned by director Gerry Mulgrew of Scotland's Communicado Theatre Company to mark the 400th anniversary of the death of Mary Queen of Scots, but also as a piece of political theatre addressing Thatcher-era Scotland and Britain. From its outset the drama cackles a complex note of Scottish difference. Though set substantially in an independent sixteenth-century nation, it is very conscious (like Scotland for most of its history) of that nation's relationship with England's cultural power. Linguistically, the play establishes from its opening words a refusal to toe the line of standard English. Its initial utterance is not, 'Country: Scotland. What is it like?', but 'Country: Scotland. Whit like is it?'[69] Throughout, Lochhead's fidelity to heightened rhythms and idioms of Scots speech sounds a note of Scottish independence. Sometimes non-Scottish audiences have found this hard to handle, but Lochhead insists it is part of her play's meaning. Determinedly, she told the *Guardian* in 1987, 'This can't be made into Mary Queen of Surbiton. If people can't hear what's being said, I suggest that they're not listening.'[70] Her play's spiritedly rhetorical displaying of Scotland may be one reason why, sharing a stage with James Robertson and other supporters of independence, including Alex Salmond, Lochhead chose to read from it as her contribution to the launch of the Scottish independence referendum's 'Yes' campaign in Edinburgh in the summer of 2012. Yet La Corbie's words are no triumphalist celebration of Scottishness. Like the play that they introduce, they contain clear notes of disturbance and challenge.

La Corbie's opening speech has a marked Scottish accent, but refuses to define Scotland in any single, reductive way. The country is presented as urban as well as rural; industrial and royal; rich as well as poor. It is a nation whose temporal boundaries are seen as extending far beyond that late sixteenth century when the play is notionally set. Edinburgh's Princes Street had not been built then, while the bargain-basement stalls of Glasgow's inner-city Paddy's Market come from Lochhead's own childhood rather than from the time of Mary Queen of Scots.

> Country: Scotland. Whit like is it?
> It's a peatbog, it's a daurk forest.
> It's a cauldron o' lye, a saltpan or a coal mine.
> If you're gey lucky it's a bricht bere meadow or a park o' kye.
> Or mibbe . . . it's a field o' stanes.
> It's a tenement or a merchant's ha'.
> It's a hure house or a humble cot. Princes Street or Paddy's Merkit.
> It's a fistfu' o' fish or a pickle o' oatmeal.
> It's a queen's hamper o' roast meats and junkets.
> It depends. It depends . . . [71]

Like gender identity, Scotland's identity in this drama is presented as depending substantially on point of view. But Scotland is regarded too in the play as depending to a considerable degree on England, even as the text articulates what we hear as cultural independence. Tensions between notional independence and national dependence characterise much of what happens. The play's Scotland is uneasy: proud but addicted to its own past, and so unable to move on.

> Ah dinna ken whit like *your* Scotland is. Here's mines.
> National flower: the thistle.
> National pastime: nostalgia.[72]

This drama offers a critique, not a celebration, of Scottishness. In so doing, it follows partly in the wake of MacDiarmid's *A Drunk Man Looks at the Thistle*, where the national flower is both exciting and strangulating. Lochhead is certainly aware of MacDiarmid as a poet from an earlier generation who supported Scottish independence and was the greatest user of the

Scots tongue in modern verse; but she has spoken too of the 'implicit, incredible sexism' in *A Drunk Man Looks at the Thistle*, and said that when she was young,

> Most of the young writers certainly in Glasgow that I knew at that time, we all agreed very much with MacDiarmid about the oppressive power of English English, but instead of being attracted towards the things that he had done I think at that time there was an enormous attraction towards American poetry. You know it was all William Carlos Williams, [Robert] Creeley and the breath, the voice [. . .][73]

This emphasis on the grain of the speaking voice in Lochhead's work – her poetry as well as her drama – was probably quickened by a vernacular aesthetic of Williams's 'American grain'.[74] But Lochhead's grain was and is emphatically Scottish, and her wariness of MacDiarmid has not stopped her from exploring Scots language and identity, albeit through a voice that, unlike MacDiarmid's, is often angularly chatty.

Moving between poetry and prose, Scots and English, the opening speech of *Mary Queen of Scots Got Her Head Chopped Off* makes use less of end-rhymes than of rhymes and chimes concealed within the lines. It winks towards the old Scots ballad 'The Twa Corbies', incorporated later into the play; but it takes the French for crow – 'le corbeau' – and regenders it as the female-sounding Scots-French 'La Corbie', producing an androgynous 'ambiguous creature' who presents a Scotland both bleak and dangerous, hinting (as if hint were needed after the drama's title) at the violence to follow. From the very beginning, linked to jokey rhymes like those found in children's chanted insults, there is a mixture of play and suppressed violence. La Corbie's words conjure up a balladic past and articulate a distinct culture, fusing these with present-day phenomena and locutions such as 'road accidents'.

> National weather: smirr, haar, drizzle, snow.
> National bird: the crow, the corbie, le corbeau, moi!
> How me? Eh? Eh? Eh? Voice like a choked laugh. Ragbag o' a burd in ma black duds, a' angles and elbows and broken oxter feathers, black beady een in ma executioner's hood. No braw, but Ah think Ah ha'e a sort of black glamour.

Do I no put ye in mind of a skating minister, or, on the other fit, the parish priest, the dirty beast.
My nest's a rickle o' sticks.
I live on lamb's eyes and road accidents.[75]

This, then, is the voice of the play's '"*chorus*"' – Lochhead puts that word inside inverted commas in her opening stage direction. The voice is vernacular, spiky and alert to nuance. La Corbie doesn't say 'on the other hand, the parish priest', but 'on the other fit' – calling to mind such locutions as 'kicks wi' the left foot': a Scottish sectarian expression indicating that the person referred to is a Roman Catholic. The politics of sectarianism are very much part of the politics of Lochhead's nation.

Right from the start, then, national identity, gender (La Corbie speaks not of 'a king's banquet' but 'a queen's banquet'), sectarianism and violence are articulated; before there is any mention of Queen Elizabeth or Mary Queen of Scots we are encouraged to tune into themes that will be given embodied expression in the ensuing play. The language is neither Shakespearian nor present-day 'Queen's English'. Staging and stage directions call on Brechtian stagecraft and on traditions of music-hall and circus. The play's second stage direction morphs La Corbie from chorus (associated with Greek theatre or with more modern dramas such as T. S. Eliot's *Murder in the Cathedral*) into circus ringmistress: '*Laughing*, LA CORBIE *cracks whip for* THE ENTRANCE OF THE ANIMALS. *In a strange circus our characters, gorgeous or pathetic, parade* [. . .]'[76]

Animality too is part of this play. Most of all in presenting her protagonists as circus characters – performers – La Corbie encourages audiences to be very aware they are watching a 'show', an interpretative version of political and personal history, not a historical re-enactment. The onstage action is fluid, subject to dangerous alteration. Relations between these 'Twa queens', and between their two nations, are revealed throughout as unstable, even unequal.

But no equal kingdoms, naebody in their richt mind would insist on that. For the northern kingdom was cauld and sma'. And the people were low-statured and ignorant and feart o' their lords and poor! They were starvin'. And their queen was beautiful and tall and fair and . . . Frenchified. The other kingdom in the island was large, and prosperous [. . .] at the mouth of her greatest river, a great port, a glistening city that sucked all wealth to its centre [. . .][77]

Mixing prejudice, fairytale, jokiness and traditional stereotypes, this passage again signals how identity gets constructed; it calls to mind, too, older as well as more recent debates about Scotland and England, and Thatcher-era notions of a 'North-South divide' within Britain. These debates' rhetoric and substance have not gone away. Indeed the play stages political contentions whose conclusion is still being worked out.

In writing about Mary Queen of Scots, Lochhead takes as her subject the only famous Scottish woman many people can name. *Mary Queen of Scots Got Her Head Chopped Off* is a feminist drama not because it blazons female triumph but because it dramatises an issue which has made society, and particularly Scottish society, uneasy: what John Knox viewed as a threat, the 'regiment of women' – female empowerment.[78] Lochhead's play is set in a period when Scotland enjoyed independence; it was written when, for the first time in history, the British monarch and the British prime minister were women. Rather than simply voicing opposition to a Thatcher government perceived as anti-Scottish, the play stages in a sharply Scottish context issues shared by many people in the 1980s and in other eras. Its women seek to achieve a redefining of gender roles so they may remain discernibly female at the same time as asserting a right to take on roles (including career roles) often seen as the preserve of men. More recently Lochhead has made no secret of her support for Scotland's national independence; at least as important in this play is its articulation of the struggle for women to achieve a form of gender independence, most pressingly (but far from exclusively) within the confines of Scottish society.

What *Mary Queen of Scots Got Her Head Chopped Off* says about this issue is, as the title suggests, bleak. Fed up with the 'terrier'-like behaviour of infighting Scots lords around her, yet sexually attracted to one of the most rapacious of them, James Hepburn, Earl of Bothwell, Mary seems trapped in arguments and disputes from the Scottish past. She is enmeshed, too, in a gender politics that scarcely acknowledges the rights of women

– even to enjoy peace and privacy.[79] In Act I, scene ii, she tells Bothwell,

> I dinna want to hear your history!
> *(A drumbeat.)*
> Bothwell, as well as queen I am widow. And maiden. And I would hae all unprotectit women in my realm honoured in their privacy![80]

'Privacy' may sound an oddly weak word here, but it is a commodity that Mary and Elizabeth lack. Neither of them has what Virginia Woolf termed 'a room of one's own'. Everyone wants something from them. They are constantly harassed and lobbied. Even their sex lives seem public property. Watched by an on-stage audience on her wedding-night with Darnley, Mary, with her 'lang rid hair' and her 'brooch o' red-gowd wire', is allowed erotic experience; but it is a disconcertingly public experience, that of a national celebrity.[81]

By the end of Act II, scene v, the regnant Mary, reduced to abject helplessness, can only appeal to Bothwell for help. Plotting for her own survival and that of her son, at this point she sees her only hope in appealing to a sexually rapacious and violent man who represents a predatory masculinity just as oppressive as that of John Knox. Ironically, this queen, ruling an independent Scotland, is pressed into subjugation; there seems no space for female independence. Lochhead's play raises questions about the relationship between female empowerment and national independence that have grown more insistent in the twenty-first century. In 2014 for all that SNP Deputy First Minister Nicola Sturgeon, independent MSP Margo MacDonald, Johann Lamont (leader of the Labour Party in Scotland) and Ruth Davidson (leader of the Scottish Conservatives) play a full part in argument, it remains awkwardly obvious that the majority of public participants in and commentators on Scotland's referendum debate are men. Moreover, considerably fewer women than men support independence. While Lochhead has made clear her support for Scottish political independence, her best known work highlights how difficult it is for a woman to identify with ideals of independence in a world where the odds – in terms of national and gender politics alike – seem weighted against her.

Lochhead's Mary regains briefly a position of dominance, both as monarch and married woman. In one of the scenes of powerful intercutting which characterise the drama, we see Mary and Elizabeth on stage at once. Their apparent togetherness is compromised as Elizabeth eyes a photograph of Mary's baby, and regards the Scottish queen with what sounds like envy.

> I do think it's hard to think of her so happy and me not! Dark deeds, bloody murders, plots against her life and throne, and she wins out again and again [. . .] All her people love her, she has a husband, a fine healthy son.
> *(Pause.)*
> Such is the wheel of fortune! [. . .]⁸²

Elizabeth makes Mary sound here like a feminist heroine who manages to have it all. Yet the emphatic mention of 'the wheel of fortune' is ominous. For that famous medieval emblem of change and mutability does not stand still; whatever or whoever is at its top is likely to be brought low as the wheel turns. Elizabeth's repetition of this figure of speech perhaps even indicates that she knows this and wishes for it. Her words indicate less a sisterly instinct than a persistent sense of rivalry.

Ultimately, Mary is unable to resist her desire or her doom. Soon, in a single line, we hear how her subjects, suspecting their queen of complicity in Darnley's murder, have turned against her. 'Burn the hoor!' they chant.⁸³ Heightening the play's sense of inescapability, La Corbie's revoicing of that traditional ballad, 'The Twa Corbies', presents the timeless mercilessness of slaughter and exploitation.

> Aye, his lady's ta'en another mate
> So he shall be oor dinner sweet
> And ower his white banes when they are bare
> The wind shall blaw for ower mair.⁸⁴

The play's final scene may appear to reduce the drama to a focus on Protestant/Catholic sectarianism; but the theme of gender, especially the topic of an oppressive yet also self-loathing, frightening male misogyny persists in Wee Knoxxy's 'Ah doan't like lassies'.⁸⁵ The outlook for women in this Scotland seems dire; or at least the play confronts that political possibility. Its final scene, entitled 'Jock Thamson's Bairns', alludes to a proverbial Scots saying (often invoked by politicians), 'We're a' Jock Tamson's bairns', meaning that underneath everything we all belong to one egalitarian human family.[86] Yet the on-stage reperforming of the story of Mary Queen of Scots in modern children's games suggests repetition of the past in a community whose 'national pastime' is 'nostalgia'. Entrapment in history, fought against by Alasdair Gray's protagonists, is what powers the continuing performance of Mary's doomed narrative:

> (*Very quietly*) Mary Queen of Scots got her head chopped off.
> Mary Queen of Scots got her ... head ... chopped ... off.[87]

With this concluding chant from La Corbie we reach a termination that seems enacted from generation to generation. The play ends in total blackout after a blood-red moment.

Lochhead's drama foregrounds a society where independence seems impossible for women; where sectarianism seems bred in the bone; and where Scottish independence is condemned to be snuffed out, thanks to the dominance of the Thatcher-like Elizabeth and the triumph of the male axeman, finally played by James Hepburn. With all its emphasis on performance and cyclic reperformance, the drama implicitly challenges its audience to break out of this cycle and perform things differently. It asks us whether or not we want to be trapped in the national, religious and gender politics that led to the Union of the Crowns, to the institutionalisation of sectarianism, and to the continuing entrapment of women; or whether we might find a different way to live.

Black Watch and Dunsinane

Twenty years after the first performance of *Mary Queen of Scots Got Her Head Chopped Off*, the cultural commentator Joyce McMillan was forced to conclude that though 'Liz Lochhead and many others have striven to put female experience at the centre of Scottish theatre', nonetheless, 'When the chips are down [...]

it still seems to take some variation on the macho workplace drama – the all-male cast, the threat of violence, and the sense of a fierce, wounded, victimized, aggressive-defensive masculinity softened by fast-talking humour – to propel a show somewhere close to the national psyche.' McMillan was reflecting on the astounding impact of Gregory Burke's drama for the National Theatre of Scotland, *Black Watch*. That play, like Lochhead's, connects Scotland's past and present, though it does so in very different circumstances. *Black Watch* was rejected as 'too parochial' for inclusion in the Edinburgh International Festival. Just seven months after its first performance at the Fringe in 2006, McMillan was confident that 'in terms of global impact and sheer audience demand [. . .] *Black Watch* is the single most successful piece of theatre ever produced in this country'.[88]

In his Director's Note to the 2007 published edition of *The National Theatre of Scotland's 'Black Watch'*, John Tiffany, whose directing contributed greatly to the play's success as it toured the world from Los Angeles to Sydney, acknowledges the inspiration of earlier 'visceral and riotous shows such as *Mary Queen of Scots Got Her Head Chopped Off*'.[89] Yet where Lochhead's Scottish history play was difficult for audience members at its American premiere, *Black Watch*, focusing on Scottish military history but mostly centred on the Iraq War, was more immediately and powerfully accessible. Prefacing his text, Gregory Burke signals his awareness of the regiment as 'a tribe', and of that group's 'appeal to the male psyche's yearning for a strong identity'.[90] Yet, unlike Lochhead's, his ultimate interest is much less in the relationship between gender, power and nation than in the intense solidarity of the regimental tribe where 'Bullying's the fucking job.'[91]

Aggressively masculine, *Black Watch* exhibits, too, a clear awareness of present-day Scottish politics and tensions between Westminster and Holyrood leaders. Drawing heavily on interviews and transcripts, unusually among Scottish dramas it depicts contemporary politicians. Along with BBC interviewer John Humphrys, its characters include Geoff Hoon (a Labour minister who was then Britain's Defence Secretary), as well as Alex Salmond who vehemently opposed the Iraq War:

Alex Salmond I think it will give way to a wave of anger as Scotland and the Black Watch families compare and contrast the bravery of our Scottish soldiers with the duplicity and chicanery of the politicians who sent them into this deployment.

John Humphrys Is that anger justified, Mr Hoon?

Geoff Hoon No, it is not, and I'm afraid the leader of the Scottish Nationalists' comments demonstrate clearly there are no depths to which he will not sink to seek [sic] – and I can't understand why he does this, I cannot understand why someone should seek to take political advantage about the tragic deaths of three brave men and their interpreter.

Alex Salmond These are professional soldiers, they'll do their job, regardless of the danger, they're among the finest infantry soldiers in the world, but we and I believe that this deployment was political in its nature, we think the request was political, during the American presidential election.[92]

From the play's earliest performances, First Minister Salmond showed his enthusiasm for it. Unionist politicians expressed horror that theatre figures such as actors Ewan McGregor and Ashley Jensen were given tickets for *Black Watch* at Salmond's behest. Conservative Unionist MSP John Lamont complained that Salmond was 'mixing it with celebrities to further his plans for separation'.[93] *Black Watch*, however, is not by any means a piece of straightforward propaganda. The play's soldiers know that politically and militarily they are 'in the shite'.[94] Respect for military professionalism is fused with an ironic awareness of parallels between Scotland's past and present-day conflict in Iraq. So, for instance, in a set-piece, Lord Elgin, before picking up the historic sword of Robert Bruce, addresses the regiment: 'Now as you know, my ancestor led his men at Bannockburn and is buried nearby at Dunfermline Abbey. He led his men in a fight for freedom from the tyranny of a foreign power and the need then, as now, for Scotsmen to serve their country in its hour of need is as great.'[95] Asking 'wha'll follow a Bruce?', this modern military man seeks to lead his professional fighters into battle; but soldiers such as Rossco, Granty and Cammy are more cynical than the leader expects, and ask 'How much?' Lord Elgin protests,

This is Robert the Bruce's sword.
Rossco Well, get Robert the fucking Bruce tay go way you then.
Cammy Aye.
Lord Elgin Bannockburn
  Beat.
Freedom
  Beat.
Robert the Bruce and that?
Granty We're still wanting fucking paid.[96]

Bannockburn is not presented as ignoble, but modern professional soldiers, even those urged to overthrow a tyrant, need to
be remunerated. In *Black Watch* appropriation of the rhetoric
of Bannockburn by the British Army is seen as suspect; the clear-
sightedness of Salmond emerges as more honestly credible.

This play avoids glamorising either Bannockburn or the
Scottish past: 'When Scotland was an independent nation we
were fucking mercenaries tay half ay fuckin Europe.'[97] Violent,
balletic and spectacularly staged, *Black Watch* is most engaged
with the politics of twenty-first-century globalised warfare. As
Cammy says about the Iraqis, 'We're invading their country and
fucking their day up'; and as one of his officers puts it later,

> **Officer** It takes three hundred years to build an army that's admired
> and respected around the world. But it only takes three years pissing
> about in the desert in the biggest western foreign policy disaster ever
> to fuck it up completely.
> *Beat.*
> But you didn't hear that from me.
> *Beat.*
> We could be off to Afghanistan next. It's going to be exactly the
> same. Kandahar. Helmand province. It's the only place on the planet
> that might be slightly more dangerous than here.[98]

In Burke's hard-hitting drama, first staged when the British
Government was discussing the abolition of the Black Watch as
a regiment even as its soldiers were dying in Iraq, the appropriation of Bannockburn for British imperial causes – common in
the late nineteenth and early twentieth centuries – is decisively
unpicked. While the play is focused more on international than
on Scottish national politics, and though it is made clear that the
soldiers fight ultimately not for the nation (whether Britain or

Scotland) but for their regiment, nonetheless it is the assessment of the war given by Salmond that seems vindicated. Implicitly, *Black Watch* questions the politics and morals of British Unionist politicians. Salmond is no Bannockburn hero; but at least he is not the one trying to twist the legacy of Bannockburn to bolster an overseas military débâcle.

In *Black Watch* distinctively Scottish politics plays a subsidiary part, and in performance the choreography and physical energy of the performers may be at least as striking as the words they speak or shout. Less dependent on physical display in its staging, the more recent historical drama *Dunsinane* by David Greig focuses clearly on Scottish independence, but the Iraqi and Afghan conflicts are a pressing off-stage presence. First performed by the Royal Shakespeare Company, then presented by the National Theatre of Scotland in 2011 after publication by Faber the preceding year, *Dunsinane* is set in the medieval nation of *Macbeth*. Written partly in verse and partly in prose, Greig's play can be seen as a sort of sequel to Shakespeare's. It begins with an English army entering Scotland to overthrow the 'tyrant' Macbeth and establish 'a new and peaceful order' (nominally headed by Malcolm) in a wildly fractured nation whose customs and habits of mind, it soon emerges, are considerably different from those of the invaders.[99] Parallels with the US-led, British-supported interventions in Iraq and Afghanistan are evident; but it was the play's specific relationship with contemporary Scottish politics which made headlines in 2011 when Scotland's most senior civil servant, Sir Peter Housden, was attacked by Unionist politicians for recommending to Scottish Office colleagues that they watch *Dunsinane* to further their understanding of Scottish politics.

For the English army in Greig's play, Scotland is difficult to comprehend. The invaders know the locals 'don't want us to be here'. In Scotland 'nothing is solid', meanings are unexpected.[100] Almost echoing Edwin Morgan's phrase 'Nothing not giving messages', the English general Siward, worried about secret signals, states that, 'In this country anything can contain a message.' The recalcitrant natives are hard to manage: 'Their grudge keeps them warm.'[101] Nevertheless, the English are sure a rational solution can be found to the Scottish problem. As

Siward puts it, 'There are plenty of disputes to be unravelled. But if we persevere I believe that we can make a picture of the world which everyone agrees true.'[102] Yet as the situation on the ground develops, such a picture fails to develop. Characters speak different languages, most obviously English and Gaelic; there seem not just divisions between English and Scots, but also among the Scots themselves.

Gruach, the queen (known to Shakespeare's audiences as Lady Macbeth, but never called that in *Dunsinane*), enters into a sexual relationship with Siward. Always she manages to remain elusive, maintaining the upper hand through what is perceived as a kind of magic that the English rationalist invader does not fully understand. Increasingly out of his depth, Siward is nonplussed when confronted by a Scottish parliament with its complex weaving of loyalties.

> **Macduff** [. . .] The Isles are demonstrating their primary allegiance is to Norway, not to England. They want you to know how unimportant you are. That's their message.
>
> **Siward** But I didn't – I don't understand the message.
>
> **Macduff** It's not important that the message arrives, what matters is that it's been sent.[103]

At times *Dunsinane* has a grim humour. When the English soldier Egham, frustrated by the Scots who seem to want to fight everyone including themselves, asks Siward, 'Do you think burning them helps?', Siward's reply is simply, 'It shows we're determined.'[104] The English long to leave, provided that ceding power can be presented as something other than defeat; they cannot understand the 'networks of obligation' and 'delicate filigree' of counterbalancing allegiances among the Scots who surround them.[105] When a local girl kills first an English soldier, then herself, this suicide attack unsettles the invaders further; it confirms that for Siward the indigenous population is an incomprehensible 'mystery'. After Siward orders the killing of a lad who may or may not be the queen's son, heir to a disputed Scotland, Malcolm warns Siward that, 'by killing this boy you have given him eternal life'.[106] His slaughter strengthens the Scots' determination to resist domination. The play ends with scenes set in winter in a snowy land where the saltire flies from every castle. English soldiery ask repeatedly, 'Why are we here?' Their leaders search for an exit strategy. Siward comes to acknowledge, as he puts it to the queen, 'You can't defeat me, Gruach, and I can't defeat you.'[107] Yet it is Gruach who appears the stronger and utters the play's last word – 'Go' – as a boy soldier follows Siward into the whiteout of the snow.[108]

Dunsinane's final word can be read as a formal joke, countering the most famous ending in modern drama: in *Waiting for Godot* the words 'Let's go' are followed by the stage direction '*They do not move*.'[109] Greig's play has a dramatic wit that does not only depend on its relationship with Shakespeare's *Macbeth*. Yet more obviously *Dunsinane* concludes with a Scottish queen who has maintained her independence and, it would appear, that of her country against apparently overwhelming odds. Though *Dunsinane* repeats aspects of the rhetoric of battle that dominates *Black Watch*, it reinstates a sense of the complexities of gender in Scottish power relations. Greig's historical play differs in many ways from Lochhead's *Mary Queen of Scots Got Her Head Chopped Off*, however, not least in the way it grants apparent victory both to a powerful femaleness and to a version of Scottish independence.

The plotting of Greig's drama seems more obviously a commentary on the Iraqi and Afghan conflicts than on twenty-first-century Scottish politics. It is both, but the overseas resonances are more sustainable: no army has invaded present-day Scotland. Nor, set centuries before Bannockburn, is this a Bannockburn play. Inevitably and ostensibly, however, like *Macbeth* before it, *Dunsinane* invites audiences to ponder relations between England and Scotland, and to contemplate Scottish independence. Where for Shakespeare the latter was clearly something bloodily atrocious and to be avoided at all costs, for Greig Scottish independence, however hard to fathom, is something that will outlast attempts – however bloody and/or well intentioned – to suppress it.

That *Dunsinane* sparked a contemporary Scottish political spat shows the play's ability to impact on the twenty-first-century independence debate. As the *Scotsman* reported in 2011, a 'furious row [. . .] erupted over the role of Scotland's top civil servant' after Sir Peter Housden, Alex Salmond's permanent secretary, had been to see *Dunsinane* and recommended in a message to Scottish civil service officials that they attend a performance. 'To my mind,' he told colleagues, 'it does genuinely speak to our present condition as a nation.'[110] Along with other remarks by Housden, this was seized on by Unionist politicians and by political commentators as evidence that the English-born civil servant had ' "gone native" '. The leaders of all three main Unionist opposition parties in Scotland – Labour, Conservatives and Liberal Democrats – made official complaints: Sir Peter's comments indicated that he was promoting SNP policies. In Scotland the tabloid *Scottish Sun* ran a story headed 'The Civil War' which quoted both Housden's remarks on *Dunsinane* and the then Scottish Labour leader Andy Gray's accusation that Housden had 'broken the cardinal rule of the Civil Service and gone native'.[111]

Outside Scotland, London-based papers such as the *Daily Telegraph* reported Housden's comments on *Dunsinane*, mentioning that political figures including Lord Forsyth (Michael Forsyth, Conservative Secretary of State for Scotland during the Thatcher era) had tabled a question in the House of Lords asking whether it was now part of the duties of Sir Peter's post to 'include preparing the break up of the United Kingdom'.[112] Matters were referred to the head of the British Civil Service who ruled that civil servants had to 'support the elected government of the day' and that Housden's comments 'should not be seen as inconsistent with the civil service code'. This failed to satisfy the leader of the Conservatives in Scotland, who protested that 'It was not "relevant support to ministers" to suggest to civil servants that they spend their free time visiting a play about the occupation of Scotland in reference to "our present condition as a nation".'[113] Though, in the wake of his remarks on *Dunsinane*, Housden was cleared of wrongdoing, in 2012 reports in the *Telegraph* stated that 'the permanent secretaries from all the Whitehall departments no longer discuss Scotland if Sir Peter Housden, the Scottish Executive's permanent secretary, is present'.[114] This reporting, using the term 'Scottish Executive' rather than 'Scottish Government', is itself clearly politically loaded towards the Unionist side – a further indication, perhaps, of how sensitive all 'messages' now are in the context of Scottish independence.

The political row over *Dunsinane* indicates that the relationship between literature and politics can become febrile in today's Scotland. Yet this volatility could be exaggerated. What is obvious is that a number of writers have raised the matter of Scottish independence in the context of the wars in Iraq and Afghanistan. Part of the motivation here may be to highlight the fact that these were wars in which Scotland as a nation lacked any specific say: the Scottish Government (though wishing, for instance, to rid Scotland of nuclear weapons) has no control over UK foreign or defence policy. Linking Scottish independence to these overseas wars highlights issues about national sovereignty both at home and abroad, as well as reminding audiences that debates about political independence belong to a global rather than a purely Scottish agenda.

Though it is not appropriate to discuss at any length here, similar questions were raised by the collaborative 2011 exhibition *Body Bags / Simonides* which was published as *Simonides* and toured in Scotland, England and the USA under that title between 2011 and 2013. In the book version an essay entitled 'Simonides and the War on Terror' prefaces Scots-language versions of two dozen poems and fragments by the poet of the most famous ancient Greek epitaphs for the dead in battle. Simonides's work was produced during the Persian Wars when the city states of ancient Greece fought against an empire that encompassed the territories we now know as Iran, Iraq and Afghanistan. While *Simonides* is not reducible to party politics, and is less visceral than *Black Watch* and *Dunsinane*, through language and context it raises questions about power, authority and independence.

Ootlin, tell oor maisters this: *Stranger*
We lig here deid. We did as we were telt.[115]   *lie*

Black Watch, *Dunsinane* and *Simonides* register shifts in contemporary Scottish politics with varying degrees of obliquity. Yet the topic is also dealt with head-on in a much more extensive work of fiction. More ambitiously, directly and fully than any other twenty-first-century novel to date, this book has discussed and provoked discussion about Scottish independence.

And the Land Lay Still

Published in 2010, James Robertson's sweeping novel *And the Land Lay Still* takes its title from one of Edwin Morgan's *Sonnets from Scotland*. In Morgan's 'The Summons', the land lies still at what seems an end-point, a Decemberish moment; yet this turns out to herald a reawakening when 'a far horn grew to break that people's sleep'.[116] Robertson quotes Morgan's entire sonnet as the epigraph to his 670-page narrative. The novel tells the story of modern struggles to achieve Scottish political devolution, and of the wider independence movement. Influenced at times by Grassic Gibbon and by Alasdair Gray, it offers a clear yet complex stranding of tales. Throughout there is an alertness to the way stories are made, altered and come to assume a satisfying shape.

Robertson's metaphor for this shaping imagination is photography. His Scottish protagonist, Michael Pendreich, is both a photographer and the son of a famous photographer. He is arranging an exhibition of his father's work, spanning five decades of Scottish life. Michael's personal history and activities intersect with other stories to present a panorama of modern Scotland – male and female, straight and gay, nationalist and Unionist, old and young, from the people of mining communities to aristocratic Tory grandees. Recent literary critics usually assume Walter Scott's legacy is tethered inevitably to an imperial past. Proving them wrong, by fusing Sir Walter's narrative technique and historical grasp with the Modernist and postmodern social attentiveness of Gibbon and Gray, Robertson (who wrote a doctoral thesis on Scott) achieves an amplitude and understanding of history that fits the social upheavals of Scotland's present and recent history.[117] Yet whereas Scott worked ultimately from a Unionist perspective, Robertson writes from a vantage point sympathetic towards Scottish independence. Hailed by Irvine Welsh as 'a landmark for the novel in Scotland', his book was described as 'outstanding' and 'important' by Alex Salmond.[118] Unsurprisingly, its politics have been censured by Unionist politicians.

Sometimes, perhaps, Robertson includes too much political material, as if his novel were aspiring to be a text-book on Scottish history. Yet that impulse is itself Scott-like, attuned to Scott's alertness to stories within stories and to his presentation of the history and culture of an entire society. It also makes the narrative readily accessible for non-Scottish as well as Scottish readers. Born in Kent, Robertson's 'thoroughly Scottish' family moved to Stirlingshire when he was six; he was then educated at the private Glenalmond College in Perthshire, 'a Scottish boarding school modelled on the English public school system'.[119] Later, in the 1980s, Robertson was involved with the left-wing, nationalist magazine *Radical Scotland*. A former bookseller and director of a Scots-language publishing imprint, he offers an insider's understanding as well as a novelistic and historical analysis of Scottish nationalism.

This author has met and corresponded with several generations of pro-independence activists – from Lillias Forbes, last surviving member of J. H. Whyte's 1930s St Andrews circle, to twenty-first-century politicians; he was writer-in-residence at the Scottish Parliament. His novel is astute in portraying early nationalists as eccentric figures, not all of them Scottish, whose perspective on Scottish independence could appear risible, yet who, in the longer term, came to represent an influential way of thinking about the available possibilities. So Monsieur Lucas, Michael Pendreich's 'dishevelled, shambling, straggle-haired' French teacher 'in deepest Perthshire', is introduced shortly after mention of Hugh MacDiarmid, a '"wild-haired poet"' notorious for having called Prime Minister Sir Alec Douglas-Home '"a zombie"'.[120] At school, M. Lucas impresses Michael as 'so unbalanced as to be a member of the Scottish National Party'; the Frenchman, excited by SNP candidate Winnie Ewing's 'famous victory at the Hamilton by-election in 1967', tells his classes 'stories of Wallace and Bruce and the Black Douglas so that they would have a true understanding of the history of their country'. He embodies a determined spirit of 'resistance'.[121]

Years later, in 1978, Michael's father, the photographer Angus Pendreich, celebrated for his unusual 'Angus Angle', photographs the now elderly M. Lucas attending a pro-independence rally at King Robert the Bruce's famous battlesite. Present at this gathering, Michael finds it disappointing: 'It seemed to Mike that the air at Bannockburn was failing to lift the saltires or make the lions rampant; the pipes and drums sounded thin and plaintive, and the speeches, relayed through a ropy PA system, sounded rather anxious than celebratory.' M. Lucas is now blind; he does not want Michael to take his picture; he represents a kind of tenacity. Later, Michael opens a newspaper and sees that his father, the more assured and bloody-minded photographer, has ignored M. Lucas's wishes and has photographed him at Bannockburn nevertheless:

> And there, taking pride of place and a full page to himself, was M. Lucas, perched on his shooting stick in his absurd kilt with all the trimmings, his hair unkempt and with ice cream running down his chin, and if you didn't know you wouldn't realize he was blind but you'd guess there was something not right about his vision. There was litter scattered around him and hints of flags and tartan at the edge of the picture, and he sat among this debris like King Lear, mad and proud.[122]

Michael is incensed at his father's photograph. Jealously, however, he recognises its genius. In the arc of the book, this picture, taken shortly before the 1979 Scottish referendum, exemplifies the old-style image of the Scottish nationalist as crazed eccentric, a pathetic but determined presence at Bannockburn: a Lear-like loser, not a Bruce-like winner. Yet Robertson shows how the determination represented by M. Lucas helps secure devolution in the long term, and moves Scotland decisively in the direction of independence. Michael Pendreich realises that 'One of the unintended effects of Margaret Thatcher's revolution [. . .] was to destroy Scottish loyalty to the British state.'[123]

Tracking the shift of independence from the eccentric margins to the political mainstream, *And the Land Lay Still* is a complex, nuanced, but also welcoming novel. Robertson's other fictions show a readiness to tackle painful themes in Scottish history such as religious extremism in *The Fanatic* (2000), slavery in *Joseph Knight* (2003) and the Lockerbie terrorist atrocity in *The Professor of Truth* (2013). Yet, despite the controversy caused by this last novel, *And the Land Lay Still* is his most ambitious book. It is alert to other stories of Scottish independence – from the English Tory and former British government minister Douglas Hurd's popular novel of imagined terrorist violence *Scotch on the Rocks* (televised by the BBC in the 1970s, and probably intended as Unionist propaganda) to the dreams of 'Lallans-spouting poets' such as MacDiarmid, whose monitoring by British Government intelligence services is alluded to in the narrative.[124] As the years pass, Michael Pendreich attends several parties at the Old Town Edinburgh home of Jean Barbour, where people who care about 'the "Scottish question"' gather in a cosmopolitan company including many 'left-leaning nationalists' and 'nationalist-inclined socialists'.[125] Edinburgh is the book's epicentre. At Barbour's home, or in the Scottish capital's pubs and streets, political arguments are staged. Alert to issues of class, the novel includes 1970s clashes between the Labour left (to whom the SNP are 'Tartan Tories') and those who sympathise with independence; often laced with irony, these contentions deploy familiar reference points:

> 'The last thing the Scottish worker needs is to be diverted from the class struggle by pipe dreams about independence.'
> 'What about Vietnam?' Mike said. 'Or Ireland? I take it you're not opposed to them being independent countries?'
> Greatcoat rolled his eyes at the biker. 'Listen to Robert the Bruce,' he said. 'That's totally fucking different. I mean, come *on*, man!'
> The biker seemed in two minds about whose view to favour. Duffelcoat was staring at the smoke-yellowed ceiling.
> 'It's just that I've noticed,' Mike said, 'that there's always one rule for Scotland when it comes to independence, and another rule for everyone else.'[126]

Chronicling and to some extent celebrating the political imagination, Robertson's novel is interested in how national narratives and the imaginings of fiction may spur one another. Change is vital to the imagining of nation and narration alike. As Jean Barbour tells Michael, 'Stories aren't static [. . .] They grow, they shrink, they change with the retelling.'[127] To some extent a transference of Edwin Morgan's metamorphic imagination to the realm of political prose fiction gives Robertson's novel an energy to match its range. His book's emphasis on needing to 'Trust the story' represents an impulse to rely on literary imagining – and on the multi-stranded tale of the nation itself. Like Morgan, Michael Pendreich seems committed to Scottish independence, yet not quite a party man: '"I'm not in any party," Mike said, "I've thought about joining the SNP, because I believe in independence, but I prefer being, well, independent."'[128] Pendreich, like Robertson, is an artist, sensing alongside political commitment a duty to the freedom of his art. His is the position of many modern Scottish writers.

Moving between rural, small-town and city communities, Robertson's novel with its gay protagonist crosses class, race and gender boundaries. His characters range from small-town shopkeeper Saleem Khan to white working-class ex-miners and a Highland land-owner; the independent-minded author of the preface to the catalogue of Michael's father's photographs has learned from feminist thought and from contemporary journalism before producing her volume of essays, *The Other Lady Macbeth*. *And the Land Lay Still* shows how art may speak to and from a range of situations within the contemporary nation, while also drawing on earlier sources. Reflecting on the Union, one of Robertson's characters argues, '"Bought and sold for English gold. Burns was right about that."'[129] This contention is set within larger wrangling over Scotland's place in the British Empire and in postcolonial struggles. Some characters in the book think the closeness of literary imaginations to the cause of independence can be an electoral drawback welcomed by Unionists: 'The more Scottish Nationalism is associated in the minds of the people with Grieve [MacDiarmid] and others like him, the less likely that it'll ever have any kind of mass appeal.'[130] Robertson's British Government spooks rejoice in nationalists' invocations of the 1320 Declaration of Arbroath and MacDiarmid's poetry – because these seem to them out of touch with contemporary reality. Yet author and protagonist alike understand how such cultural references can also resonate to shape modern debates about identity, politics and culture.

Towards the end of *And the Land Lay Still* is a section set just before the 1997 devolution referendum which led to the establishment of a devolved Scottish parliament: 'Mike went out to vote thinking of M. Lucas and his prophecy at

Bannockburn, that a time to accept would come, and that when it did the ghosts of history would whisper in people's ears. And so it turned out.'[131] This memory of a modern-day rally at Bannockburn is presented as underpinning Robertson's protagonist's vote; but, though occasionally strained, his novel is well aware that nostalgia (including nostalgia for Unionism) is a temptation both for Scottish literature and Scottish politics. The coming of devolution is shown neither as necessary end-point nor as a backward look but as something that may contribute to a continuing process. Pendreich and his former lover Adam Shaw argue about recent politics.

'Thatcher won after all, in spite of everything. That's what I think.'
'How can you say that?' Mike said. 'Her own party chucked her out. She fought against devolution all the way, and we beat her. And the Tories won't be back in power for years.'
'They don't have to be. Blair and Brown are gonnae dae it aw for them. It's true. The market is king. So what aboot this parliament of oors? It's twenty years ower late. It's like we fought our way tae the bar just in time for the barman tae tell us he's stopped serving.'
'No,' Mike protested. 'I don't feel that. We're at the start of something new and different. It *can't* be like it was before.'
Adam laughed. 'Like it was in the olden days, ye mean?'
'The olden days,' Mike said. 'My mother used to go on about them. The Middle Ages, knights in armour and no plumbing is what she meant.'
'Aye, and ye ken what it means noo? It means no that lang ago. When I was young. It's me that's middle-aged, and you're no that far behind me. We're frae the olden days just the same as Robert the Bruce and Bonnie Prince fucking Charlie.' The rain came on stronger and a gust of wind tried to jerk the umbrella out of Adam's hand. 'I think I'll dae what he did, go into exile,' he said. 'I'm sick of this weather apart frae onything else.'
In the station they stood on the long, almost empty platform waiting for Adam's train.
'What aboot you?' he said. 'What'll you dae?'
'I'm not going anywhere,' Mike said. 'I'm sticking around to see what happens.'[132]

The narrative ends in the present day. Mike opens the exhibition of his father's photographs, which chart the course of modern Scottish history in the period before devolution. For Mike the exhibition marks both a new start in his life and a moment in the development of a nation apparently heading for further political change. Just as Mike the photographer has arranged pictures, so Robertson the novelist has set in order a national narrative. Mike's final realisation is that now new 'connections will be made, and he understands that it has fallen to him to make them'.[133]

When, in support of independence, the 'Yes Scotland' campaign was launched in 2012, its published list of supporters included James Robertson as well as Alasdair Gray, Liz Lochhead, David Greig and other writers.[134] As far as the coming together of Scottish independence and literary imagination goes, matters are reaching a political crescendo. From authors as different as Ewan Morrison, Meaghan Delahunt and Iain Banks has come widespread support for independence among the literary community, though that does not and should not mean that Scottish writers make this one issue central to their work. The writer's job is to imagine all sorts of things, not to straitjacket art for the purposes of political propaganda. In 2012 Scotland's Makar, Liz Lochhead, caused a stir when she said with characteristic forthrightness that 'if there was a referendum [on independence] tomorrow, I'd vote yes.'[135] Later, in a talk at the Scottish Poetry Library, she tried to make clear that she was speaking as an individual, rather than trying to politicise the role of 'Makar', but the idea that poetry and politics might go together is scarcely new in Scottish cultural life. Nor is it something to back away from.

Some months before Lochhead spoke, the *Observer* asked several Scottish writers for their views on the Anglo-Scottish Union. Among the five published responses in its issue of 28 August 2011, four (from Iain Banks, Janice Galloway, David Greig and A. L. Kennedy) inclined towards Scottish independence; only Shena Mackay said simply, 'I don't know.' Many other writers have joined the debate, including Scotland's most influential novelist, James Kelman, who makes it clear that, although he does not regard himself as a nationalist, he is '100% in favour of independence'.[136] Kelman writes constantly about kinds of independence, but not the sort trumpeted by nationalists. It is hard to imagine him sharing a platform with Alex Salmond. Yet he is unequivocal about what is needed as Scotland moves towards its independence referendum.

Scottish history is not nice history. It's the history of subjection. We are so used to tipping the hat to our superiors. And that's still the way things are, unfortunately. How many other countries do we know, how many cultures in the world do we know where there's a debate about 'should we determine our own existence or not?' Such inferiority, it's shocking. Independence is not an economic decision, it is a decision to do with self-respect. How we determine our own existence, this is what we do as adults for goodness sake, it's our culture, ultimately it concerns survival. And we'll see it literally, if the independence movement is set back again, emigration as usual, for those able to do it, spiritual demoralization for others.

When his interviewer hoped that more intellectual weight would be put into the independence campaigning, Kelman responded,

I think it's up to us, up to the public, that discourse should go that way. I'm not saying it's being deliberately manipulated, but the way the discourse is at present, it's almost like, how many people in Scotland even know that those in favour of independence are not necessarily nationalists? Of course more so in England. It's said of me, that I'm a nationalist. I'm continually having to deny that I am a nationalist but at the same time I'm 100% in favour of independence. They don't get it [. . .] Here's an interesting thing. Alan Warner and Louise Welsh, Alasdair Gray, Keith Dickson and myself were on a panel in Montpelier in the south of France two or three months ago. Each one of us favours independence, and not one of us is a Scottish Nationalist, not as far as I know. Each of us has a different position, yet each of us favours independence.[137]

These and other authors' expressions of support for independence are particularly interesting since in their imaginative writing many have expressed little or no interest in the independence *v.* Unionism debate. It seems possible to find a few Scottish writers who back Unionism. Though he now professes neutrality, the distinguished crime writer Ian Rankin seemed to lend his support to Gordon Brown a few years ago, while Allan Massie has consistently backed the Unionist cause, as has Andrew O'Hagan whose 1999 novel *Our Fathers* elegised the Scottish Labour politics of an earlier era. However, vocal supporters of Unionism among the Scottish literati, and particularly among those who reside in Scotland, are notably scarce. Perhaps our age of declared austerity, recessionary economics and Scottish nationalist resurgence has moved us into a closer alignment with the 1930s Scotland of MacDiarmid, J. H. Whyte and *The Modern Scot*; except that where once the nationalists were a bohemian fringe, now they are in government.

It would be obtusely reductive if, having noted the responses of Kennedy, Banks, Kelman and others to questions about the British Union, one then read all their work in the light of those responses. Especially in a time of intensifying focus on Scottish politics, even poets, novelists and dramatists who support independence must assert, too, the independent-mindedness of art: writing can be (but need not be) politically engaged. Noticeably, several important Scottish writers have either other political fish to fry – or none at all: John Burnside, for instance, shows little interest in Unionism or independence, maintaining that his ideological stance is 'deep ecologist/anarchist'; in prose Don Paterson has trashed the bureaucratic mumbo-jumbo of arts administrator Andrew Dixon's Creative Scotland, and hastened Dixon's resignation as that organisation's leader, but Paterson's poetry avoids political engagement with the topic of independence.[138] As artists, Kennedy, Galloway, Burnside and Paterson are distinguished not least for setting aspects of modern Scotland alongside preoccupations of world literature from Rilke to Mary Oliver. My own imagination is sometimes more stubbornly and parochially political, but I recognise that even when a poet expresses political commitments, he or she must also 'Keep at a tangent' as Seamus Heaney puts it.[139] To restrict one's writing to the single theme of Scottish independence would be damagingly small-minded; yet I find the issue of independence too imaginatively exciting to ignore.

I have not written this book to insist that all a country's writers should engage with one specific political issue, or to suggest that this topic dominates the history of Scottish literature. Over the centuries authors from Scotland and beyond have engaged with Scottish independence, but the topic has mattered at least as much to minor figures as to great poets like Burns and MacDiarmid. Designedly or not, all have played a part in constructing a resilient and adaptable 'political imaginary'. It is a long, long time since Bannockburn. But there remains a place, surely, not just for ambitious panoramically-minded novelists but also for poets to go on articulating the link between Scottish independence and the literary imagination, sounding at this moment in the early twenty-first century a continuing note of reveille:

> Wake up, new nation,
> Stretch yourself. It's time
> To fling the covers back, and sing,
> Alarm-clock loud, a sharpened trill of song
> Greeting the daylight now that dawn has broken,
> You who have slept so long – too long –
> With one eye open.[140]

Bannockburn 2014

From the multi-authored 'political variety show' planned by the National Theatre of Scotland for the run-up to the 2014 referendum to books by individual writers with political resonances, the independence debate has focused imaginative attention.[141] While some continue to denounce invocations of myth and history – whether of Robert the Bruce or Margaret Thatcher – others, at times, relish them. In recent decades the most frequently sung song about Bannockburn has not been Burns's 'Scots, Wha Hae' but folksinger Roy Williamson's 1967 'Flower of Scotland', that unofficial Scottish national anthem popularised at rugby matches and other sporting events, and more widely disseminated through YouTube, Wikipedia and other internet sites than on paper. Sung by singers as different as Princess Anne and working-class Glasgow schoolchildren, this rousing chant celebrates how Scots encountered 'Proud Edward's army, / And sent them homeward / To think again'. Acknowledging that 'those days are past', the song also calls on Scots to 'rise' and 'be the nation again'.[142] Its language is plain, and can lapse into touristic cliché as it invokes Scots' 'wee bit hill and glen', but Williamson's song has achieved a popularity that is impressively resilient, and it confirms the centrality of Bannockburn as a symbolic point of reference.

While not aiming to replace 'Flower of Scotland', but perhaps seeking subtler poetic responses, for 2014, in one of the largest acts of poetic commissioning carried out in the modern nation, the National Trust for Scotland commissioned ten Scottish poets to write poems marking Bannockburn's 700th anniversary. After a public vote and judgments from a panel including the Scottish Makar, Liz Lochhead, one of the ten poems was chosen for prominent display. The year 2014 sees it inscribed on the inner face of the hundred-metre-long circular rotunda beam surrounding the flagpole that marks the site of the Bannockburn Borestone where Bruce is said to have raised his standard at the beginning of the battle. The poets commissioned were John Burnside, Robert Crawford, Douglas Dunn, Alec Finlay, Valerie Gillies, Kathleen Jamie, William Letford, Aonghas MacNeacail, Tom Pow and Robin Robertson. Our brief was 'to evoke the significance of the Bannockburn landscape in ways which will touch and inspire 21st century visitors and enhance the contemplative mood of this place of commemoration', and the winning poem, by Kathleen Jamie, is now the most affirmative modern addition to the battlesite.[143]

Though the present book has had little to say about cyberculture, it is striking that when the poems were first published online and made available for the public to vote on, several poets, in the prose statements accompanying their poems, emphasised that their work should not be read as in any way triumphalist. Where earlier celebrants had sung Bannockburn as a victory of the Scots over the English, the writers for this 2014 anniversary project stressed instead the site's universal meaning. So, for instance, John Burnside, moved by a statement from dissident Chinese artist Ai Weiwei ('If someone is not free, I'm not free'), wrote in his poem that 'nobody is free till each is free'. While readers might be tempted to relate these words to the 1320 Declaration of Arbroath, Burnside in his prose invokes instead the famous 'Red Clydeside' political leader John Maclean, appointed consul for Soviet Affairs in Great Britain after the 1917 Russian Revolution. Striving to avoid 'kneejerk patriotism' and 'twee ghost-spotting', Douglas Dunn, too, builds into his poem a criticism of patriotic rhetoric, writing of a nobleman who urges Scots soldiers to fight at Bannockburn, 'The more he spoke, the less he had to say.'

If Burnside and Dunn are critical of the nobility, a republican accent is heard in Alec Finlay's Bannockburn poem-inscription, which speaks of 'FREE CITIZENS', rather than subjects, and warns against the tyranny of myth, suggesting that if myth itself becomes tyranny it must be driven out. Like Kathleen Jamie's poem, Finlay's alludes to Hamish Henderson's song 'Freedom Come All Ye', as well as to Burns's republican 'A Man's a Man For A' That'. Even when, as all seem to have done, the poets drew on historical reading and research into the history and representation of Bannockburn, they refused to be confined by these. King Robert the Bruce would have had little time for republicanism, but several of the poems, including Aonghas MacNeacail's with its image of the tree of liberty, seem to long for a country that has moved beyond royalty. One exception may be Valerie Gillies, whose celebration of 'a crown on a helmet' seems unironic, and whose research included rereading Barbour's *Bruce*.

Gillies is not the only poet to have felt the pull of details from older Bruce narratives. William Letford, in his accompanying prose piece, recalls hearing the story of Bannockburn in some detail when he was a second-year pupil at the tellingly named Wallace High School in nearby Stirling; nimbly and even-handedly, his history teacher liked to act out both parts in the duel between Bruce and the English nobleman Henry De Bohun, struck dead on horseback by a blow from Bruce's axe. The final word of Letford's poem – 'welcome' – appears unironic. It recognises, surely, that Bannockburn with its new Visitor Centre, is now, and has long been, a tourist site more than a battlesite. Letford's anecdote about his teacher backs up Aonghas MacNeacail's contention that 'no child can go through a Scottish education without gaining some knowledge of the Battle of Bannockburn', but MacNeacail's poem, mixing Gaelic, Latin, Scots and English, encourages readers to reflect on the multi-stranded inheritance of Scottish culture as well as hinting at the richness of the literary inheritance in the Bannockburn story.

Reinterpreted, that wealth persists and still resonates in the year of the 2014 referendum on Scottish independence. Though some of the commissioned Bannockburn poems seem to minimise the bloodiness of the battle, Tom Pow, who read or reread Edwin Morgan's translation of Robert Baston's 1314 eyewitness poem on the carnage, and who invokes, too, the World War I poetry of Wilfred Owen, quotes as his epigraph the line from Morgan's Baston, 'How can I sing of so much blood'. Pow's Bannockburn poem includes 'blood-flecked linnets' which 'Flit between the mouths of the dead and the dying'. Like several other poems, this one sets side by side the peacefulness and beauty of the present-day 'soft landscape' with the past suffering for which it is so famous. Determined 'to resist any simplistic nationalism', and wanting 'to re-position the battle of Bannockburn in the *continuum* of Scots history: as a memorial to the past that looks to the future', Robin Robertson looks out as far as Canada, hinting at the scattered Scottish diaspora; his poem also mentions 'Culloden', and wants Bannockburn to represent 'The same cause and course for everyone'. Bannockburn can have a universal resonance, but it was about *Scotland* having an independent future and, however inclusive modern poets may wish to be, it seems odd to sidestep that specific issue. At the same time, how can one make such a point in the twenty-first century without appearing narrow-minded or Anglophobic?

This is the dilemma faced by all ten poets. It would not have troubled Scottish writers in 1314 or for centuries afterwards, but at the time of the 2014 referendum it is insistent. Surely the best and most moving poetic solution to the dilemma is that arrived at by the assured literary imagination of Kathleen Jamie. From the beginning, she writes in the prose piece composed to go with her poem, she was determined to engage with 'the Scottish literary tradition'. She wanted to make towards it 'More than a nod – a profound bow'. Her poem quotes from or alludes to a number of writers and singers. She sees it as invoking, among others, the ballads, Robert Burns, the twentieth-century poet Violet Jacob and the lyricist of the 'Freedom Come All Ye', Hamish Henderson. Elsewhere, Jamie, like so many other Scottish authors, has made clear her support for twenty-first-century Scottish political independence, and her prose piece winks towards the modern anthem 'Flower of Scotland' in its concluding words 'sent Edward homeward to think again'. Her poem, however, in singing a landscape that belongs 'to none but itself', a terrain in which all humans are transient, mentions neither Robert Bruce nor Scottish independence. Instead, letting the land sing and have the last word, it offers a challenge to the reader, whether at Bannockburn itself or much further afield, and whether in the year 2014 or beyond:

> *'Come all ye,'* the country says
> *You win me, who take me most to heart.*

In these lines, concisely and magnificently, Jamie, through a subtly measured act of literary imagination, turns both the battle of Bannockburn and modern arguments over Scottish independence from a contest into an expression of love.

Notes

Introduction

1. Robert Burns, 'Such a Parcel of Rogues in a Nation', in Robert Crawford and Christopher MacLachlan (eds), *The Best Laid Schemes: Selected Poetry and Prose of Robert Burns* (Edinburgh: Birlinn; Princeton: Princeton University Press, 2009), 145.
2. Branimir Anzulović, *Heavenly Serbia: From Myth to Genocide* (London: Hurst and Company, 1999).
3. Miodrag Pavlović, *The Slavs beneath Parnassus*, trans. Bernard Johnson (London: Angel Books, 1985), 46.
4. Anzulović, *Heavenly Serbia*, 51, 61, 92, 113.
5. Ibid., 113.
6. Tom Nairn, *The Break-Up of Britain* (London: New Left Books, 1977).
7. Burns, in Crawford and MacLachlan (eds), *The Best Laid Schemes*, 154.
8. See Marilyn Reizbaum, 'Canonical Double Cross: Scottish and Irish Women's Writing', in Karen Lawrence (ed.), *Decolonizing Tradition* (Chicago: University of Illinois Press, 1992), 165–90; and Stefanie Lehner, '"Dangerous Liaisons": Gender Politics in the Contemporary Scottish and Irish ImagiNation', in Michael Gardiner, Graeme Macdonald and Niall O'Gallagher (eds), *Scottish Literature and Postcolonial Literature* (Edinburgh: Edinburgh University Press, 2011), 221–33.
9. See Craig Buchanan, 'The Scottish Parliament – A Novel Institution', in Caroline McCracken-Flesher (ed.), *Culture, Nation, and the New Scottish Parliament* (Lewisburg, PA: Bucknell University Press, 2007), 57–75.
10. Benedict Anderson, *Imagined Communities* (London: Verso, 1983); Homi K. Bhabha (ed.), *Nation and Narration* (London: Routledge, 1990).

11. Daniel O'Rourke (ed.), *Dream State: The New Scottish Poets* (Edinburgh: Polygon, 1994).

12. Robert Crawford, *Scotland's Books* (London: Penguin, 2007); Roderick Watson, *The Literature of Scotland*, 2nd edn, 2 vols (Basingstoke: Palgrave Macmillan, 2007); Ian Brown (gen. ed.), *The Edinburgh History of Scottish Literature*, 3 vols (Edinburgh: Edinburgh University Press, 2007); Marco Fazzini (ed.), *Alba Literaria* (Venice: Amos Edizioni, 2005); Douglas Gifford (ed.), *Scottish Literature* (Edinburgh: Edinburgh University Press, 2002).

13. Pierre Nora, 'Between Memory and History: *Les Lieux de Memoire*', *Representations*, 26 (Spring 1989), 7.

14. Jan Assmann, 'Collective Memory and Cultural Identity', trans. John Czaplicka, *New German Critique*, 65 (1995), 132.

15. Jürgen Habermas, *The Structural Transformation of the Public Sphere*, trans. Thomas Burger with the assistance of Frederick Lawrence (Cambridge: Polity Press, 1989); Peter Sloterdijk, *Spheres: Volume 1*, trans. Wieland Hoban (Los Angeles: Semiotext(e), 2011).

16. James Mitchell, Lynn Bennie and Rob Johns, *The Scottish National Party: Transition to Power* (Oxford: Oxford University Press, 2012), 154.

17. Robert Crawford, *Devolving English Literature* (1992; 2nd edn, Edinburgh: Edinburgh University Press, 2000).

18. It is interesting to consider Scotland's political unconscious in the context of Adam Phillips, *Missing Out* (London: Hamish Hamilton, 2012).

19. See W. H. Auden, 'In Memory of W. B. Yeats', in *Collected Shorter Poems* (London: Faber and Faber, 1966), 142; see also Peter Robinson, *Poetry, Poets, Readers* (Oxford: Oxford University Press, 2002).

20. For works by Anderson and Bhabha see n. 8 above; Robert Young, *Colonial Desire* (London: Routledge, 1995) and *The Idea of English Ethnicity* (Malden, MA: Blackwell, 2008); Gilles Deleuze and Félix Guattari, *Kafka: Toward a Minor Literature*, trans. Dana Polan (Minneapolis: University of Minnesota Press, 1986).

21. See especially Cairns Craig, *Out of History* (Edinburgh: Polygon, 1996) and *The Modern Scottish Novel* (Edinburgh: Edinburgh University Press, 1999); Leith Davis, *Acts of Union* (Stanford: Stanford University Press, 1999); Ian Duncan, *Scott's Shadow* (Princeton: Princeton University Press, 2007); Susan Manning, *Fragments of Union* (Basingstoke: Palgrave Macmillan, 2002); Murray Pittock, *The Invention of Scotland* (London: Routledge, 1991), *Scottish and Irish Romanticism* (Oxford:

Oxford University Press, 2008) and *The Road to Independence?* (London: Reaktion, 2008); Alan Riach, *Representing Scotland in Literature, Popular Culture, and Iconography* (Basingstoke: Palgrave Macmillan, 2005); Janet Sorensen, *The Grammar of Empire* (Cambridge: Cambridge University Press, 2001); Katie Trumpener, *Bardic Nationalism* (Princeton: Princeton University Press, 1997).

22. For more on this see the first chapter of Crawford, *Devolving English Literature*, as well as Robert Crawford (ed.), *The Scottish Invention of English Literature* (Cambridge: Cambridge University Press, 1997).

23. Les Murray, *Selected Poems* (Manchester: Carcanet, 1986), 39 ('Sidere Mens Eadem Mutato').

24. See Eleanor Bell, *Questioning Scotland* (Basingstoke: Palgrave Macmillan, 2004); Eleanor Bell and Gavin Miller (eds), *Scotland in Theory* (Amsterdam: Rodopi, 2004); Penny Fielding, *Scotland and the Fictions of Geography* (Cambridge: Cambridge University Press, 2009); Michael Gardiner, *The Cultural Roots of British Devolution* (Edinburgh: Edinburgh University Press, 2004), *From Trocchi to Trainspotting* (Edinburgh: Edinburgh University Press, 2006) and *The Constitution of English Literature* (London: Bloomsbury, 2013); Graeme Macdonald, 'Postcolonialism and Scottish Studies', *New Formations*, 59.1 (2006), 116–31.

25. Michael Gardiner, Graeme Macdonald and Niall O'Gallagher (eds), *Scottish Literature and Postcolonial Literature* (Edinburgh: Edinburgh University Press, 2011).

26. Lorna Burns, *Contemporary Caribbean Writing and Deleuze* (London: Continuum, 2012); also Lorna Burns and Birgit M. Kaiser (eds), *Postcolonial Literatures and Deleuze* (Harmondsworth: Palgrave Macmillan, 2012).

27. Stefanie Lehner, '"Dangerous Liaisons"', in Gardiner et al. (eds), *Scottish Literature and Postcolonial Literature*, 230; despite some lapses into jargon, this is a valuable essay.

28. Robert J. C. Young, 'Scots' goal must be postcolonial nationhood', *Scotsman*, 15 August 2010 (accessed online); Archie Stirling, Letter: 'How wrong to see Scotland as a colony', *Scotsman*, 17 August 2010 (accessed online); Keith Brown, 'A dash of cold water can bring a nation to its sense of history', *Scotsman*, 18 August 2010 (accessed online).

29. Brown, ibid.

30. See notes above for details of the works by Pittock and Fielding; see also Marinell Ash, 'William Wallace and Robert the Bruce: The Life and Death of a National Myth', in Raphael Samuel and Paul Thompson (eds), *The Myths We Live By* (London:

Routledge, 1990), 83–94; Graeme Morton, *William Wallace* (Stroud: Sutton Publishing, 2001); Cairns Craig, *Intending Scotland* (Edinburgh: Edinburgh University Press, 2009); Carla Sassi, *Why Scottish Literature Matters* (Edinburgh: Saltire Society, 2005); Hugh Trevor-Roper, *The Invention of Scotland* (New Haven, CT: Yale University Press, 2008); Fiona Stafford, *The Sublime Savage* (Edinburgh: Edinburgh University Press, 1988).

31. Gavin Bowd, *Fascist Scotland: Caledonia and the Far Right* (Edinburgh: Birlinn, 2013).
32. Tacitus, *The Agricola and the Germania*, trans. H. Mattingly, rev. S. A. Handford (Harmondsworth: Penguin Books, 1970), 76, 24, 23.
33. See Douglas S. Mack, *Scottish Fiction and the British Empire* (Edinburgh: Edinburgh University Press, 2006).
34. Alasdair Gray, *Why Scots Should Rule Scotland* (Edinburgh: Canongate, 1992).
35. James Kelman, 'The SRB Interview', *Scottish Review of Books*, 8.3 (2012), 9.

Chapter 1

1. Robert Baston, *Metrum de Praelio apud Bannockburn / The Battle of Bannockburn*, trans. Edwin Morgan (Edinburgh: The Scottish Poetry Library with Akros Publications and The Mariscat Press, 2004), 7.
2. Robert Crawford and Mick Imlah (eds), *The Penguin Book of Scottish Verse* (London: Penguin Classics, 2006), 12, 13, 32, 33.
3. Colin Kidd, *Subverting Scotland's Past* (Cambridge: Cambridge University Press, 1993), 15.
4. Gaelic text from Carolyn Proctor, *Ceannas nan Gaidheal* (Armadale: Clan Donald Lands Trust, 1985), 16; English version from Robert Crawford, *Full Volume* (London: Jonathan Cape, 2008), 26.
5. Roger A. Mason, 'Scotching the Brut: Politics, History and National Myth in Sixteenth-Century Britain', in Roger A. Mason (ed.), *Scotland and England, 1286–1815* (Edinburgh: John Donald, 1987), 62.
6. Roger A. Mason, 'Chivalry and Citizenship: Aspects of National Identity in Renaissance Scotland', in Roger Mason and Norman Macdougall (eds), *People and Power in Scotland* (Edinburgh: John Donald, 1992), 53.
7. Alexander Grant, 'Aspects of National Consciousness in Medieval Scotland', in Claus Bjorn, Alexander Grant and Keith

J. Stringer (eds), *Nations and Patriotism in the European Past* (Copenhagen: Academic Press, 1994), 74.

8. Walter Bower, *Scotichronicon*, Volume VI, ed. D. E. R. Watt et al. (Aberdeen: Aberdeen University Press, 1991), 367.

9. Baston, *Metrum de Praelio*, trans. Morgan, 7.

10. *The Poems of Laurence Minot*, ed. Richard H. Osberg (Kalamazoo: Medieval Institute Publications, 1997), 'Now for to tell yow will I turn / of the batayl of Banocburn', accessed online at www.lib.rochester.edu/camelot/teams/minot.htm (January 2013); see also David R. Carlson, *John Gower* (Cambridge: D. S. Brewer, 2012), 20ff.

11. Baston, *Metrum de Praelio*, trans. Morgan, 26, 27.

12. Ibid., 15, 11, 17, 22, 23, 28, 29.

13. D. E. R. Watt (ed.), *Scotichronicon*, I, 123.

14. Sally Mapstone, 'The *Scotichronicon*'s First Readers', in Barbara Crawford (ed.), *Church, Chronicle and Learning in Medieval and Early Renaissance Scotland* (Edinburgh: Mercat Press, 1999), 33, 39.

15. *Scotichronicon*, VI, 363.

16. Ibid., 364 (my translation).

17. See *Scotichronicon*, VI, 363–5.

18. Ibid., 358 (my translation).

19. Sir James Ferguson, *The Declaration of Arbroath* (Edinburgh: Edinburgh University Press, [n.d.]), 8, 9.

20. Alexander Grant, *Independence and Nationhood* (London: Edward Arnold, 1984), 30; R. James Goldstein, *The Matter of Scotland* (Lincoln: University of Nebraska Press, 1993), 97.

21. J. R. Philip, 'Sallust and the Declaration of Arbroath', *Scottish Historical Review*, XXVI (1947), 75–8; see also Edward J. Cowan, 'Identity, Freedom and the Declaration of Arbroath', in Dauvit Broun, R. J. Finlay and Michael Lynch (eds), *Image and Identity* (Edinburgh: John Donald, 1998), 38–68.

22. *Sallust*, trans. J. C. Rolfe (Cambridge, MA: Harvard University Press, 1931), 57 and 58–9.

23. *Scotichronicon*, VI, 319.

24. Ibid., 353.

25. 'The Epitaph of Robert the Bruce', in Thomas Owen Clancy (ed.), *The Triumph Tree* (Edinburgh: Canongate Classics, 1998), 306 and 307.

26. See Goldstein, *The Matter of Scotland*, 330, n. 12.

27. John Barbour, *The Bruce*, ed. A. A. M. Duncan (Edinburgh: Canongate Classics, 1997), 47 (my glossary).

28. Ibid., 69.

29. Ibid., 81.

30. Ibid., 115 and 163.

31. Ibid., 191.
32. Ibid., 133, 135.
33. Ibid., 233–9.
34. Sally Mapstone, *The Advice to Princes Tradition in Scottish Literature, 1450–1500* (unpublished DPhil thesis, University of Oxford, 1986).
35. Mason, 'Chivalry and Citizenship', 56.
36. Barbour, *The Bruce*, ed. Duncan, vii (Preface).
37. The passage and its gloss are quoted from Crawford and Imlah (eds), *Penguin Book of Scottish Verse*, 43, where it appears under the title 'In Praise of Freedom'.
38. Barbour, *Bruce*, ed. Duncan, 461, 463.
39. Goldstein, *The Matter of Scotland*, 141.
40. Barbour, *Bruce*, ed. Duncan, 425.
41. Ibid., 451.
42. Text and glossing from Crawford and Imlah (eds), *Penguin Book of Scottish Verse*, 44.
43. Barbour, *Bruce*, 137.
44. Bower, *Scotichronicon*, VI, 94.
45. Ibid., 241.
46. See James E. Fraser, '"A Swan from a Raven": William Wallace, Brucean Propaganda, and *Gesta Annalia* II', *Scottish Historical Review*, LXXXI.1 (April 2002), 2.
47. Bower, *Scotichronicon*, VI, 94–5.
48. Ibid., 241.
49. Ibid., 62, 63.
50. Ibid., 243.
51. Quoted in Goldstein, *The Matter of Scotland*, 217.
52. On the significance of Blind Hary's name see John Balaban, 'Blind Hary and *The Wallace*', *Chaucer Review*, 8.3 (1974), 241–51.
53. Ann McKim, 'Introduction' to her edition of Blind Hary, *The Wallace* (Edinburgh: Canongate Classics, 2003), xvii.
54. R. James Goldstein, '"I will my process hald"', in Priscilla Bawcutt and Janet Hadley Williams (eds), *A Companion to Medieval Scottish Poetry* (Cambridge: D. S. Brewer, 2006), 37.
55. Hary's *Wallace*, ed. Matthew P. McDiarmid (Edinburgh: William Blackwood and Sons for the Scottish Text Society, 1968), 2 vols, I, 1.
56. R. James Goldstein, 'Blind Hary's Myth of Blood', *Studies in Scottish Literature*, XXV (1990), 73.
57. Nicola Royan, 'Writing the Nation', in Michael Hattaway (ed.), *A Companion to English Renaissance Literature and Culture* (Malden, MA: Blackwell, 2000), 704.

58. Elizabeth Walsh, 'Hary's Wallace: The Evolution of a Hero', *Scottish Literary Journal*, 11.1 (May 1984), 7.
59. Kylie Murray, 'Dream Vision and Scottish Identity: The Epic Case of William Wallace', in Kassandra Conley et al. (eds), *Proceedings of the Harvard Celtic Colloquium, 29: 2009* (Cambridge, MA: Harvard University Press, 2011), 185 and 188–9.
60. Hary's *Wallace*, ed. McDiarmid, I, 5.
61. Ibid., I, 67.
62. Ibid., I, 118, 179 and 211.
63. Text and glosses from Crawford and Imlah (eds), *Penguin Book of Scottish Verse*, 76–7.
64. Hary's *Wallace*, ed. McDiarmid, I, 185.
65. Alan Riach, 'Wallace Triptych, II. Abstract', in Lesley Duncan and Elspeth King (eds), *The Wallace Muse* (Edinburgh: Luath Press, 2005), 130.
66. Ibid., I, 190; for a wider political context, see Roger A. Mason, 'Kingship, Tyranny and the Right to Resist in Fifteenth-Century Scotland', *Scottish Historical Review*, 66 (1987), 125–51.
67. Hary's *Wallace*, ed. McDiarmid, I, 235.
68. Ibid., II, 38, 39.
69. W. A. Craigie, 'Barbour and Harry as Literature', *The Scottish Review*, XXII (1893), 199; Hary's *Wallace*, ed. McDiarmid, II, 54, 55, 56; see also Mapstone, 'The *Scotichronicon*'s First Readers', 41–3.
70. Hary's *Wallace*, ed. McDiarmid, II, 57.
71. Ibid., II, 77 and 120.
72. Ibid., II, 115.
73. Walsh, 'Hary's Wallace: The Evolution of a Hero', 18.
74. Mair, *Historia*, Lib. IV, cap. xv, cited in McDiarmid (ed.), *Hary's 'Wallace'*, I, xxx; Mason, 'Scotching the Brut', 66.
75. Hector Boece, *Hystory and Croniklis of Scotland* (Edinburgh: Thomas Davidson [?1540]), 480.
76. Crawford and Imlah (eds), *Penguin Book of Scottish Verse*, 97; the surviving fragments of the 1509 *Wallace* are in the Mitchell Library, Glasgow (S. R. 341201) and Cambridge University Library (Syn 3.50.3).
77. See *The Complaynt of Scotland*, ed. A. M. Stewart (Edinburgh: Scottish Text Society, 1979), 50.
78. Mason, 'Scotching the Brut', 71.
79. George Buchanan, *History of Scotland*, trans. anon., 2 vols, 3rd edn (London: J. Bettenham for D. Midwinter and A. Ward, 1733), I, 321.
80. Roger Mason (ed.), *A Dialogue on the Law of Kingship among the Scots* (Aldershot: Ashgate, 2004), xxxiv, lxv.

81. King James VI, *Basilicon Doron*, ed. James Craigie, 2 vols (Edinburgh: Blackwood for the Scottish Text Society, 1944–50), I, 4.
82. Ibid., I, 70, 74, 149.
83. William Shakespeare, *Macbeth*, ed. Sylvan Barnet (New York: Signet Classics, 1963), 122 (V,iii,56); see also Peter R. Roberts, 'The Business of Playing and the Patronage of Players at the Jacobean Courts', in Ralph Houlbrooke (ed.), *James VI and I* (Aldershot: Ashgate, 2006), 81–105; and Sally Mapstone, 'Scottish Kingship: A Case History', in Sally Mapstone and Juliette Wood, *The Rose and the Thistle* (East Linton: Tuckwell Press, 1998), 158–94.
84. The fullest treatment is Gustavo Secchi Turner's 2006 Harvard University PhD thesis, *The Matter of Fact: 'The Tragedy of Gowrie' (1604) and its Contexts*.
85. John Kerrigan, *Archipelagic English: Literature, History, and Politics, 1603–1707* (Oxford: Oxford University Press, 2008), 111–12.
86. Ibid., 99.
87. Shakespeare, *Macbeth*, ed. Barnet, 112 (IV,iii,189, 190).
88. Ibid., 111 (IV,iii,164–5).
89. King James VI, *Basilicon Doron*, I, 134.
90. William Shakespeare, *Richard II*, ed. Kenneth Muir (New York: Signet Classics, 1963), 66, 67 (II,i,40, 50).
91. Buchanan, *History of Scotland*, I, 322.
92. Ibid., I, 325.
93. Ibid., I, 341.
94. *Apollos of the North*, ed. and trans. Robert Crawford (Edinburgh: Polygon, 2006), 48, 49.
95. Ibid., 54, 55.
96. [Blind Hary], *The Actis and Deidis of [. . .] Schir William Wallace* (Edinburgh: Robert Lekprevik, 1570), 184.
97. Compare the versions of these lines in Anne McKim (ed.), *The Wallace: Selections* (Kalamazoo: Medieval Institute Publications for TEAMS, 2003), 98–100 with the text in *The Actis and Deidis of the Illuster and Vailzeand Campioun, Schir William Wallace, Knicht of Ellerslie* (Edinburgh: Robert Lekpreuik, 1570), 66, 68.
98. Henrie Charteris, 'Vnto the Gentil Reider', [Preface to] *The Lyfe and Actis of the Maist Illvster and Vailzeand Campiovn William Wallace, Knicht of Ellerslie, Mainteiner and Defender of the Libertie of Scotland* (Edinburgh: Henrie Charteris, 1594), [i, iii, iv, vii, ix, xiii, xiv].
99. George M. Brunsden, 'Aspects of Scotland's Social, Political and Cultural Scene in the Late 17th and Early 18th Centuries, as Mirrored in the Wallace and Bruce Tradition', in Edward J.

Cowan and Douglas Gifford (eds), *The Polar Twins* (Edinburgh: John Donald, 1999), 78 and 89.

100. See Jenny Wormald, 'The Union of 1603', in Roger A. Mason (ed.), *Scots and Britons* (Cambridge: Cambridge University Press, 1994), 18–20.
101. Keith M. Brown, 'The Vanishing British Kingship and its Decline, 1603–1707', in Mason, (ed.), *Scots and Britons*, 84.
102. [Blind Hary], *The Life and Acts of* [. . .] *Sir William Wallace* (Edinburgh: Andro Hart, 1611), [ii].
103. Patrick Gordon, *The Famous Historie of the Renouned and Valiant Prince Robert surnamed the Bruce* (Dort: George Waters, 1615), preface.
104. Ibid., Preface and Z iiij.
105. Ibid., Preface.
106. Ibid., A a iii.
107. Ibid., A iiij ('To the Author' by A. Gordone).
108. [Andro Hart], 'The Printer's Preface', to *The Actes and Life of the Most Victoriovs Conqverovr, Robert Brvce, King of Scotland* (Edinburgh: Andro Hart, 1616), i, ii and iii.
109. Ibid., xx, xxi.
110. Ibid., xi–xii.
111. Ibid., xvii–xviii.
112. Brunsden, 'Aspects of Scotland's Social, Political and Cultural Scene', 79–81.
113. *The Life and Acts of the Most Famous & Valiant Champion Syr William Wallace, Knight of Ellerslie: Maintainer of the Libertie of Scotland* (Edinburgh: Andro Hart, 1618), [i, iv, viii].
114. For statistics on editions of *The Bruce* see R. McKinlay, 'Barbour's Bruce', *Records of the Glasgow Bibliographical Society*, VI (1920), 35–6; there is some disagreement over the exact number of printings of Hary's *Wallace*, but see Graeme Morton, *William Wallace* (Stroud: Sutton Publishing, 2001), 38 and 164, n. 33 for listings and details of further bibliographical scholarship.
115. *The Lyfe and Acts of the Most Famous and Valiant Champion, Sir William Wallace, Knight of Ellerslie: Mayntayner of the Libertie of Scotland* (Aberdene: Edward Raban, 1630), [i]. This and the other editions mentioned are available in full-text form on the electronic database *Early English Books Online*.
116. Morton, *William Wallace*, 35.
117. 'The Printer to the Reader', in *The Life and Acts of the Most Famous and Valiant Champion, Sir William Wallace* (Edinburgh: Robert Bryson, 1645), [i].
118. On Walter Scott's sceptical intention to read the *Valliados* in 1817, see *The Letters of Sir Walter Scott*, ed. H. J. C.

Grierson, 10 vols (London: Constable, 1932–7), IV, 442; on Hary and *The Valiant Scot*, see J. S. Carver, 'The Valiant Scot', in Allison Gaw (ed.), *Studies in English Drama, First Series* (Philadelphia: University of Pennsylvania, 1917), 77–9, and Kerrigan, *Archipelagic English*, 91–114.

Chapter 2

1. Robert Crawford, *Devolving English Literature*, 2nd edn (Edinburgh: Edinburgh University Press, 2000), Chaps 1–3.
2. Robert Crawford (ed.), *The Scottish Invention of English Literature* (Cambridge: Cambridge University Press, 1997).
3. William Forbes, *A Pil for Pork-Eaters: or, a Scots Lancet for an English Swelling* (Edinburgh: James Watson, 1705), 9.
4. John Arbuthnot, *The History of John Bull*, ed. Alan W. Bower and Robert A. Erickson (Oxford: Clarendon Press, 1976), 49–50.
5. G. Wilson, 'An Heroic Ballad, On the Memorable Battle of Bannockburn', in Thomas Evans, *Old Ballads* (London: T. Evans, [1777]), 249.
6. Robert Burns, *Poems and Songs*, ed. James Kinsley, 3 vols (Oxford: Clarendon Press, 1968), I, 323 (hereafter cited simply as *Poems*); see also Robert Crawford (ed.), *Heaven-Taught Fergusson* (East Linton: Tuckwell Press, 2003), 7.
7. Robert Fergusson, *Poems* (Edinburgh: Walter and Thomas Ruddiman, 1773), 51.
8. *The Fingal of Ossian* (London: J. Robson, B. Law, and E. and C. Dilley, [1777]), 108–9, n.
9. David Hume, *The History of England* (London: T. Cadell, [1770]), 357.
10. See manuscript note opposite title page of British Library copy of *The Acts and Deeds of the Most Famous and Valiant Champion Sir William Wallace* (Edinburgh: n.p., 1758) (ESTC No. T107015), available digitally through Eighteenth Century Collections Online; but see also Matthew P. McDiarmid, 'Introduction' to his edition of Hary's *Wallace*, 2 vols (Edinburgh: William Blackwood for the Scottish Text Society, 1968), I, xii.
11. See David McCordick (ed.), *Scottish Literature, an Anthology*, vol. I (New York: Peter Lang, 1996), 852, 854.
12. 'Familiar Epistles between W--- H------ and A--- R------', in Allan Ramsay, *Poems* (Edinburgh: The Author, 1720), 179, 192, 193, 174.
13. *James Watson's Choice Collection of Comic and Serious Scots Poems*, ed. Harriet Harvey Wood, vol. I (Edinburgh: The Scottish Text Society, 1977), i (Watson's preface).

14. [William Hamilton], *A New Edition of the Life and Heroick Actions of the Renoun'd Sir William Wallace* (Glasgow: William Duncan, 1722), title page.

15. *The Life and Acts of the Most Famous and Valiant Champion Sir William Wallace* (Edinburgh: Gedeon Lithgovv, 1648), [1].

16. Ibid., the First Book, Chap. I (n.p.).

17. William Hamilton, *Blind Harry's Wallace*, intro. Elspeth King (Edinburgh: Luath Press, 1998), 1.

18. See Gerard Carruthers, 'Hamilton, William, of Gilbertfield', *ODNB*.

19. Hary's *Wallace*, ed. McDiarmid, I, 140; Hamilton, *Wallace*, intro. King, 79.

20. Ibid., 2, 3.

21. Ibid., 3.

22. Ibid., 6.

23. Ibid., 19, 18, 20.

24. Ibid., 23, 24.

25. Ibid., 24, 25, 27, 32.

26. Ibid., 33.

27. Ibid., 40.

28. Ibid., 41.

29. Ibid., 44, 47, 48, 55.

30. Ibid., 64.

31. Ibid., 67.

32. Ibid., 99, 110, 111.

33. Ibid., 123, 121; Blind Harry, *The Wallace*, ed. Anne McKim (Edinburgh: Canongate Classics, 2003), 198.

34. Hamilton, *Wallace*, intro. King, 123, 124.

35. Ibid., 135.

36. Ibid., 144.

37. Ibid., 153.

38. Ibid., 176, 177.

39. Ibid., 183.

40. Ibid., 193.

41. Ibid., 195, 198, 196.

42. Ibid., 201.

43. Ibid., 218, 220.

44. Ibid., 222.

45. Carruthers, 'Hamilton, William', *ODNB*.

46. George M. Brunsden, 'Aspects of Scotland's Social, Political and Cultural Scene in the Late Seventeenth and Early Eighteenth Centuries', in Edward J. Cowan and Douglas Gifford (eds), *The Polar Twins* (Edinburgh: John Donald, 1999), 93.

47. John Hervey, *The Life and Martial Achievements of that Valiant Hero, Robert Bruce*, appended to *A New Edition of the Life and*

Heroick Actions of the Renown'd Sir William Wallace (Dundee: H. Galbraith, 1770), 374, 378, 382, 384, 390.

48. Brunsden, 'Aspects', 93 and 94 (quoting *The Bruciad*).
49. *The Acts and Life of the Most Victorious Conqueror Robert Bruce* (Glasgow: A. Carmichael and A. Miller, 1737), title page.
50. John Barbour, *The Life and Acts of the Most Victorious Conqueror Robert Bruce* (Edinburgh: [n.p.], 1758), title page.
51 *The Letters of Robert Burns*, ed. J. De Lancey Ferguson; 2nd edn ed. G. Ross Roy, 2 vols (Oxford: Clarendon Press, 1985), I, 135–6.
52. Hamilton, *Wallace*, intro. King, 196.
53. Burns, *Letters*, I, 62.
54. Hamilton, *Wallace*, intro. King, 14.
55. Burns, *Poems*, I, 95.
56. *Robert Burns's Commonplace Book 1783–85*, ed. James Cameron Ewing and Davidson Cook (Fontwell: Centaur Press, 1965), 36.
57. Burns, *Poems*, I, 106.
58. Ibid., I, 109.
59. Hamilton, *Wallace*, intro. King, 81.
60. Burns, *Poems*, I, 151–2.
61. Ibid., I, 283.
62. Burns, *Letters*, I, 62.
63. James Thomson, *The Seasons and the Castle of Indolence*, ed. James Sambrook (Oxford: Clarendon Press, 1972), 112, 113.
64. Burns, *Letters*, I, 83.
65. *Robert Burns and Mrs Dunlop, Correspondence*, ed. William Wallace (London: Hodder and Stoughton, 1898), 4; see also p. 6.
66. Burns, *Letters*, I, 84–5, 86.
67. Burns, *Poems*, I, 153.
68. John Pinkerton (ed.), *Ancient Scotish Poems*, 2 vols (Edinburgh: William Creech, 1786), I, xxx.
69. Burns, *Letters*, I, 91.
70. Buchan's letter is quoted in John Pinkerton (ed.), *The Bruce*, 2 vols (London: H. Hughs, 1790), I, vii–viii.
71. Burns, *Letters*, I, 151.
72. 'Adair's Account of the Stirlingshire Tour', in Raymond Lamont Brown (ed.), *Robert Burns's Tours of the Highlands and Stirlingshire 1787* (Ipswich: The Boydell Press, 1973), 53.
73. Ibid., 53–4.
74. Burns, *Letters*, I, 112.
75. Burns, *Poems*, I, 332–3.
76. James Currie (ed.), *The Works of Robert Burns*, 4 vols (London: T. Cadell and W. Davies, 1801), I, 139.
77. Burns, *Poems*, I, 375 and III, 1255.

78. Burns, *Poems*, I, 376; Burns, *Letters*, II, 280.
79. Burns, *Poems*, I, 376–7.
80. Burns, *Letters*, I, 342 and II, 246.
81. Burns, *Poems*, I, 444.
82. Burns, *Poems*, II, 529–30.
83. Burns, *Poems*, I, 396.
84. Burns, *Letters*, I, 441.
85. Burns, *Poems*, II, 869, 871.
86. Burns, *Poems*, I, 459; Brown, *Burns's Tours*, 18.
87. See, e.g., the 1745 piece, 'A Curious Poem to the Memory of Sir William Wallace', quoted in Brunsden, 'Aspects', 97.
88. Burns, *Letters*, I, 464.
89. Burns, *Letters*, II, 18.
90. Burns, *Poems*, II, 544.
91. Burns, *Poems*, II, 546.
92. Burns, *Poems*, I, 484, 488.
93. Burns, *Letters*, I, 423.
94. Francis Grose, *The Antiquities of Scotland*, 2 vols (London: Hooper and Wigstead, 1797), II, 41.
95. Ibid., II, 27.
96. Burns, *Letters*, II, 64.
97. Henry, commonly called Blind Harry, *The Metrical History of Sir William Wallace*, 3 vols (Perth: R. Morison, 1790), I, dedication.
98. Ibid., I, 5–6.
99. Ibid., I, 8, 11.
100. Ibid., I, 6.
101. Burns, *Letters*, II, 64.
102. Pinkerton (ed.), *The Bruce*, I, vi, vii, x.
103. Ibid., II, 3, 6, 7.
104. Ibid., I, x and II, 20.
105. Ibid., II, 130, 129.
106. Burns, *Poems*, II, 763.
107. Burns, *Letters*, II, 24.
108. Ibid,; cf. Roger Lonsdale (ed.), *The Poems of Gray, Collins, and Goldsmith* (London: Longman, Green and Co., 1969), 694.
109. Burns, *Letters*, II, 24.
110. Burns, *Poems*, II, 613, 637.
111. Burns, *Poems*, III, 1403.
112. Hamilton, *Wallace*, intro. King, 212, 213.
113. See Robert Crawford, 'America's Bard', in Sharon Alker, Leith Davis and Holly Faith Nelson (eds), *Robert Burns and Transatlantic Culture* (Farnham: Ashgate, 2012), 101–3.
114. Burns, *Poems*, II, 643–4.
115. Burns, *Letters*, II, 269.

116. Burns, *Letters*, II, 276.
117. Burns, *Letters*, II, 236.
118. Burns, *Letters*, II, 238.
119. Joseph Ritson (ed.), *Scotish Songs*, 2 vols (London: J. Johnson and J. Egerton, [1794]), I, xcii.
120. Burns, *Poems*, II, 707–8.
121. Sir David Dalrymple, *The Annals of Scotland* (London: J. Murray, 1779), 93, 94; James Boswell, *An Account of Corsica* (Glasgow: Robert and Andrew Foulis, 1768), epigraph.
122. Liam McIlvanney, *Burns the Radical* (East Linton: Tuckwell Press, 2002).
123. Burns, *Poems*, II, 763.
124. Marilyn Butler, 'Burns and Politics', in Robert Crawford (ed.), *Robert Burns and Cultural Authority* (Edinburgh: Edinburgh University Press, 1997), 102.
125. Burns, *Letters*, II, 236 (to George Thomson [about 30 August 1793]).
126. See Graeme Morton, 'The Most Efficacious Patriot', *Scottish Historical Review*, LXXVII.2 (October 1998), 244.
127. George Galloway, 'On the Earl of Buchan presenting General Washington (Jan. 3 1792) with a Box', in Lesley Duncan and Elspeth King (eds), *The Wallace Muse* (Edinburgh: Luath Press, 2005), 48, 49.
128. Burns, *Poems*, II, 733.
129. Burns, *Poems*, II, 734.
130. Henry Mackenzie, unsigned essay in *The Lounger*, repr. in Donald A. Low (ed.), *Robert Burns, the Critical Heritage* (London: Routledge and Kegan Paul, 1974), 70.
131. Burns, *Poems*, II, 770.

Chapter 3

1. Robert Galloway, *Poems, Epistles and Songs, Chiefly in the Scottish Dialect* (n.p.: E. Miller, [1792]), 79.
2. Quoted also in *The Proceedings, at Large, on the Trial of John Horne Tooke, for High Treason* (London: J. S. Jordan, 1794), this passage is quoted here from *The Trial of Thomas Hardy for High Treason* (London: Martha Gurney, [1795]), 208.
3. Henry Siddons, *William Wallace, or The Highland Hero*, 2 vols (London: G. and T. Wilkie, 1791), I, 90.
4. Ibid., II, 42, 57.
5. Ibid., II, 175.
6. Ibid., II, 174.
7. Ibid., II, 175–6.

8. Stephen Gill, 'Wordsworth and Burns', in David Sergeant and Fiona Stafford (eds), *Burns and Other Poets* (Edinburgh: Edinburgh University Press, 2012), 157.
9. William Wordsworth, *The Prelude*, ed. J. C. Maxwell (Harmondsworth: Penguin, 1971), 46.
10. Elspeth King, 'Wallace Place Names', in her edition of William Hamilton of Gilbertfield, *Blind Harry's Wallace* (Edinburgh: Luath Press, 1998), 224.
11. [John Finlay], *Wallace; or, the Vale of Ellerslie* (Glasgow: R. Chapman, 1802), 33.
12. Robert Southey, *The Poetical Works* (London: Longman, 1844), 128.
13. *The Poems of John Keats*, ed. Miriam Allott (London: Longman, 1977), 27.
14. See Robert Crawford, *Devolving English Literature*, 2nd edn (Edinburgh: Edinburgh University Press, 2000).
15. Alexander Fraser Tytler, *Elements of General History, Ancient and Modern*, 2nd edn, 2 vols (Edinburgh: William Creech, 1803), II, 117, 288, 321.
16. T. C. Smout, *A Century of the Scottish People, 1830–1950* (London: Collins, 1986), 236.
17. Sir Walter Scott, *Selected Poems*, ed. Thomas Crawford (Oxford: Clarendon Press, 1972), 122, 123.
18. Ibid., 123.
19. Robert Tannahill, 'The Lament of Wallace, After the Battle of Falkirk', in Lesley Duncan and Elspeth King (eds), *The Wallace Muse* (Edinburgh: Luath Press, 2005), 56.
20. [Anon.,] *The Shade of Wallace: A Poem* (Glasgow: n.p., 1807), n.p.
21. Scott to Joanna Baillie (20 February 1810) in *The Letters of Sir Walter Scott*, ed. Herbert J. C. Grierson, 12 vols (London: Constable, 1932–7), II, 302; James Hogg, *Anecdotes of Scott*, ed. Jill Rubenstein (Edinburgh: Edinburgh University Press, 1997), 71.
22. Hogg, *Anecdotes*, 71.
23. Walter Scott, *Ivanhoe*, intro. H. J. C. Grierson (London: Collins, 1970), 44.
24. Stuart Kelly, *Scott-land* (Edinburgh: Birlinn, 2010); Ann Rigney, *The Afterlives of Walter Scott* (Oxford: Oxford University Press, 2012). To be fair, Wallace is mentioned on p. 142 of Rigney's book, though its index does not pick this up.
25. Walter Scott, *Poetical Works* (London: Marcus Ward, n.d.), 48, 49.
26. Ibid., 64.
27. Ibid., 103, 102.

28. Walter Scott, *Waverley*, ed. P. D. Garside (Edinburgh: Edinburgh University Press, 2007), 60, 320, 323.
29. Walter Scott, *Tales of a Grandfather* (London: Adam and Charles Black, 1898), xxiii, 1, 2.
30. Ibid., 4.
31. For Scott's slightly scornful reference to Wallace at the Carron, see *The Letters of Sir Walter Scott*, ed. Grierson, VI, 15.
32. Walter Scott, *Tales of a Grandfather*, 58–9.
33. Ibid., 67.
34. Ibid., 74.
35. Leigh Hunt, *The Poetical Works* (London: Routledge, Warne and Routledge, 1860), 128.
36. Horatio Waddington, *Wallace, A Poem* (Cambridge: n.p., 1815), 6, 8, 4.
37. Kathryn Sutherland, 'Holford, Margaret', *ODNB*.
38. [Margaret Holford], *Wallace* (London: T. Cadell and W. Davies, 1809), iv, v, viii.
39. Ibid., viii, 4, 7.
40. Ibid., 16, 25, 34, 191.
41. Charles Strong, 'Miss Holford', *Sonnets*, 2nd edn (London: Walter and Maberly, 1862), n.p. (Sonnet LXXXVII).
42. [Holford], *Wallace*, 228.
43. Anon., 'Sir William Wallace', in Duncan and King (eds), *The Wallace Muse*, 32.
44. Judith Bailey Slagle, 'Margaret Holford, Joanna Baillie, and the "Terrible Beauty" of William Wallace', *Keats-Shelley Journal*, LIX (2010), 120.
45. [Holford], *Wallace*, 192, 228, 229.
46. Slagle, 'Margaret Holford, Joanna Baillie, and the "Terrible Beauty" of William Wallace', 120.
47. Ina Ferris, *The Achievement of Literary Authority* (Ithaca, NY and London: Cornell University Press, 1991); Katie Trumpener, *Bardic Nationalism* (Princeton: Princeton University Press, 1997), 291.
48. See Jane Porter, *The Scottish Chiefs* (Boston, MA: Lee and Shepherd, 1877), xvii.
49. Jane Porter, *The Scottish Chiefs*, 3 vols (New York: Thomas Y. Crowell, n.d.), xlvi ('Postscript' to the 'Retrospective Preface to the Illustrated Edition', dated May, 1840).
50. Thomas McLean, 'Nobody's Argument: Jane Porter and the Historical Novel', *Journal for Early Modern Cultural Studies*, 7.2 (Fall/Winter 2007), 98.George Galloway, *The Tears of Poland*, 'Introduction', cited in McLean, 'Nobody's Argument', 98.
51. George Galloway, *The Tears of Poland*, 'Introduction', cited in McLean, 'Nobody's Argument', 98.

52. Devoney Looser, 'The Porter Sisters, Women's Writing, and Historical Fiction', in Jacqueline M. Labbe (ed.), *The History of British Women's Writing, 1750–1830* (Basingstoke: Palgrave Macmillan, 2010), 239, 243–4.
53. Ibid., 250, n. 16.
54. Graeme Morton, 'The Scottish Nation of Jane Porter in her International Setting', in Jodi A. Campbell, Elizabeth Ewan and Heather Parker (eds), *The Shaping of Scottish Identities* (Guelph: Centre for Scottish Studies, 2011), 235–49.
55. See Carol Anderson and Aileen M. Riddell, 'The Other Great Unknowns', in Douglas Gifford and Dorothy McMillan (eds), *A History of Scottish Women's Writing* (Edinburgh: Edinburgh University Press, 1997), 183–5; also Andrew Hook, 'Jane Porter, Sir Walter Scott, and the Historical Novel', *Clio* 5.2 (Winter 1976), 181–92, which argues Porter's work did not influence Scott though it may have conditioned the reception of his fiction; and Fiona Price, 'Resisting "the Spirit of Innovation": The Other Historical Novel and Jane Porter', *Modern Language Review*, 101.3 (July 2006), 638–51, which argues challengingly that Porter's work, with its interest in conflict and disruption, should prompt a rethinking of our ideals of the historical novel as a genre.
56. Walter Scheps cites the 1810 Philadelphia edition of Holford's poem in his 'William Wallace and his "Buke": Some Instances of their Influence on Subsequent Literature', *Studies in Scottish Literature*, VI (1969), 230.
57. Holford, *Wallace*, 19.
58. Jane Porter, *The Scottish Chiefs*, 3 vols (Exeter: Abel Brown, 1827), I, [i, ii, iii].
59. Thomas Campbell, *Complete Poetical Works*, ed. J. Logie Robertson (Oxford: Oxford University Press, 1907), 169, 170.
60. Porter, *The Scottish Chiefs* (Boston: Lee and Shepherd, 1877), iii ('Retrospective Introduction' of 1831).
61. Francis James Child (ed.), *The English and Scottish Popular Ballads*, 5 vols (1882–98; repr. New York: Dover, 2003), III, 274.
62. Porter, *The Scottish Chiefs* (1877), x.
63. James Grahame, *Wallace: A Tragedy* (Edinburgh: Archibald Constable, 1799).
64. Ian Dennis, *Nationalism and Desire in Early Historical Fiction* (Basingstoke: Macmillan, 1997), 17.
65. Dennis, *Nationalism and Desire*, 19–20.
66. Jane Porter, *The Scottish Chiefs*, Complete Edition (New York: New York Publishing Company, 1895), 604.
67. Dennis, *Nationalism and Desire*, 24.

68. Ibid., 28.
69. Ibid., 38.
70. Marinell Ash, 'William Wallace and Robert the Bruce', in Raphael Samuel and Paul Thomson (eds), *The Myths We Live By* (London: Routledge, 1990), 92 (Ash is quoting Dobie).
71. Munro's manuscript is now in the Stirling Smith Art Gallery and Museum; these two watercolours are reproduced in Duncan and King (eds), *The Wallace Muse*, figs [15] and [19].
72. The Boston Public Library copy can be found on the 'Internet Archive' full-text website; the copy presented at the Mod now belongs to the present writer; extracts from the graphic novel version appear as figures [24] and [25] in Duncan and King (eds), *The Wallace Muse*; Scheps, 'William Wallace and his "Buke"', 235.
73. Kate Douglas Wiggin, 'Introduction', in Jane Porter, *The Scottish Chiefs*, ed. Kate Douglas Wiggin and Nora Archibald Smith (New York: Charles Scribner's Sons, 1921), v, vii, vi.
74. Porter, *The Scottish Chiefs*, Complete Edition (1895), 23.
75. Ibid., 23, 24.
76. Porter, *The Scottish Chiefs* (1827), I, [ii].
77. Porter, *The Scottish Chiefs* (1895), 33.
78. Ibid., 36.
79. Ibid., 125.
80. Ibid., 57, 268.
81. Ibid., 388.
82. William Wordsworth, *The Poetical Works* (London: Frederick Warne, n.d.), 157.
83. Porter, *The Scottish Chiefs* (1895), 160.
84. Ibid., 178.
85. Ibid., 184.
86. Ibid., 190.
87. Ibid., 200.
88. Ibid., 201, 214.
89. Ibid., 215.
90. Ibid., 433.
91. Ibid., 304.
92. Ibid., 330.
93. Ibid., 438.
94. Ibid., 453.
95. Ibid., 455.
96. Ibid., 490.
97. Ibid., 504.
98. Ibid., 538, 560.
99. Ibid., 607.
100. Ibid., 690, 696, 706.

101. Ibid., 706.
102. Hary's *Wallace*, ed. Matthew P. McDiarmid (Edinburgh: William Blackwood for the Scottish Text Society, 1969), II, 121; Porter, *The Scottish Chiefs* (1877), iv, xi.
103. Porter, *The Scottish Chiefs* (1895), 708.
104. Ibid., 718.
105. Ibid., 721 and 726.
106. Ibid., 730.
107. Ibid., 736.
108. Ibid., 737.
109. 2 Samuel I: xxiii.
110. [Anon.,] *Washingtoniana* (Petersburgh, VA: Blandford Press, [1800]), 62–3.
111. Ibid., 63.
112. *The History of the Life, Adventures, and Heroic Actions, of the Celebrated Sir William Wallace* (New York: William W. Crawford, 1820), title page.
113. *Poems of Freneau*, ed. Henry Hayden Clark (New York: Hafner Publishing Co., 1968), 32, 179–80.
114. James Paterson, *Wallace, the Hero of Scotland* (New York: Virtue and Yorston, [1869]), xxii.
115. C. E. Walker, *Wallace: A Tragedy* (London: W. Simpkin, R. Marshall, 1823), 23.
116. Ibid., 23–4, 56.
117. Ibid., prologue.
118. William Barrymore, *Wallace: The Hero of Scotland* (Boston, MA: William V. Spencer, [?1856]), 4, 7, 30.
119. Graeme Morton, 'The Most Efficacious Patriot', *Scottish Historical Review*, LXXVII.2 (October 1998), 237.
120. S. M. [Menella Bruce Smedley], *Lays and Ballads from Ancient History* (London: James Burns, [1845]), table of contents and facing illustration.
121. Nancy Moore Goslee, 'Contesting Liberty', *Keats-Shelley Journal*, 50 (2001), 57; Linda Colley, *Britons: Forging the Nation, 1707–1837* (New Haven, CT: Yale University Press, 1992).
122. Goslee, 'Contesting Liberty', 63.
123. Ibid., 49, 52.
124. Felicity Dorothea Browne Hemans, *The Works,* 6 vols. (Edinburgh: Blackwood, 1839), I, 342, 344, 345, 346, 351.
125. Janet Hamilton, *Poems* (Glasgow: Thomas Murray, 1863), 64, 65.
126. *The Times*, 4 December 1856.
127. Arthur Hugh Clough, *The Bothie*, ed. Patrick Scott (St Lucia: University of Queensland Press, 1976), 9.

128. See Graeme Morton, *Unionist-Nationalism* (East Linton: Tuckwell Press, 1999), 133–54.
129. Murray G. H. Pittock, *The Invention of Scotland* (London: Routledge, 1991), 113.
130. Morton, *Unionist-Nationalism*, 139.
131. 'The Sad Scottish lion lists its grievances', *Punch*, XXV (1853), 39; 'A Growl from the Scottish lion', *Punch*, XXV (1853), 179.
132. William McGonagall, 'A Summary History of Sir William Wallace', in Duncan and King, ed., *The Wallace Muse*, 64.
133. Randall Wallace, *Braveheart* (1995; repr. London: Penguin, 1997), ix.
134. Randall Wallace, quoted in Elspeth King, 'Introduction', in William Hamilton of Gilbertfield, *Blind Harry's Wallace* (Edinburgh: Luath Press, 1998), xxii.
135. Ibid., xxii, xxiii.
136. Wallace, *Braveheart*, 76.
137. Francis William Lauderdale Adams, *Songs of the Army of the Night*, 2nd edn (London: William Reeves, 1892), text of poem available online at <adc.library.usyd.edu.au/data-2/adasong.pdf>
138. Les Murray, 'The Physical Diaspora of William Wallace', in Duncan and King (eds), *The Wallace Muse*, 110.
139. Wallace, *Braveheart*, 5.
140. Walter Bower, *Scotichronicon*, vol. 6, ed. D. E. R. Watt et al. (Aberdeen: Aberdeen University Press, 1991), 94.
141. King, 'Introduction', in Hamilton, *Blind Harry's Wallace* (1998), xxii.
142. Gary Kelly, 'Introduction', in Kelly (ed.), *Varieties of Female Gothic*, 6 vols (London: Pickering and Chatto, 2002), IV: Jane Porter, *The Scottish Chiefs*, vii.
143. Jane Porter, *The Scottish Chiefs*, 5th edn, 4 vols (London: Longman, Hurst, Orme, Brown, and Green, 1825), II, 206.
144. Hamilton, *Blind Harry's Wallace*, 162.
145. *Braveheart*, dir. Mel Gibson (Icon Productions, 1995).
146. Wallace, *Braveheart*, 273.
147. Ibid., x.
148. Ibid., 128, 144.
149. David Kinloch, 'Braveheart!', in *Un Tour d'Écosse* (Manchester: Carcanet, 2001), 74.
150. Colin McArthur, *Brigadoon, Braveheart and the Scots: Scotland in Hollywood Cinema* (London and New York: I. B. Tauris, 2003), 5 and 123.
151. Ibid., 152, 157.
152. Ibid., 186.

153. Ibid., 159, 209, 151.
154. Ibid., 5.
155. Ibid., 126.
156. Rory Reynolds, 'A Very Danish Drama Packs a Special Punch in Edinburgh', *Scotsman*, 4 February 2013, 8–9; see also front-page photograph.
157. Nicola Sturgeon, quoted in Magnus Linklater, 'Nippy sweetie who is keen on the right blend of nationalism', *Times*, 16 February 2013, 41.

Chapter 4

1. See Scott Lyall, *Hugh MacDiarmid's Poetry and Politics of Place* (Edinburgh: Edinburgh University Press, 2006).
2. See Richard Griffiths, *Patriotism Perverted* (London: Constable, 1998).
3. Gavin Bowd, *Fascist Scotland* (Edinburgh: Birlinn, 2013), 13.
4. Bowd, *Fascist Scotland*, 131.
5. John Stuart Blackie, *A Song of Heroes* (Edinburgh: Blackwood, 1890), 103, 111, 119, 120, 124.
6. John Walker (ed.), *The Scottish Sketches of R. B. Cunninghame Graham* (Edinburgh: Scottish Academic Press, 1982), 1.
7. Theodore Napier in *Scottish Highlander*, 11 June 1896, and *Montrose Review*, 22 May 1896, quoted in Graeme Morton, *William Wallace, Man and Myth* (Stroud: Sutton Publishing, 2001), 119-20.
8. Napier, *Scottish Highlander*, 21 May 1896, quoted in Morton, *Wallace*, 122.
9. Murray Pittock, *The Invention of Scotland* (London: Routledge, 1991), 130.
10. Cunninghame Graham, quoted on the website of Siol nan Gaidheal http://www.siol-nan-gaidheal.org/rbcg.htm (accessed 12 January 2012).
11. Lewis Spence, *The Story of William Wallace* (Oxford: Oxford University Press, 1919), 4 and 92.
12. Lewis Spence, 'The Prows o' Reekie', in Robert Crawford and Mick Imlah (eds), *The Penguin Book of Scottish Verse* (London: Penguin Classics, 2006), 396.
13. See Bowd, *Fascist Scotland*, 154, 143.
14. See especially Margery Palmer McCulloch (ed.), *Modernism and Nationalism* (Glasgow: Association for Scottish Literary Studies, 2004); and Margery Palmer McCulloch, *Scottish Modernism and its Contexts 1918–1959* (Edinburgh: Edinburgh University Press, 2009).

15. Lewis Spence, *The National Party of Scotland* (Glasgow: The National Party of Scotland, 1928), 3–4, 7.
16. Often reproduced, this photograph appears, e.g., in Alan Bold, *MacDiarmid: Christopher Murray Grieve, A Critical Biography* (London: John Murray, 1988).
17. Hugh MacDiarmid, *Complete Poems 1920–1976*, ed. Michael Grieve and W. R. Aitken, 2 vols (Manchester: Carcanet, 1993), II, 1200.
18. Hugh MacDiarmid, *Albyn*, ed. Alan Riach (Manchester: Carcanet, 1996), 132.
19. Hugh MacDiarmid, *The Raucle Tongue, Vol. I*, ed. Angus Calder, Glen Murray and Alan Riach (Manchester: Carcanet, 1996), 29.
20. MacDiarmid, *Complete Poems*, II, 1204.
21. Ibid., II, 1207, 1208.
22. MacDiarmid, *Albyn*, 150, 151.
23. Hugh MacDiarmid, *The Raucle Tongue, Vol. II*, ed. Angus Calder, Glen Murray and Alan Riach (Manchester: Carcanet, 1997), 125.
24. Ibid., 133–4.
25. Andro Linklater, *Compton Mackenzie* (London: Chatto and Windus, 1987), 222.
26. MacDiarmid, *Complete Poems*, I, 17, with my glosses added.
27. John Jamieson's 'Address to Cartlane Craigs' is reprinted in Lesley Duncan and Elspeth King (eds), *The Wallace Muse* (Edinburgh: Luath Press, 2005); see also Susan Rennie, *Jamieson's Dictionary of Scots* (Oxford: Oxford University Press, 2012).
28. MacDiarmid, *Complete Poems*, I, 23.
29. Ibid., I, 31.
30. Ibid., I, 27.
31. Ibid., I, 36.
32. Ibid., I, 40.
33. Robert Crawford, 'MacDiarmid, Burnsians, and Burns's Legacy', in David Sergeant and Fiona Stafford (eds), *Burns and Other Poets* (Edinburgh: Edinburgh University Press, 2012), 182–94.
34. MacDiarmid, *Complete Poems*, I, 72, 75.
35. Matthew Hart, *Nations of Nothing But Poetry* (New York: Oxford University Press, 2010), 51–78.
36. MacDiarmid, *Complete Poems*, I, 84.
37. Ibid., I, 88.
38. Ibid., I, 106.
39. Ibid., I, 114.
40. Ibid., I, 138–9.
41. Ibid., I, 144.

42. Ibid., I, 153.
43. Ibid., I, 165.
44. Ibid.
45. Ibid., I, 157.
46. Ibid., I, 159.
47. Ibid., I, 162.
48. Ibid., I, 160.
49. Ibid., I, 164, 166, 167.
50. Ibid., I, 189. 190.
51. Ibid., I, 192, 194.
52. Ibid., I, 203.
53. Ibid., I, 223.
54. Ibid., I, 228.
55. Ibid., I, 273.
56. Hugh MacDiarmid, *Selected Prose*, ed. Alan Riach (Manchester: Carcanet, 1992), 3.
57. MacDiarmid, *Complete Poems*, I, 236, 223.
58. Edwin Muir, *Scott and Scotland* (1936; rpr. Edinburgh: Polygon, 1982), 2, 7.
59. Edwin Muir, *The Complete Poems*, ed. Peter Butter (Aberdeen: Association for Scottish Literary Studies, 1991), 100 ('Scotland 1941').
60. Lewis Grassic Gibbon, quoted in Hugh MacDiarmid, *Lucky Poet* (1943; rpr. London: Jonathan Cape, 1972), 71.
61. Hugh MacDiarmid and Lewis Grassic Gibbon, *Scottish Scene* (London: Jarrolds, 1934), 82.
62. MacDiarmid, *Complete Poems*, I, 264.
63. MacDiarmid and Gibbon, *Scottish Scene*, 328.
64. Ibid., 329.
65. Ibid.
66. Ibid., 335, 347.
67. Lewis Grassic Gibbon, *A Scots Quair* (1946; repr. London: Pan, 1982), *Sunset Song*, 2–3.
68. Lewis Grassic Gibbon, *A Scots Quair* (1946; repr. London: Pan, 1982), *Grey Granite*, 34–5.
69. Ibid., 149.
70. Ibid., 220.
71. Hamish Henderson, 'Scotland's Alamein', *Voice of Scotland*, July 1947.
72. Norman MacCaig, quoted from memory by Geoff Dutton, in Timothy Neat, *Hamish Henderson: A Biography, Volume 1, The Making of the Poet* (Edinburgh: Polygon, 2007), 211.
73. Hamish Henderson, 'The Role of the Artist in Society' (1949 lecture), quoted in Neat, *Hamish Henderson, Vol. 1*, 235.
74. Neat, *Hamish Henderson, Vol. 1*, 227.

75. Hamish Henderson, 'The John Maclean March', quoted in Neat, *Hamish Henderson, Vol. 1*, 229.
76. MacDiarmid took this phrase from G. Gregory Smith; see Smith in McCulloch (ed.), *Modernism and Nationalism*, 6.
77. See Bowd, *Fascist Scotland*, 161.
78. Lyall, *Hugh MacDiarmid's Politics of Place*; W. N. Herbert, *To Circumjack MacDiarmid* (Oxford: Oxford University Press, 1992); Herbert in Robert Crawford et al., 'Hugh MacDiarmid: A Disgrace to the Community', *PN Review*, 89 (January–February 1993), 21–2.
79. MacDiarmid, *Complete Poems*, I, 428.
80. Ibid., I, 429.
81. Ibid., I, 431.
82. Tom Normand, *The Modern Scot* (Aldershot: Ashgate, 2000).
83. Biographical information has been pieced together largely from the following online resources: Marc Van Campenhondt, 'Rene de Kerchove et L'*International Maritime Dictionary*: Genèse d'un Ouvrage de Référence', 3rd International Conference on Maritime Terminology (Lisbon: 23–4 June 2003): 1 (2003) www.terministi.org/kerchove. pdf (accessed 19 November 2011); *Catalogue of Officers and Graduates of Columbia University from the Foundation: Barnard College, 1903–4 Graduates in Arts* (Maisie Saville Shainwald); 'Michael Dreicer dies at his summer home', *New York Times*, 27 July 1921; 'Influenced beauty on Fifth Avenue: Michael Dreicer set an example for commercially attractive buildings', *New York Times*, 31 July 1921; *Who's Who in New York (City and State) 1909* (Shainwald, Ralph Louis); Joseph Parrish Thompson, *The National Cyclopaedia of American Biography*, vol. 16 (Shainwald, Ralph Louis); also websites of the National Gallery of Art, Washington; of the National Galleries of Scotland; and of the Smith Andersen North Gallery, San Anselmo, California (Don Whyte pages) as well as Deerfield Academy, Massachusetts (Library and Book Endowment Funds: In Memory of James Huntington Whyte).
84. 'Influenced beauty on Fifth Avenue', *New York Times*, 31 July 1921.
85. Michael Stenton and Stephen Lees, *Who's Who of British Members of Parliament*, vol. III (Brighton: Harvester Press, 1979), 376; engagement notice (Maisie Dreicer), *Scotsman*, 27 October 1923, 8.
86. Smith Andersen North (Don Whyte pages), accessed 19 November 2011.
87. Normand, *Modern Scot*, 37; for the duration of Whyte's time at Cambridge I am grateful to J. Cox of Cambridge University Archives.

88. *Trinity Magazine*, June 1929, 46.
89. Magpie and Stump Debating Society minute book, 1927–October 1930, 72 (Wren Library, Trinity College, Cambridge, REC.8.12).
90. Smith Andersen North (Don Whyte pages), accessed 19 November 2011.
91. 'A Film of Edinburgh', *Scotsman*, 13 April 1931, 7.
92. Hugh MacDiarmid, 'Clan Albainn', in *Selected Prose*, ed. Alan Riach (Manchester: Carcanet, 1992), 54, 55.
93. [Hugh MacDiarmid] cited in Bowd, *Fascist Scotland*, 135.
94. *The Correspondence between Hugh MacDiarmid and Sorley MacLean*, ed. Susan R. Wilson (Edinburgh: Edinburgh University Press, 2010), 193 (MacDiarmid to MacLean, 8 March 1941). Though the editor identifies MacDiarmid's 'Maude [sic] Ramsay' as a princess, I suspect MacDiarmid meant 'Maule Ramsay', since 'Maule' was one of the notorious Captain Ramsay's forenames and Captain Ramsay would have seemed to MacDiarmid a more appropriate choice for Hitler's ruler of Scotland.
95. MacDiarmid, 'Clan Albainn', in *Selected Prose*, ed. Riach, 56.
96. Hugh MacDiarmid, *New Selected Letters*, ed. Dorian Grieve, Owen Dudley Edwards and Alan Riach (Manchester: Carcanet, 2001), 61 (MacDiarmid to Valda Trevlyn, 27 May 1933) and 122.
97. Normand, *The Modern Scot*, 42.
98. Margery Palmer McCulloch, *Scottish Modernism and its Contexts*, 23.
99. James H. Whyte, 'The Danger of Caution', in McCulloch (ed.), *Modernism and Nationalism*, 345.
100. Edwin Muir, 'Literature in Scotland', in McCulloch (ed.), *Modernism and Nationalism*, 99.
101. Lillias Scott Forbes, 'The Home of *The Modern Scot*', in Robert Crawford (ed.), *The Book of St Andrews* (Edinburgh: Polygon, 2005), 86.
102. Hugh MacDiarmid, 'Whither Scotland, V', in *The Raucle Tongue, II*, 270.
103. Edwin Muir, *Selected Letters*, ed. P. H. Butter (London: Hogarth Press, 1974), 70 (to James Whyte, 10 September 1931).
104. Hugh MacDiarmid, *The Letters*, ed. Alan Bold (London: Hamish Hamilton, 1984), 442.
105. James H. Whyte, letter to William McCance, 25 April 1932, quoted in Normand, *The Modern Scot*, 39.
106. Sorley MacLean, conversation with the present writer, around 1990.
107. Willa Muir, *Belonging*, quoted in Crawford (ed.), *The Book of St Andrews*, 90.

108. 'Lectures Intended for Candidates for the Qualifying Examination in Law', *Cambridge University Reporter 1928–29*, 66 (Wren Library, Trinity College, Cambridge, 325.G.2.57).
109. James H. Whyte to F. Marian McNeill (1934), letter in the National Library of Scotland quoted in Normand, *The Modern Scot*, 173, n. 1; 'Magazines', *Scotsman*, 1 May 1930, 2.
110. Compton Mackenzie, 'The National Party', *The Modern Scot*, I.4 (1931), 28, 29.
111. J. H. Whyte, 'Nationalism in the East', *The Modern Scot*, II.3 (1931), 220.
112. A. T. Cunninghame [John Tonge], 'Scottish Nationalism and Imperialism: England's Crisis', *The Modern Scot*, II. 2 (1931), 124, 126.
113. [Hugh MacDiarmid], 'The Little White Rose of Scotland', *The Modern Scot*, II. 2 (1931), 127.
114. [J. H. Whyte], 'Editorial Notes: The Background of Present-Day Nationalism, I', *The Modern Scot*, II.4 (1932), 266, 267, 269.
115. [J. H. Whyte], 'Editorial Notes: The Background of Present-Day Nationalism, II', *The Modern Scot*, III.2 (1932), 5, 6, 7, 8.
116. [J. H. Whyte], 'Editorial Notes: The Background of Present-Day Nationalism, III', *The Modern Scot*, III.3 (1932), 92.
117. [J. H. Whyte], 'Editorial Notes: The Background of Present-Day Nationalism, IV', *The Modern Scot*, III.4 (1932), 194, 195, 196.
118. Ibid., 197 (Baird's painting of MacColla is now in the Scottish National Portrait Galley, Edinburgh); [J. H. Whyte], 'Editorial Notes: The Background of Present-Day Nationalism, V', *The Modern Scot*, IV.1 (1933), 282.
119. Ibid., 284, 286.
120. [James H. Whyte], 'Editorial Notes: Scottish Nationalism, I', *The Modern Scot*, IV.1 (1934), 5, 6, 8.
121. [James H. Whyte], 'Editorial Notes: Scottish Nationalism, IV', *The Modern Scot*, IV.4 (1934), 271; and 'Editorial Notes: Scottish Nationalism, II', *The Modern Scot*, IV.2 (1934), 94, 96, 97, 99.
122. [James H. Whyte], 'Editorial Notes: Scottish Nationalism, III', *The Modern Scot*, IV.3 (1934), 181, 183, 184.
123. See Bowd, *Fascist Scotland*, 20.
124. Julia Melvin, letter to the present writer, 12 October 2011.
125. Willa Muir, quoted in Crawford, *The Book of St Andrews*, 90–1.
126. Edwin Muir, *Complete Poems*, ed. Butter, 100; [James H. Whyte], 'Editorial Notes: The Catholic Irish in Scotland', *The Modern Scot*, V.4 (1935), 224, 226.
127. [James H. Whyte], 'Editorial Notes: [Retrospect and Prospect]', *The Modern Scot*, VI.4 (1936), 287.
128. Willa Muir, 'Mrs Grundy in Scotland' (1936), in *Imagined*

Selves, ed. Kirsty Allen (Edinburgh: Canongate Classics, 1996), 86.

129. [James H. Whyte], 'Editorial Notes: This Affligit Realm', *The Modern Scot*, VI.3 (1936), 187.
130. 'Island Funeral', *Scotsman*, 19 April 1936, 8.
131. James H. Whyte to Hugh MacDiarmid, 25 June [1936], in John Manson (ed.), *Dear Grieve* (Glasgow: Kennedy and Boyd, 2011), 155.
132. MacDiarmid, *Letters*, ed. Bold, 853, 851, 854 (to Whyte, 1 July 1936).
133. Whyte to MacDiarmid, 10 September 1936, in Manson (ed.), *Dear Grieve*, 173.
134. MacDiarmid, *Letters*, ed. Bold, 157 (to Soutar, 21 December 1936).
135. Whyte to MacDiarmid, 27 September 1936, in Manson (ed.), *Dear Grieve*, 175.
136. Smith Andersen North (Don Whyte pages), accessed 19 November 2011.
137. Normand, *The Modern Scot*, 62. His brother Donald, a successful photographer, died in California in 1989.
138. Alexander Moffat and Alan Riach with Linda MacDonald-Lewis, *Arts of Resistance* (Edinburgh: Luath Press, 2008), 50–2; Moffat's painting is reproduced on p. 51 as plate 1.35.
139. Sorley MacLean, *Caoir Gheal Leumraich / White Leaping Flame*, ed. Christopher Whyte and Emma Dymock (Edinburgh: Polygon, 2011), 134, 135.
140. Norman MacCaig, *Collected Poems* (London: Chatto and Windus, 1990), 226.
141. H. J. Rose, reference for Young, quoted in 'Douglas Young: A Memoir', in Clara Young and David Murison (eds), *A Clear Voice* (Loanhead: Macdonald Publishers, c. 1975), 19.
142. Eric Linklater, *Manifesto*, East Fife By-Election, 1933 (Edinburgh: National Party of Scotland, 1933), quoted in Michael Parnell, *Eric Linklater* (London: John Murray, 1984), 138.
143. Douglas Young, letter to Hugh Seton-Watson, quoted in Bowd, *Fascist Scotland*, 159.
144. Home Office report of 25 August 1943, quoted in Bowd, *Fascist Scotland*, 177.
145. Douglas Young, from *Chasing an Ancient Greek* (1950), repr. in Young and Murison (eds), *A Clear Voice*, 76.
146. Aristophanes and Douglas Young, *The Puddocks*, 2nd edn (Tayport: The Author, 1958), 9.
147. Eliot, Bowra, Morgan and others are quoted in Aristophanes and Young, *The Puddocks*, 50, 51.
148. 'Douglas Young: A Memoir', 20.

149. Douglas Young, *St Andrews* (London: Cassell, 1969), 263.

150. James Robertson, *And the Land Lay Still* (London: Hamish Hamilton, 2010), 572.

151. K. J. Dover, 'William Laughton Lorimer', *Proceedings of the British Academy*, LIII (1967), 437, 443.

152. R. L. C. Lorimer, 'Editor's Introduction', in *The New Testament in Scots*, trans. William Laughton Lorimer (Edinburgh: Southside for the Trustees of the W. L. Lorimer Trust, 1983), xii, xiv. Though he had not yet published his Aristophanes translations, by 1947 Young had already published some translations from Greek into Scots as part of his 1943 collection *Autran Blads*.

153. Lorimer, *The New Testament in Scots*, xiii.

154. Ibid., 298. Readers seeking an English translation may wish to look up 1 Cor. 4: 7, in the New Testament.

155. Lorimer, *The New Testament in Scots*, 455.

156. See Young and Murison (eds), *A Clear Voice*, 159–60; also Barbara E. Crawford, 'Obituary: Ronald Gordon Cant', in *Proceedings of the Society of Antiquaries of Scotland*, 130 (2000), 1–5.

157. David Torrance, *Salmond* (Edinburgh: Birlinn, 2010), 27; G. W. S. Barrow, *Robert Bruce and the Community of the Realm of Scotland* (Edinburgh: Edinburgh University Press, 1976), 3, 13.

158. Ibid., inside back cover.

159. Ibid., 9, 13.

160. Ibid., 85, 97.

161. Ibid., 112.

162. Ibid., 119, 129, 166.

163. Ibid., 234.

164. Ibid., 243.

165. Ibid., 261, 274.

166. Ibid., 322, 328.

167. Ibid., 426, 428.

168. Ibid., 428, 254.

169. Torrance, *Salmond*, 27.

170. 'Interview: Alex Salmond, why he is a fan of Douglas Hurd', *Fife Today*, 2 August 2010, accessed online at http://fifetoday.co.uk/lifestyle/entertainment/interview-alexsalmond

171. Torrance, *Salmond*, 28.

172. Ibid.

173. Ibid., 25, 45.

174. Ibid., 38–9.

175. Young, *St Andrews* (1969), quoted in Young and Murison (eds), *A Clear Voice*, 144.

176. Salmond, quoted in Torrance, *Salmond*, 25.

177. Torrance, *Salmond*, 22 (quoting R. S. Thomas, who quotes William Power).
178. MacDiarmid, *Complete Poems*, I, 75; Alex Salmond's New Year Message, 31 December 2011, accessed online on Scottish National Party website at <http://www.snp.org/blog/post/2011/dec/alex-salmonds-new-year-message>.
179. Ibid.
180. 'Alex Salmond has been re-elected to the post of First Minister at the Scottish Parliament', STV News, 18 May 2011, accessed online at <http://news.stv.tv/politics/250329–alex-salmond-re-elected-as-first-minister>.
181. Ibid.
182. Ibid.

Chapter 5

1. C. J. Sansom, *Dominion* (London: Mantle, 2012), 586, 593.
2. James Robertson, *And the Land Lay Still* (London: Penguin, 2010), 119.
3. Irvine Welsh, *Trainspotting* (1993; rpr. London: Minerva, 1994), 78.
4. Ibid., 198, 202, 228.
5. See 'Declaration of Calton Hill' entry on Wikipedia at <http://en.wikipedia.org/wiki/Declaration_of_Calton_Hill > (accessed 12 August 2012).
6. Irvine Welsh, interview with Jeremy Paxman on BBC TV's *Newsnight*, 17 April 2012, available online at <www.youtube.com/watch?v=6_Pbw9_1400> (accessed 12 August 2012). See also, e.g., 'Irvine Welsh: I love England but Scotland should be independent nation', *Daily Record*, 8 April 2012, available online at <http://www.dailyrecord.co.uk/news/politics/irvine-welsh-i-love-england-but-scotland-1118811> (accessed 12 August 2012).
7. Neal Ascherson, *Stone Voices* (London: Granta, 2002).
8. Tom Gordon, 'Revealed: Better Together's £2m war chest . . . and who donated it', *Sunday Herald*, 7 April 2013, 6.
9. Sansom, *Dominion*, 593.
10. C. J. Sansom, quoted in Phil Miller, 'Scots author condemns dangerous SNP in book', *Sunday Herald*, 13 October 2012, available online at http://www.heraldscotland.com/news/home-news/scots-author-condemns-dangerous-snp-in-book.19134105 (accessed April 2013).
11. Edwin Morgan, *Essays* (Cheadle Hulme: Carcanet New Press, 1974), 158–65.

12. Edwin Morgan, 'The Coin', *Collected Poems* (Manchester: Carcanet, 1990), 454.
13. Edwin Morgan, *A Book of Lives* (Manchester: Carcanet, 2007), 9.
14. Ibid., 10.
15. Ibid., 12.
16. The unpublished works and scrapbooks are all among the Edwin Morgan Papers (hereafter EMP), Special Collections Department, Glasgow University Library.
17. Edwin Morgan, *Beowulf* (Aldington: Hand and Flower Press, 1952), viii; for more on Morgan's *Beowulf* see Chris Jones, *Strange Likeness* (Oxford: Oxford University Press, 2006).
18. W. S. Graham, letter to Tony Lopez, 30 March 1981, cited in Tony Lopez, *The Poetry of W. S. Graham* (Edinburgh: Edinburgh University Press, 1989), 63.
19. Morgan, *Collected Poems*, 30.
20. Ibid., 350.
21. See Robert Baston, *Metrum de Praelio apud Bannockburn / The Battle of Bannockburn*, trans. Edwin Morgan (Edinburgh: The Scottish Poetry Library with Akros Publications and The Mariscat Press, 2004), which is discussed in Chapter 1 of the present book.
22. Morgan, *Essays*, 89.
23. Ibid., 89.
24. Ibid., 97.
25. Ibid.
26. Morgan, *Collected Poems*, 434.
27. Ibid., 202.
28. Interview with Edwin Morgan by Robert Crawford, *Verse*, 5.1 (February 1988), 33.
29. Morgan, *Collected Poems*, 203.
30. See *Deor*, ed. Kemp Malone, 3rd edn (London: Methuen, 1961).
31. Morgan, *Collected Poems*, 536.
32. Edwin Morgan, 'Sculptures', unpublished 1939 poem, EMP.
33. While MacCaig spoke to me about his support for the SNP, see also 'Patriot' in his *Collected Poems* (London: Chatto and Windus, 1990), 266.
34. Morgan, *Collected Poems*, 267.
35. Ibid., 336.
36. Ibid., 268.
37. Ibid., 408.
38. Ibid., 291.
39. Ibid., 522.
40. Ibid., 154.
41. Ibid., 233.

42. Morgan, *Essays*, 7.
43. Morgan, *Collected Poems*, 248.
44. Ibid., 167.
45. Ibid., 532.
46. Nicholas Jacobs, 'Divided by One Language?', *Balliol College Annual Record*, 1985, 80.
47. Morgan, *A Book of Lives*, 14.
48. Alasdair Gray, *Why Scots Should Rule Scotland* (Edinburgh: Canongate, 1992), 17.
49. Ibid., 15, 16.
50. Ibid., 63.
51. Alasdair Gray, 'Settlers and Colonists', in Scott Hames (ed.), *Unstated: Writers on Scottish Independence* (Edinburgh: Word Power Books, 2012), 108.
52. Gillian Bowditch, 'Free-dumb', *Sunday Times*, 23 December 2012, 18.
53. Arthur Meikle gave an account of the schoolboy Gray to the present writer during a conversation in St Andrews, 10 July 1990, and in a letter of 26 October 1990. For a fuller account, see Robert Crawford, 'Introduction', in Robert Crawford and Thom Nairn (eds), *The Arts of Alasdair Gray* (Edinburgh: Edinburgh University Press, 1991), 1–9.
54. Ibid., 155.
55. Arthur E. Meikle, letter to the present writer, 26 July 1990.
56. Alasdair Gray, *Lanark, A Life in Four Books* (Edinburgh: Canongate, 1981), 82.
57. Alasdair Gray, *Unlikely Stories, Mostly* (Edinburgh: Canongate, 1983), 121; 'Gray Talking with Donaldson', *Verse*, 1 (October 1984), 33.
58. Gray, *Unlikely Stories, Mostly*, 133.
59. Alasdair Gray, *1982, Janine* (London: Jonathan Cape, 1984), 65–6.
60. Gray, *Lanark*, 190, 83.
61. Ibid., 484.
62. Ibid., 498.
63. Ibid., 560–1.
64. Gray, *Why Scots Should Rule Scotland*, 63.
65. Rodge Glass, *Alasdair Gray: A Secretary's Biography* (London: Bloomsbury, 2008), 291.
66. See Eddie Barnes, 'Salmond unveils one Bella of a festive card', *Scotsman*, 14 December 2011, 18.
67. Liz Lochhead in *Time Out*, 16–23 September 1987, quoted in Anne Varty, 'Scripts and Performances', in Robert Crawford and Anne Varty (eds), *Liz Lochhead's Voices* (Edinburgh: Edinburgh University Press, 1993), 163.

68. Alan Hulme, *Manchester Evening News*, 28 September 1991, quoted in Varty, 'Scripts and Performances', 163.
69. Liz Lochhead, *'Mary Queen of Scots Got Her Head Chopped Off' and 'Dracula'* (London: Penguin, 1989), 11. Throughout, I cite this first published version of the play, rather than the more recent version.
70. Liz Lochhead in *Guardian*, 22 September 1987, quoted in Varty, 'Scripts and Performances', 163.
71. Lochhead, *Mary Queen of Scots*, 11.
72. Ibid.
73. Liz Lochhead in Robert Crawford et al., 'Hugh MacDiarmid: A Disgrace to the Community', *PN Review*, 89 (January-February 1993), 21-2.
74. William Carlos Williams, *In the American Grain* (1925; repr. New York: New Directions, 1956).
75. Lochhead, *Mary Queen of Scots*, 11-12.
76. Ibid., 12.
77. Ibid.
78. John Knox's famous *First Blast of the Trumpet against the Monstrous Regiment of Women*, a denunciation of female rule, was published in 1558.
79. Lochhead, *Mary Queen of Scots*, 27.
80. Ibid., 28.
81. Ibid., 37, 38.
82. Ibid., 58-9.
83. Ibid., 60.
84. Ibid., 61.
85. Ibid., 65.
86. Ibid., 63.
87. Ibid., 67.
88. Joyce McMillan, 'Frontline Scotland', *Scotsman Review*, 16 March 2007, 4; Brian Ferguson, 'Why Festival rejected Black Watch', *Scotsman*, 9 April 2013, 21.
89. John Tiffany, 'Director's Note', in Gregory Burke, *The National Theatre of Scotland's 'Black Watch'* (London: Faber and Faber, 2007), xii.
90. Burke, *Black Watch*, viii, vii.
91. Ibid., 4.
92. Ibid., 8-9.
93. Tom Peterkin, 'Salmond looks for winning ticket with celebrities', *Scotsman*, 10 August 2012, 6.
94. Burke, *Black Watch*, 17.
95. Ibid., 25-6.
96. Ibid., 26-7.
97. Ibid., 30.

98. Ibid., 38, 49, 71.
99. David Greig, *Dunsinane* (London: Faber and Faber, 2010), 27–8.
100. Edwin Morgan, *Nothing Not Giving Messages*, ed. Hamish Whyte (Edinburgh: Polygon, 1990); Greig, *Dunsinane*, 39, 53.
101. Greig, *Dunsinane*, 62, 41.
102. Ibid., 48.
103. Ibid., 79.
104. Ibid., 95.
105. Ibid., 108.
106. Ibid., 120, 125.
107. Ibid., 129, 133.
108. Ibid., 138.
109. Samuel Beckett, *Waiting for Godot* (1956; repr. London: Faber and Faber, 1975), 94.
110. Tom Peterkin, '£185,000-a-year mandarin accused of "going native"', *Scotsman*, 1 October 2011 (accessed online).
111. Andrew Nicoll, 'The Civil War', *Scottish Sun*, 1 October 2011 (accessed online).
112. Auslan Cramb, 'Sir Gus O'Donnell told Scotland's most senior civil servant has become "craven follower" of Alex Salmond', *The Daily Telegraph*, 1 October 2011 (accessed online).
113. 'Under-fire mandarin wins GOD's forgiveness', *Scotsman*, 8 October 2011 (accessed online).
114. Simon Johnson, 'Mandarins "freeze out" Alex Salmond's civil servant from independence talks', *Daily Telegraph*, 7 February 2012 (accessed online).
115. Robert Crawford and Norman McBeath, *Simonides* (Edinburgh: Easel Press, 2011), XIV.
116. Edwin Morgan, 'The Summons', quoted in James Robertson, *And the Land Lay Still* (London: Penguin, 2010), epigraph.
117. Stuart Kelly, *Scott-land* (Edinburgh: Polygon, 2010); Ann Rigney, *The Afterlives of Walter Scott* (Oxford: Oxford University Press, 2012).
118. 'Irvine Welsh enjoys a sweeping look through a Scottish lens at a turbulent era', *Guardian*, 24 July 2010 (accessed online); 'Books of 2010: Authors, actors, politicians, sports stars and more reveal their top reads of the year', *Scotland on Sunday*, 14 December 2010.
119. Robertson, quoted in James Campbell, 'A Life in Writing: James Robertson', *Guardian*, 14 August 2010 (accessed online).
120. Robertson, *And the Land Lay Still*, 21, 19, 17.
121. Ibid., 21, 22.
122. Ibid., 114, 18.
123. Ibid., 36.

124. Ibid., 46, 49, 267.
125. Ibid., 64, 585.
126. Ibid., 53.
127. Ibid., 101.
128. Ibid., 107.
129. Ibid., 164.
130. Ibid., 269.
131. Ibid., 617.
132. Ibid., 619.
133. Ibid., 671.
134. Tom Gordon, 'McConnell's chief of staff among first 100 to sign up for independence', *Herald*, 27 May 2012 (accessed online).
135. Liz Lochhead, 'The SRB Interview', *Scottish Review of Books*, 8.1 (2011), 14.
136. James Kelman, 'The SRB Interview', *Scottish Review of Books*, 8.3 (2012), 9.
137. Ibid., 8–9.
138. John Burnside, interviewed by Rosemary Goring in 'Sympathy for the Devil', Glasgow *Herald* Arts Supplement, 26 January 2013, 8; see Don Paterson, 'A Post-Creative Scotland', in Hames (ed.), *Unstated*, 156–64.
139. Seamus Heaney, *Station Island* (London: Faber and Faber, 1984), 94.
140. Robert Crawford, *Testament* (London: Cape, 2014), forthcoming.
141. Brian Ferguson, 'Independence "variety show" planned for tour of Scotland', *Scotsman*, 9 April 2013, 21.
142. See <en.wikipedia.org/wiki/Flower_of_Scotland> (accessed in January 2013).
143. This and all other quotations that follow are taken from the Rotunda Beam Inscription Project Website http://www.battle-ofbannockburn.com/Rotunda-Beam-Inscription/ (accessed in December 2012).

Index

References indicating main sections for authors are in **bold**.